Crim

C000128795

Justice

2000

STRATEGIES FOR A NEW CENTURY

Michael Cavadino is a senior lecturer in law. He is the author of *The Penal System: An Introduction* (with James Dignan), *The Law of Gravity: Offence Seriousness and Criminal Justice*, and *Mental Health Law in Context: Doctors' Orders?* among other works.

Iain Crow is a lecturer in law. He was previously head of research at the National Association for the Care and Resettlement of Offenders (NACRO), where he was involved with a wide range of research on offenders, and criminal justice policy. He took up his present post in 1989, and has carried out research on the Criminal Justice Act 1991 and recent developments in the youth court. His particular interests have included the employment and training of offenders and fine default and enforcement, and his earlier publications have included *Unemployment, Crime and Offenders* and *Aspects of Credit and Debt*. He is also writing a book on the treatment and rehabilitation of offenders.

James Dignan is a senior lecturer in law. He is the author of *The Penal System: An Introduction* (with Michael Cavadino) and has written extensively on the theoretical, practical and policy-related issues raised by the development of restorative justice. He is a member of SINRJ (an independent forum of experts in restorative justice).

The authors are all at the Centre for Criminological and Legal Research, University of Sheffield.

Criminal Justice 2000
Strategies for a New Century

Published 1999 by
WATERSIDE PRESS
Domum Road
Winchester SO23 9NN
Telephone or Fax 01962 855567
E-mail:watersidepress@compuserve.com
Online Bookstore: www.watersidepress.co.uk

First reprint 2001

ISBN Paperback 1 872 870 77 5

Cataloguing-in-Publication Data A catalogue record for this book can be obtained from the British Library.

Printing and binding Antony Rowe Ltd, Chippenham.

Criminal Justice 2000

STRATEGIES FOR A NEW CENTURY

Michael Cavadino
Iain Crow
James Dignan

Criminal Policy Series Editor Andrew Rutherford

WATERSIDE PRESS
WINCHESTER

Preface

In terms of criminal justice in Britain the twentieth century began on a fairly optimistic note. Winston Churchill, a youthful 'New Liberal' home secretary, set forth a bold reform agenda which was both rational and humane. Eighty years later, and to the surprise of some political commentators, much of that early reductionist spirit seemed to be alive and well. But during 1992-93 the Conservative government and the Labour Party, as the government in waiting, engaged in an unprecedented transformation of political perspectives on crime and criminal justice. As the century drew to a close, with an activist New Labour Government at the helm the direction ahead, at best, was highly problematic. It is against this extraordinary background that Michael Cavadino, Iain Crow and James Dignan have produced this timely and remarkable exposition of the choices ahead for policy makers and practitioners in the arena of criminal justice.

The authors make their starting point the Criminal Justice Act 1991, a statute that promised to be a watershed for principled sentencing but which was unable to withstand the slings and arrows of a combative but weak government and an opposition party which had sensed, given agile footwork, that it could claim the territory for its own. The particular strength of this study is the authors' insistence that the policy choices should be explicitly set forth. Their firm grasp of the complex array of issues does not impair the clarity they bring to this task. While they are explicit about their own value preferences and their vision of a form of reparative justice, the authors are careful not to allow a polemical fervour to take over. As a result, the book will appeal to students wanting to go beyond an introductory text as well as experienced practitioners and hardened policy-makers alike. The study is also highly recommended for the expanding group of elected members, officials and active citizens involved at the sharp end of the crime and disorder strategies taking shape at the local level of government. The limitations as well as the possibilities for criminal justice need to be fully appreciated if the new initiatives on crime prevention are to be effective.

Waterside Press is delighted to augment its Criminal Policy Series with this important study by three closely informed and insightful scholars of crime and justice in Britain.

Andrew Rutherford
August 1999

Acknowledgements

We should like to thank all the many people at the four courts in the North of England who assisted our original research into the effects of the Criminal Justice Act 1991; also our co-researchers Valerie Johnston, Monica Walker and Joanna Moore; and the Nuffield Foundation who funded the research.

We also acknowledge our double debt to Andrew Rutherford, who not only provided the original foundation for the conceptual framework developed and applied in this book, but also helped shepherd it through into publication while flattering us with encouraging noises along the way.

Michael Cavadino, Iain Crow and **James Dignan**
August 1999

Criminal Justice 2000
Strategies for a New Century

CONTENTS

Foreword

This book—written at a time when the 'New Labour' government's criminal justice strategy is taking shape—is an attempt to analyse past developments in criminal justice policy in such a way that it is possible to take a rational look at the options for the future. We are not in the business of forecasting what will happen, or setting out a precise policy agenda. Rather we are looking at frameworks and general directions for policy development. Ironically this intention is pretty well all that is left of the book we originally anticipated writing some five years or more ago.

The book has its origins in a research project we were involved in to study the impact of the Criminal Justice Act 1991. The project studied what happened between 1991 (before the Act was implemented) and 1993 (the year after the Act was implemented) in four areas in the North of England. The detailed results of that research have been written up in a report by ourselves and two former colleagues, Valerie Johnston and Monica Walker, *Changing Criminal Justice: The Impact of the Criminal Justice Act 1991 in Four Areas of the North of England* (University of Sheffield, 1996). Our plan at the time was to use the research as a basis for a book which looked at the wider implications of the Criminal Justice Act 1991 for the future of criminal justice in England and Wales. Two things happened to change this. The first was that, as everyone now knows, the Act was a political and public relations disaster, and within a year of its implementation key sections of it were repealed. Although the Criminal Justice Act 1991 contained provisions which have had an enduring effect on criminal justice, its significance was rapidly eroded by Michael Howard's programme to introduce a more overtly punitive criminal justice policy.

The second thing that happened was that, as a result of these developments, we realised that the book that needed to be written should not take a single piece of legislation as its focus, but instead should take a broader look at the development of criminal justice policy, of which legislative provisions are only a part. For example, it is not always necessary to pass new laws in order to affect the size of the prison population; it can certainly be increased (and maybe could also be reduced) by the kind of messages that magistrates and judges get from the government. It is not necessary to legislate in order to ensure that resources of the right kind are available in order to address crime and offending. New laws are not needed to get agencies working together in new and constructive ways. Nor is it necessary to legislate in order to have an impact on public perceptions and attitudes towards the management of crime and offenders.

We therefore set about considering various broad strategies and strands which have run through criminal justice policy for much of this century, with a view to looking at the prospects for a new century. Certain elements of the work we did in relation to the Criminal Justice Act 1991—on fines, community penalties and custody—have exerted an influence on this book. We have also drawn on earlier work by Andrew Rutherford, and acknowledge our indebtedness to a framework which he first created. But we think we have developed an approach which builds on his earlier analysis.

We unashamedly express a preference for a criminal justice policy which goes in one direction rather than another. We reject an approach which is purely punitive and which increases the likelihood of social exclusion. We favour moving in the direction of restorative justice—a philosophy which emphasises reparation, rebuilding and reintegration—as holding out the best prospects for a twenty-first century criminal justice system which will not only be better capable of managing crime and offending, but will also be based on the fundamental principles of human rights. Whether or not you agree with us, we hope you will find something in this book to help you reflect on the course which criminal justice has taken in the final years of the twentieth century, and consider what the prospects are for the twenty-first.

Michael Cavadino
Iain Crow
James Dignan

August 1999

CHAPTER 1

Introduction: 'I Didn't Get Where I Am Today . . .'

It is tempting to consider how one might reshape the criminal justice system. All of us have probably mused at some time how we might alter this, get rid of that, or introduce something else. Some get more chance to put their ideas into practice than others; the ones that get to do it most are Home Secretaries. Whether you do it from an armchair in Anytown or from behind a desk in Queen Anne's Gate you have to contend with what is already there and what has already happened. Our intention is that this book should look forward to the prospects and possibilities for criminal justice policy for a new century. But we are not starting with a blank sheet; the options available for the future are bound to reflect to some degree the legacy of the past, and in particular the recent past. The purpose of this chapter is to set a background by situating criminal justice policy towards the end of the twentieth century in the context of recent developments, as a basis for considering a strategy for the future.

In doing this an initial consideration is where to start. This is partly a matter of where to start chronologically, but it is also about where one starts from conceptually. For many who are concerned with criminal justice this means considering the objectives of criminal justice including retribution, incapacitation, deterrence, rehabilitation and reparation.[1] At any one time criminal justice policy consists of a mixture of objectives. In the UK, as in most other Western societies, one rarely finds a purely retributivist or purely rehabilitative approach. The British *penchant*, in particular, has tended to be for a blend of approaches to criminal justice rather than a pure doctrine. However, at different times the proportions of the different ingredients has varied. Thus, for some time from around the middle of the century until the early 1970s the prospects for the treatment and rehabilitation of offenders were the focus of attention. This did not mean, however, that there were no retributive, deterrent or restorative elements in the ways that criminals were dealt with. The 1990s saw a swing towards a more overtly punitive response to crime, but some treatment programmes and attempts to find and promote 'what works' continued. So care needs to be exercised to avoid adopting a crude and stereotypical conception of criminal justice policy. Nonetheless, we argue that it is possible to identify three broad strategic approaches which have characterised recent criminal justice policy, and we argue that in moving forward towards the twenty-first century there is an important choice to be made about which strategy will form the basis for future policy. Therefore, before looking at the recent history of criminal justice policy, we need to briefly explain what these three strategies are.

THREE STRATEGIES FOR CRIMINAL JUSTICE

A government—were it sufficiently unwise—could try to do without a strategy for criminal justice. But government cannot avoid having a *policy*, even if that policy were only one of complete *laissez faire*[2]—of leaving everything in criminal justice alone and allowing whatever happens to happen. Although, as we shall see in later chapters, governments have at times let things slide along in a manner very similar to this, the results of such a (non-)policy at present would be disastrous. For it would leave untouched the current trends of an ever more steeply rising prison population, ever more stretched penal resources, plummeting morale among criminal justice staff, simmering unrest among prison inmates and chronic dissatisfaction with criminal justice among the general public.

Another kind of policy which does not amount to a strategy is what Tony Bottoms has called 'penological pragmatism': muddling along, responding to developments in an *ad hoc* manner and trying to manage the criminal justice system by a succession of tinkering adjustments and minor reforms 'with no clear philosophical or theoretical basis'.[3] British politics has a traditional tendency to this kind of piecemeal, pragmatic approach, which some might even praise as suiting the moderate, empirical British temperament. Yet it is almost as prone as the *laissez faire* approach to simply let things slip downhill at an ever-increasing rate. Desperate situations require measures which, if not actually desperate, are less complacent than this. When the ship is heading straight for the iceberg at top speed, more than a light touch on the tiller is called for. We need a positive turn in a clear and definite new direction in other words, a strategy.

In this book, we will be referring to three general (or 'ideal-type') strategies. We elaborate them more fully, and justify our own preferences, in *Chapter 2*.

Strategy A is a *highly punitive* approach embodying what might be called 'law and order ideology':[4] the attitude that offenders should be dealt with as severely as possible. A governmental strategy based on this attitude would involve making criminal justice harsher and more punitive at every stage and in every respect—very much like the programme pursued by Michael Howard when he was Conservative Home Secretary between 1993 and 1997.

The '*managerialist*' Strategy B seeks to apply administrative and bureaucratic mechanisms to criminal justice in an attempt to make the system as smooth-running and cost-effective as possible.

Strategy C seeks to protect and uphold the *human rights* of offenders, victims and potential victims of crime. It seeks to minimise punishment and to ensure fairness and humane treatment within the criminal justice system. *Restorative justice*—the movement which seeks to respond to crime with positive measures whereby offenders make reparation for the harm they have done and both offenders and victims are reconciled with the community as a whole[5] is one manifestation of a Strategy C approach although, as we shall see more fully in *Chapter 2*, there is more than one view about the implications of human rights for criminal justice. Some adherents of Strategy C particularly favour attempts to *reform* offenders, while others espouse a philosophy of '*just deserts*' whereby punishment is strictly proportional to the seriousness of the offence.

Readers may not be surprised to learn that our own preferred approach is to reject Strategy A and to favour Strategy C (especially its 'restorative justice' version). Perhaps less predictably, we also see an important rôle for aspects of Strategy B. Again, the reasons for this are spelt out more fully in *Chapter 2*; but stated briefly we believe that, as long as human rights are made central to government policy, there is much to be said for the use of managerialist techniques in the service of these moral ends, to ensure that human rights are being preserved and protected effectively and efficiently. It is this judicious mixture of Strategies B and C, with Strategy C as the fundamental goal of policy, which this book is concerned to explain and advocate.

A RECENT HISTORY OF CRIMINAL JUSTICE POLICY

A large part of recent criminal justice policy is taken up by the 18 years of Conservative government from May 1979 to April 1997. Policy during this period can be seen as having undergone a series of developments, roughly corresponding to different Conservative administrations, and reflecting different aspects of the three strategies referred to above.

Travelling hopefully (pre-1979)

Although it is difficult to summarise briefly the four-fifths of the twentieth century that preceded 1979, certainly much of the period from the Second World War up to then had been characterised by what might be broadly described as a period of growing optimism about dealing with crime and offenders. Even prior to the war there was a growing impetus in Britain to get rid of corporal punishment and reduce reliance on custodial institutions, especially for young offenders. The growing influence of psychiatry and psychotherapy was making itself felt in the developing probation services which adopted a 'casework' approach towards offenders. Following the war the Criminal Justice Act of 1948 abolished corporal punishment and the approach óf most Western industrial countries towards crime and offenders centred around the 'treatment model', an approach that owed much to positivist attempts to base social science on natural science, and in this instance in particular on medical science. Whilst treatment and rehabilitation were the goals both inside and outside institutions, there was an increasing movement towards decarceration and 'alternatives to custody'. Although the treatment model was seen at the time as an enlightened approach, contrasting with the punitive and incapacitative efforts of an earlier period, it came under increasing attack during the 1970s, both theoretically and ethically. Theoretically it was criticised by what was then the 'new' school of criminological thought, which attacked the treatment model's highly individualised conception of the nature of criminal behaviour. In the early 1970s the treatment approach was also increasingly criticised on ethical grounds by those who felt that, in the name of supposedly enlightened 'treatment', due process, equity and proportionality of punishment were abused.[6] But perhaps the decisive blow was empirical, and was precipitated in 1974 by the publication of a now famous article by Martinson reporting the results of a project to study the effectiveness of a wide range of attempts to reform offenders which was interpreted as showing that 'nothing works'.[7] This article was followed by further reports[8] in a similar vein and the term 'nothing works' became the mantra of criminal justice practitioners, administrators and politicians for years to come.

The reports by Martinson and others were criticised subsequently on a number of grounds,[9] including the fact that they were based on old studies, using outdated methods, and overlooked the many positive findings which accompanied the negative ones. Indeed, Martinson subsequently retracted his original claims[10] and more recently his co-researcher Douglas Lipton has also distanced himself from Martinson's article saying that many people '. . . did not recognise the difference between the pessimistic viewpoint of the summary article and the more guarded conclusions, arrived at by my colleagues and me, which left open the possibility that rehabilitation could work'.[11] Later researchers have gone on to stress the importance of concentrating on what does work and seeking to learn from it.[12] However, the fact remains that during the mid-to-late-1970s there was a vacuum in criminal justice policy waiting to be filled. Various ideas were developed, including amongst other things the 'just deserts' approach. In contrast to the treatment model, this stresses the importance of due process in proceedings against offenders, determinate (rather than indeterminate) sentencing, and sentences where the penalty is proportional to the gravity of the offence. It was during this period, as well, that crime prevention became of increasing interest. But this was also a time when there was growing public anxiety about rising crime, particularly juvenile delinquency. Hence there was the opportunity to exploit growing disenchantment with what became regarded as trendy permissiveness and a call for a return to the 'good old days' of simple discipline and a 'clip round the ear'. Into the space created by the waning of the treatment model and the subsequent uncertainty stepped the formidable figure of William Whitelaw, the Conservative Party's Shadow Home Secretary, who arrived at the Home Office when the Conservatives took power in 1979.

A tougher regime (1979-87)

It may seem strange now, but there was a time prior to the General Election of 1979 when crime and criminal justice was not a significant party political issue. The almost universal acceptance that the treatment model offered the best hope for reducing offending probably contributed to this, and its decline may therefore be a factor in the ending of a largely bipartisan approach to criminal justice policy. But there were other factors. The Labour Governments of 1974-1979 faced a variety of problems, and opposition parties were keen to present a failure to address crime, especially juvenile crime, as part of a more general failure. William Whitelaw had had a distinguished military career, and like many of his generation recalled the days when discipline was strict, not just in the forces, but in society as a whole. The Army's military detention centre at Aldershot, the Glasshouse, became conflated with some of the ideas put forward at the time that detention centres for young offenders were introduced in 1948. The basis for toughening up detention centres has been questioned by a number of writers,[13] but the Gilbertian slogan of the 'short, sharp, shock' was resurrected in an attempt to come up with a banner that those on the right of politics could unite around.

Having played such a prominent part in the Conservative election campaign, it was inevitable that following the party's victory in the 1979 General Election a tougher regime for detention centres would be implemented. This became a feature of the first Conservative government's approach to criminal justice: a strengthening of Strategy A, 'law and order' impulses, albeit within an otherwise eclectic ideological mix.[14] When the tougher regimes initiative was evaluated, the failure of the policy to live up to expectations[15] helped to pave the way for a shift in thinking at a later date. It is ironic that this period of law and order rhetoric should have been most closely associated with William Whitelaw who, in the context of Thatcherism, was something of an old-fashioned liberal. And indeed he did attempt to balance the tough, but short, regimes for detention centres with more pragmatic solutions for dealing with a growing crisis in the prisons by attempting to introduce earlier parole for some prisoners. In this, however, he fell foul of not only the judges but of the Conservative Party Conference of 1981, and subsequently reversed the policy, paving the way for a period of expansion of prison places.

There was a feeling among sections of the criminal justice establishment, particularly magistrates, that the previous decade had seen increasing attempts to restrict the courts' sentencing powers and to hand more control to social workers and the executive part of the penal system. The Criminal Justice Act 1982 marked the beginning of a reversal of this process, freeing the courts from certain restrictions on their discretion, although section 1 of the Act also placed restrictions on the use of custodial sentences for offenders under 21 years of age. Around the same time, William Whitelaw told the House of Commons, 'We are determined to ensure that there will be room in the prison system for every person whom the judges and magistrates decide should go there',[16] a statement which heralded the most extensive prison building of the century. The government also allocated increased resources to the police. Thus, at a time when other social and economic institutions were coming under pressure to reduce expenditure, the 'law and order' budget continued to enjoy an access to resources that was almost unrestrained, on the basis that if criminals needed to be caught and incarcerated then cost should not be a consideration.

These Strategy A trends were nevertheless attenuated by pragmatic attempts to deal with the problem that the number of people in prison was growing faster than new prisons could be built. This took the form of what Tony Bottoms christened a *bifurcation* approach,[17] whereby it was held that there were many less serious offenders who did not warrant serious punishment, and that the real target of punitive sanctions should be those who committed the more serious offences involving violence and robbery. This was the line taken by William Whitelaw's successor, Leon Brittan, who significantly restricted the availability of parole for more serious offenders while allowing earlier parole for shorter term prisoners. However, as the Conservatives' second period of office came to a close two things were becoming increasingly apparent. First, the policy was not working. Crime was not being contained, let alone reduced as a consequence of a supposedly tough 'law and order' policy.

Second, this failing policy was becoming increasingly expensive to sustain. In particular, the cost of imprisonment was rising at an alarming rate. In other words, still 'nothing worked', and it cost more.

The 'Hurd approach' (1987-92)

It was this recognition that was responsible for ushering in a new phase of Conservative policy, a period characterised by even more pragmatism and containing elements of Strategies A, B and C. This was aided by the appointment of Douglas Hurd as Home Secretary in 1985 to replace Leon Brittan. Hurd was prepared to take a less doctrinal approach to criminal justice policy, but it was following the General Election of 1987 that real change became apparent. Indeed the shift in policy can be related to a defining moment that took place at a meeting of Home Office ministers and officials at Leeds Castle in September 1987. The meeting has been reported by Lord Windlesham, a former Home Office minister and Chairman of the Parole Board, who describes how initially there were echoes of the law and order rhetoric of the recent election. However, as the meeting progressed ministers and officials contemplated figures produced by the Home Office Statistical Department forecasting an increase in the prison population to 60,000 in the foreseeable future and the prospect of it reaching 70,000 by the year 2000.[18] It was resolved that 'such a situation would be intolerable, and must not be allowed to happen.[19] It was therefore essential to do something about the escalating costs of criminal justice that this would involve. Having been in power for eight years and just secured another term, it was also possible for the Conservative administration following the 1987 General Election to take a longer term perspective. This concordance of factors resulted in a growing emphasis on managerialism in criminal justice, and the framing of one of the more coherent pieces of criminal justice legislation that have been introduced in recent years. Previous Criminal Justice Acts had tended to be something of a hotchpotch of measures, assembled to respond to a variety of concerns. In the late 1980s Home Office ministers and civil servants set about the task of developing a sentencing framework underpinned by a 'just deserts' rationale.

Punishment in the Community: The Green Paper

The Green Paper of July 1988, *Punishment, Custody and the Community,*[20] had two main themes. The first was to draw attention to the disadvantages of custody:

> for . . . less serious offenders, a spell in custody is not the most effective punishment (para. 1.1)

> Overcrowded local prisons are emphatically not schools of citizenship (para. 1.6)

and

> Imprisonment is not the most effective punishment for most crime. Custody should be reserved as punishment for very serious offences, especially when the offender is violent and a continuing risk to the public. (para. 1.8)

Attention was also drawn to the high cost of custody compared with community penalties (para. 3.37). This was an important step for an administration that had hitherto adopted a largely punitive approach.

However, 'not every sentencer or member of the public has full confidence in the present orders which leave offenders in the community' (para. 1.8). Hence the second theme of the Green Paper was on emphasising supervision and punishment as key features of community penalties. It was stressed that such penalties 'are punishments, not treatments' (2.1) and there was much concern with discipline, rigour, strictness, and frequent and punctual reporting (paras. 2.3 to 2.13). What was envisaged was a continuum of punishment, the main feature of which was the restriction of freedom, with custody at the high end (3.5). Consequently there was discussion of such measures as electronic monitoring of offenders (3.17 to 3.21), discussed further in *Chapter 4.*

Thus, the Green Paper embraced a bifurcation approach to sentencing, whereby custody was to be reserved for the most serious offenders, whilst aiming to strengthen the perception of community penalties as sufficiently punitive for non-serious offenders. We call this a policy of 'punitive bifurcation' since it seeks to make community penalties more punitive at the same time as using them more extensively in place of custody for less serious cases.[21] As described in the Green Paper, this less serious category included the vast majority of non-violent offenders. The position regarding burglars is instructive in this context. The Green Paper basically placed burglars in the non-serious category stressing that 'Nearly half the burglaries reported are of offices, shops and other buildings, not houses', and proposing 'less use of custody, particularly for thieves and burglars'.[22] (By contrast, after 1993 Michael Howard was to focus particular attention on the need to incarcerate convicted burglars, culminating in section 4 of the Crime (Sentences) Act of 1997, which would have required offenders convicted of a third domestic burglary to be imprisoned for a minimum of three years). The Green Paper also discussed the need for more positive approaches to dealing with young offenders, including young adult offenders. It was stressed that 'most young offenders grow out of crime' (2.15), and that community penalties were particularly suitable for young men and women because they were likely to 'grow out of crime'.[23] (3.38).

Crime, Justice and Protecting the Public: The White Paper

The White Paper, *Crime, Justice and Protecting the Public*,[24] issued in February 1990, continued and developed the themes outlined in the Green Paper. Attention was drawn to the ineffectiveness of custody:

> Nobody now regards imprisonment, in itself, as an effective means of reform for most prisoners (para. 2.7).

In its most memorable and often quoted phrase the White Paper described imprisonment as 'an expensive way of making bad people worse'.[25] *Chapter 3* of the White Paper started by referring to the increasing use of custody since 1979, and cited the example of juvenile justice as one where the use of custody had been reduced without a discernible increase in the number of offences committed by juveniles. Hence, under the forthcoming legislation courts would have to justify the use of an expensive and ineffective resource. There was a clear commitment to reducing the use of custody: 'The Government believes a new approach is needed if the use of custody is to be reduced'.[26]

This would be done in part by making a sharper distinction between violent and sexual offences and the rest, and the use of custody would be focused on the former:

> Most crimes are not violent and for many of those who commit them, punishment in the community is likely to be better for the victim, the public and the offender, than a custodial sentence. Imprisonment makes it more difficult for offenders to compensate their victims and allows them to evade their responsibilities. (1.11)

It was also argued that 'successful re-integration of an offender into the community is easier if the offender is being punished in the community rather than in custody'.[27] This would also be achieved, as the previous Green Paper indicated, by strengthening community penalties. Henceforth these would be penalties in their own right and not, as they had often been described previously, 'alternatives' to custody. Punishments should be seen as 'restraints on liberty' which could be applied either in the community or through custodial penalties.[28]

The means by which all this was to be achieved was through the introduction of 'a new and more coherent statutory framework for sentencing', based on ensuring that criminals got their 'just desserts' (sic).[29] This was to be the central feature of the proposed legislation. An important component of this would be that, as the Court of Appeal had already said, the sentence should be appropriate for the offence before the court and an offender should not be sentenced on the basis of past offences for which he had already been punished.[30] Hence there would be a three tier hierarchy of sentences representing progressive restriction of liberty, ranging from discharges and financial penalties (the lowest tier) through 'community sentences' such as probation and community service (the middle tier) up to the top tier of imprisonment; the sentence to be based first and foremost on the seriousness of the offence, with the clear objective of reserving custody only for the most serious cases.

The Criminal Justice Act 1991 and its aftermath

The Criminal Justice Act 1991 had five main parts, covering the powers of courts to deal with offenders, early release of prisoners, children and young persons, the provision of services, and financial and other provisions. The principal measures included:

- a general (three tier) sentencing framework based on increasing degrees of restriction of liberty commensurate with the seriousness of the offence;

- limitations on courts' abilities to take account of previous convictions;

- establishing criteria for the use of custody, notably that an offence must normally be 'so serious' that custody is the only sentence that can be justified;

- allowing nonetheless for more severe sentences for violent and sexual offenders;

- introducing unit fines, which were more closely related to the means of the offender;

- introducing a combination order, combining probation with community service;

- introducing a curfew order enforced by electronic monitoring;

- abolishing the partly suspended sentence and limiting use of the suspended sentence; and

- introducing the youth court for offenders under 18 years of age.

The Act was intended to bring about a major transformation in criminal justice. Indeed the Minister of State responsible for overseeing its progress, John Patten, said of it, 'We are on the threshold of a major and lasting change in the criminal justice system'.[31] Because of this, a considerable amount of effort went into preparing the ground, not just for the Bill's passage through Parliament, but in the form of seminars and conferences being held in several parts of the country to give the opportunity for discussion. Training packages were prepared and delivered, and in respect of one of the more radical measures, the introduction of unit fines, pilot experiments were carried out at four courts to test their viability and effectiveness.[32]

Most of the provisions of the Criminal Justice Act 1991 came into force on 1 October 1992. It was widely anticipated that there would be a period of 'settling in' and that some adjustments might subsequently need to be made, perhaps in the form of Home Office circulars. That the precise consequences of legislative change could not be foreseen was borne out by the experience of earlier legislation.[33] Indeed the White Paper also acknowledged that the precise extent and nature of the consequences of the Act for sentencing were uncertain, and it pointed out that changes in the criminal justice system can easily have unintended results.[34] As a consequence, plans were developed by the Home Office to monitor the impact of the Act nationally, and by others including ourselves, to examine its impact at a local level.[35]

What happened was something very different. The Act became caught up in a period of media attention and political controversy that was quite unprecedented for criminal justice legislation. As far as the Act itself was concerned, the main foci of attention were the introduction of unit fines and the section of the Act that limited the extent to which courts could take account of offenders' previous convictions. The press carried stories of the Act being condemned by judges, and of magistrates resigning or threatening to resign. Around the same time considerable concern was being expressed about rising crime rates, some highly publicised cases of 'joy-riding', a small number of very young persistent offenders, and most tragically the murder of two year old James Bulger in February 1993 by two young boys who were themselves only just over the age of criminal responsibility. Criminal justice policy also became caught up in the fact that the government was under pressure from other directions, particularly for its economic and European policy. In September 1992, for example the government had had to withdraw from the European Exchange Rate Mechanism and the currency was effectively devalued. Members of the government that had been formed following the General Election of 1992 attacked the Act brought in by their predecessors with such vehemence that one could almost believe that it was the work of an opposition party. This created an atmosphere in which some response became inevitable, and in May 1993 the then Home Secretary, Kenneth Clarke, announced that the two most controversial sections of the 1991 Act, those concerning previous convictions and unit fines, were to be repealed.

'Prison works' (1993 to 1997)

After 1993 the Criminal Justice Act 1991 had a continuing effect on sentencing in the criminal courts. Its legacy included the three-tier framework of seriousness that governs sentencing severity, increased levels of maximum fines (even though the unit fine had gone), the combination order, a massive reduction in the use of suspended sentences of imprisonment, and the youth court. But the 1993 legislative changes were important, both in substance and as a symbolic refutation of previous policy. It was not just the Criminal Justice Act 1991 that had changed. What happened around the middle part of 1993 was the signalling of a much more general shift in criminal justice policy towards a more avowedly punitive approach. This culminated in the speech of the new Home Secretary, Michael Howard, at the Conservative Party conference in October 1993, when he announced a 27-point plan of action on law and order, and most famously stated that 'prison works'. This represented a rejection of the pre-1992 policy and a swing back to a more extreme, Strategy A, solution. The effects were dramatic. After a decline in late 1992, the prison population started to rise again in 1993. The next year saw the introduction of the Criminal Justice and Public Order Act 1994 which, amongst other things, provided for a new custodial sentence (the secure training order) for 12 to 14 year olds, and increased the maximum term of custody for 15 to 17 year olds. One of the last Acts of the Conservative administration was the passage of the Crime (Sentences) Act 1997, which provided for mandatory and minimum sentences for repeated violent and sexual offences, drug trafficking, and domestic burglary. The Act received the Royal Assent in March 1997, just prior to the General Election on May 1. This, of course, was the juncture at which Tony Blair's 'New' Labour Party won a landslide victory and took office, having pledged to be 'tough on crime and tough on the causes of crime'.

THEMES AND FEATURES OF RECENT PENAL HISTORY

Throughout the period described above there have been several features which have defined the nature of penal policy at different times. These include the use of custody, the size of the prison population, and the extent to which the prisons are, or appear to be, in a state of crisis. Thus, the shifts in Conservative government policy can be seen in terms of a growing use of custody in the early 1980s, followed by an attempt to reduce this in the late 1980s and up to 1992, followed by a sharp move up again from 1993 (see *Figure 1*).

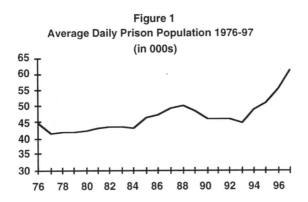

Figure 1
Average Daily Prison Population 1976-97
(in 000s)

Another theme of the period has been the attempt to get community penalties to match custody in terms of its punitive element. This comparison with custody has become the criterion by which community penalties have come to be judged, rather than by any claims to improve people or deal with the problems that underlie their offending. Hence a constant refrain has been the need for the courts and the public to have 'confidence' in community penalties. This was apparent in the various documents and discussions surrounding the Criminal Justice Act 1991, as some of the references cited earlier show. As a result the probation service and others put considerable effort into trying to satisfy this demand at that time. But when Michael Howard later took over as Home Secretary it was as though this was something still to be addressed. For example, despite the emphasis on making community penalties more acceptable to the public and sentencers around the time of the 1991 Act, the Home Office Consultation Document, *Strengthening Punishment in the Community*,[36] was still saying in 1995 that 'probation supervision is still widely regarded as a soft option'. This raises the question whether community penalties ever could or can satisfy the same kind of expectations as a custodial sentence, a question touched upon recently by Lord Chief Justice Lord Bingham of Cornhill in the following terms:

In the public mind, I think that custody is generally seen as the only truly retributive or punitive sentence. Anyone who commits a crime of any seriousness and is not sentenced to custody is generally perceived to have got away with it. This is very unfortunate because of the inherent drawbacks of imprisonment.[37]

Lord Bingham went on to conclude that there is a need to ensure that community service is rigorous and demanding, and that sentencers and the public are convinced that it is a serious punishment. But we shall return in *Chapter 4* to discuss whether this is the right way to think about punishment in the community.

A third feature has been developments in the way that different types of offence are dealt with. In particular, the recent past has been characterised by placing increasing emphasis on more serious penalties for violent and sexual offenders. At certain times (for example during Leon Brittan's period as Home Secretary, 1983-85, and again during the introduction of the Criminal Justice Act 1991) this was accompanied by making a distinction between serious offence groups and less serious, non-violent, and property offences: a bifurcation strategy. Under Michael Howard the emphasis on dealing with certain offences more severely continued, but the need to treat less serious offenders less punitively did not: the emphasis was on toughness all round. Indeed, as we have already seen, his term of office was characterised by wanting to be tougher with non-violent offenders such as burglars.

This concern with the nature of offences has been accompanied by a different concern about the number of previous convictions an offender has. Thus, from a time when courts were greatly influenced by the offender's past record, the Criminal Justice Act 1991 was intended to move sentencing policy on to a point where, because of the focus on just deserts for the current offence, there was to be relatively less reference to previous convictions. Subsequently, after 1993, increasing attention focused on repetitive offending behaviour and on persistence. The guiding beacon for this was the American 'three strikes and you're out' slogan. This concern with repeat offending found expression most obviously in the Criminal Justice and Public Order Act 1994, with its provision for secure training orders for persistent young offenders, and the Crime (Sentences) Act 1997, with its mandatory and minimum sentences for repeat offenders.

A preoccupation with young offenders has been another feature of the period under discussion. The Conservative government first came to power in 1979 offering a specific response to young offenders in the form of tougher regimes for detention centres. Subsequently the 1980s saw a shift in policy towards decarceration of the young, the development of non-custodial intermediate treatment for juveniles, and a degree of satisfaction with the fact that the use of custody for juveniles was decreasing, and that offending amongst juveniles also appeared to be on the decline. This encouraged the hope that a similar approach could be adopted towards young adult offenders. Indeed, during the late eighties there were attempts to focus more on young adult offenders, with the publication of a Home Office document[38] requiring local 'action plans' for young adult offenders. Once again 1992-93 proved to be the turning point: suddenly attention was being focused on persistent young offenders, children who kill, teenage joyriders, and children who seemed impossible to contain in custody, given such nicknames as 'Rat Boy'. A perception was created of a generation of young people out of control. The government responded with the secure training order for persistent offenders aged 12 to 14.

In reviewing this period, some mention needs to be made of the role of successive Home Secretaries. This is one of the most senior offices of state, and whoever occupies the position is more often than not regarded as a potential contender for the leadership of their party, and a possible Prime Minister. Not surprisingly, therefore, Home Secretaries tend to be strong figures who want to leave their imprint on some aspect of the job—though not all succeed. Thus William Whitelaw, a Tory 'grandee', was in charge of the Conservative government's law and order policies during their first period of office, although he was to suffer politically from the hostile reception which he received at the Conservative Party Conference in 1981, when he proposed to relieve some of the growing pressure on the prison system by extending short term prisoners' eligibility to parole. Leon Brittan sought to make his impression on policy by adopting a bifurcation strategy, making further significant changes which limited the availability of parole in certain cases. Douglas Hurd had more traditional liberal instincts and it was during his period as Home Secretary that a more pragmatic policy developed, culminating in the Criminal Justice Act 1991. It is not surprising that since leaving office Douglas Hurd has associated himself with more progressive polices than those of his successors, becoming Chairman of the Prison Reform Trust in 1997. Finally, Michael Howard's emphatic rejection of the Hurd approach, and his reversion to the more atavistic policies of punishment and retribution may be seen not only as following his own right-wing instincts but also as making his mark as a potential candidate for the Conservative leadership (unsuccessfully, as it turned out). Hence, criminal justice polices are about much more than simply finding the best way to combat crime. As we have seen, when a government is under pressure there is a temptation to play the 'law and order' card, and criminal justice policy can also be affected by the personalities involved.

Our aim here is not to prove that there have been carefully coordinated campaigns to embrace one approach to criminal justice policy rather than another during recent years. The suggestion is rather that there have been swings and shifts, which in part have reflected the fortunes of governments over time. They have also reflected the fortunes and anxieties of wider society. For this reason it is not possible to consider criminal justice policy in the later part of the twentieth century without also referring to some of the economic, social and political developments that have had an influence on that policy.

Much has been written about the relationship between economic conditions and crime,[39] and it is not our intention to develop the theme to any great extent here. However, we have presented criminal justice policy during the period 1979 to 1997 as a period of shifts and swings, consisting firstly of moves towards a Strategy A approach during the early part of the period, altering course towards a more pragmatic and indeed creative middle period containing large elements of Strategy B managerialism, before reverting to an even more explicitly punitive approach during the early 1990s. While not wanting to indulge in over-simplification, it is hard not to note that during the same period there was a severe recession in the early 1980s, with unparalleled post-war unemployment in Britain, followed by the Thatcher-Lawson boom of the mid-eighties, followed by a decline and another severe recession in the early 1990s. When societies feel insecure and under social or economic pressure, there is a tendency for them to become more aggressive and punitive and, in particular, to focus on certain groups within society who can be scapegoated for society's problems. So times of economic and social stress tend to be accompanied by the adoption of punitive approaches to crime and other social problems.[40] (United Nations Social Defence Research Institute, 1976; Hall, *et al*, 1978; Hall, 1980). Hardship tends to foster authoritarian tendencies and a wish to find scapegoats and simple solutions. Calls for more 'law and order' say more about society's anxieties, and its need to deflect these onto identifiable culprits, than about the real nature of the crime problem. Another factor is the tendency of governments—of which John Major's government was an outstanding example—to seek to distract attention from their economic failures and court popularity by promising to attack the criminal 'enemy within'.

A key feature of Conservative economic policy throughout this whole period was a move towards free market economics. This had various implications. It meant increasing privatisation and restraints on the public sector and on public expenditure. The 1980s saw most sectors of public life being subjected to cash limits, to (Strategy B-type) 'value for money' examinations, and various government departments being given agency status. For some time criminal justice was treated as an exception and evaded many of the restrictions applied elsewhere. The police and prisons, and to a lesser extent the probation service, received more money for a while, but cash limits eventually caught up with criminal justice agencies in the early 1990s. Privatisation was also a long time coming, but when it did come in the early 1990s, its adoption was rapid.

Another consequence of the economic policies of successive Conservative administrations was to look towards the world's largest free market economy, the United States, and to move in the direction of styles of working and living which were more like those in the United States than the traditional approaches of management previously found in Britain and other European countries. Along with this went the importation of much American culture, and this has been accompanied by numerous attempts to introduce US-style penal practices, especially since the Conservative government's U-turn on penal policy in 1992-93. Thus, we have seen the transplantation into Britain of developments such as the privatisation of prisons, electronic tagging, 'three strikes and you're out' sentences, 'boot camps' and so on. Britain has been urged to follow the United States in this manner—and by moving towards US levels of incarceration by American writers such as Charles Murray.[41] Hence it is not too surprising to find that the influence of American penal policy has been an increasing characteristic of developments in the UK during the period of Conservative governments. However, not all Americans agree with the policies that have been adopted in the United States. Another American writer, Elliott Currie, has argued that market societies, 'those in which the pursuit of private gain becomes the dominant organizing principle of social and economic life', are especially likely to breed high levels of violent crime, and that 'rising levels of endemic violence will provoke the beginnings of American style investment in incarceration as the dominant mechanism of mass social control of increasingly disadvantaged and volatile populations'.[42] Currie has also argued that such an investment in incarceration restricts investment in the kind of social opportunities that might help to contain crime.[43]

This brings us to the last main point in this section, but one that takes us from looking back over the best part of two decades to looking towards the future. This is the changing approach of the Labour Party since Tony Blair became Shadow Home Secretary in 1992. After successive electoral defeats the Labour Party attempted to re-form itself in ways that influenced most of its policies, usually in a direction which meant that it was able to challenge the Conservatives on their own ground. It was recognised that if the party was to be re-elected it had to appear more 'credible' to the electorate. This applied particularly to crime and 'law and order'. Increasingly the Conservatives became more vulnerable on this issue in the late 1980s and early 1990s as their policies were appearing not to work. It was Tony Blair as Shadow Home Secretary who set the tenor of future policy by being increasingly willing to be 'tough on crime and tough on the causes of crime' (see *Chapter 2*). While the latter part of the phrase suggested a recognition of the need to address the social roots of crime, there was much less emphasis on this than on clamping down on a variety of perpetrators of (mostly minor) deviant behaviour, such as beggars, graffiti artists, 'squeegee merchants' and anti-social neighbours. But the consequence of Labour's apparent acceptance of the 'law and order' (Strategy A) approach was that the Conservatives now felt that they could not be seen to be outdone by their opponents. Hence, during the mid-1990s, under Michael Howard, Conservative policy moved even further right on this issue in an attempt to put 'clear blue water' between themselves and their opponents. In this context it is not surprising that, once Labour accepted the same premises on which Conservative criminal justice policy operated, they too increasingly advanced ideas drawn from the United States, such as 'zero tolerance'. This also probably has something to do with the fact that following Labour's electoral defeat in 1992 and the success of the Democratic Presidential campaign later that year, there was a tendency for Labour to look towards the Clinton administration—which espoused Strategy A policies towards crime and offenders—for sources of inspiration.

Robocop: The coming of zero tolerance

The Labour government elected in May 1997 has declared that it has 'no interest in chanting a simplistic mantra that prison works'.[44] The new government's almost omnipresent law and order slogan was not 'prison works' but 'zero tolerance'. This is a concept which also found favour with Michael Howard but which rose to particular prominence in Britain recently thanks to its fervent espousal by both Prime Minister Tony Blair and Home Secretary Jack Straw.

'Zero tolerance'—like 'three strikes and you're out' and 'boot camps'—is a concept imported from the United States. Its origins can be traced to a famous 1982 article about policing and local anti-crime strategy by criminologists James Q Wilson and George Kelling entitled 'Broken Windows'.[45] Their thesis is based on the idea that the first broken window in a building or neighbourhood can start off a downward spiral of neglect, with petty crime and 'incivilities' leading to low-level disorder, fear of crime and in the longer run problems of serious criminal activity in the locality. Prevent that first broken window—or mend it quickly to maintain the impression that the neighbourhood is cared for—

and the whole downward spiral can be 'nipped in the bud' (a quintessential zero tolerance phrase). Prevent 'incivilities' such as graffiti, rowdiness and aggressive begging and the neighbourhood can be saved from becoming a magnet for crime and ultimately turning into a chronic high-crime area. This might sound simplistic, and certainly it is easy to mock the idea that cracking down on graffiti artists will stop them progressing to armed robbery and murder, or to point to all the other myriad factors which are known to affect crime rates and which this thesis ignores. Nevertheless, there is some evidence that these local downward spirals do indeed occur.[46]

A substantial logical leap is made from this 'broken windows' notion to the idea that what is required is 'zero tolerance' of petty crime and public incivilities in order to nip serious crime in the bud. The example most often cited is that of New York, where William Bratton became Police Commissioner in 1994 and initiated wide-ranging reforms in the Police Department. Three years later, New York's rate of officially recorded crime had fallen by 38 per cent and the homicide rate by over 50 per cent.[47] In Britain, the approach has been copied in King's Cross in London and (controversially) in Hartlepool and Middlesborough by Cleveland's high-profile Detective Superintendent Ray Mallon, who has been nicknamed 'Robocop' and has been reported to 'have the ear' of Tony Blair, Jack Straw and Michael Howard.

This book is not primarily about policing, the original and perhaps natural context of the concept of zero tolerance. We should briefly point out, though, that the famous New York success story may not be all it seems. New York's crime rates were already falling (following massive increases in previous years) before the advent of William Bratton; and other US cities experienced similar falls in crime rates around the same time without introducing more aggressive policing, or even while making policing less aggressive.[48] Recorded crime has been falling dramatically throughout the US in recent years, almost certainly due mostly to factors such as economic and demographic trends and changes in patterns of drug use.[49] This is not to say that William Bratton made no impact on crime in New York. He became Commissioner of a police department which was inefficient, lazy and even corrupt. Urban 'no-go areas' had been allowed to develop in which crime of a whole range of magnitude was largely ignored by the police, and citizens could not expect any kind of adequate service from the police.

Zero tolerance—along with other reforms initiated by Bratton—was doubtless an effective remedy for this deplorable state of maximum toleration of crime in parts of the city. But it is hardly the optimum or ideal level of policing. Taken literally, 'zero tolerance' denotes minimum police discretion in dealing with minor crime and disorder, with the police automatically implementing the most drastic enforcement response ('robotic policing', to use the cautionary phrase of one of the authors of the original 'broken windows' article).[50] As Lord Scarman warned in his report on the Brixton riots of 1981,[51] over-zealous macho policing can seriously alienate large minority sections of the population, especially the young working-class and ethnic minority males who are most likely to be targets of police attention, storing up trouble in the form of magnified urban unrest in the future. In this respect, it is disconcerting to learn that one prominent feature of 'zero tolerance' policing in Cleveland has been a massive sixfold increase in police use of their powers to stop and search people in the street[52]—the very practice which was such a major factor in provoking the Brixton riots.

Similar fears were expressed by a major Home Office review of research, *Reducing Offending*, published in July 1998. This review concluded that, although zero tolerance policing could cut crime in localised areas in the short term, there were serious question marks over its long-term impact, including whether the police are able to distinguish between firm and harsh styles of policing and the long-term effect of mass arrests for minor offences.[53]

One problem with nice snappy soundbites is that there is a temptation to use them at every possible opportunity because they make your policies sound so attractive to the casual ear. There is the danger that they may come to function as a substitute for proper examination and explanation of policies, and even that policies may end up being slogan-driven rather than principled or rational. Such a danger has been looming with 'zero tolerance' (along with 'three strikes and you're out', a slogan originally designed to appeal to sports-loving Americans with a 30-second attention span). There have certainly been some worrying signs, as 'zero tolerance' quickly seemed to become an all-purpose political catchphrase. Recently it has been used by government politicians and others to describe disparate policies relating to (*inter alia*) domestic violence, noisy neighbours, poor teachers, failing schools, beggars, 'squeegee merchants', petty crime, white collar crime in the City, juvenile crime and (no doubt) rebellious Labour backbenchers. Only some of these are subjects of this book. But our general argument as regards issues of crime and criminal justice is that the correct approach is neither zero tolerance nor maximum toleration in our responses to crime. Both principled and practical considerations call for liberal policies situated between these two extreme poles. One encouraging sign, as we write in the summer of 1998, is that following the publication of the Home Office's *Reducing Offending* review Mr Straw seems to have taken notice and is currently distancing himself from at least some aspects of 'zero tolerance'.

It remains to be seen whether this will mark a turning of the general trend of the recent past. What has happened as we approach the end of the twentieth century is that, after several decades of looking hopefully at various ways of responding to crime, we seem to have become locked into a pattern where governments seek electoral popularity by promising tougher policies towards crime, which in turn feed public beliefs and expectations that the way to deal with crime is by punitive action, usually encapsulated in pithy sound-bites. Douglas Hurd has recently complained about the way in which criminal justice legislation has been hampered by 'the bitter competition between the two main political parties for the prize of being tough on crime'.[54] The question then becomes, how does one break out of the self-reinforcing logic of this situation? It has been suggested that what is needed is a 'replacement discourse' which changes the terms of reference by which the issues are addressed.[55] This would include stressing the reintegration and inclusion of offenders rather than their punitive exclusion (see *Chapters 2* and *4*), and would mean addressing social as well as purely criminal justice matters, such as employment and education strategies. It is in this context that we hope to see a transformation towards a Strategy C approach which places particular emphasis on restorative justice. The end of the eighteenth and beginning of the nineteenth centuries saw what has been called the 'great transformation' in punishment, from 'corporal' to 'carceral' penal policies.[56] This reminds us that criminal justice can change, and gives us cause to hope that the end of the twentieth and beginning of the twenty-first centuries might witness another transformation. We recognise this is an ambitious aspiration, and we do not expect any sudden or dramatic shift, but we do think that it is possible to take some modest and practical steps in a hopeful direction.

ENDNOTES: *Chapter 1*

1 See Michael Cavadino and James Dignan, *The Penal System: An Introduction* (2nd edn, London, Sage, 1997), ch. 2 for a discussion of the aims and justifications of punishment.

2 This kind of 'penological *laissez faire*' should be distinguished from the better known policy of economic *laissez faire*, in which the free market is left as undisturbed as possible. The two kinds of *laissez faire* do not have to go together, and indeed usually do not seem to.

3 Anthony E Bottoms, 'An Introduction to "The Coming Crisis"', in Anthony E Bottoms and Ronald H Preston (eds.), *The Coming Penal Crisis: A Criminological and Theological Exploration* (Edinburgh, Scottish Academic Press, 1980), 1-24 at p. 4.

4   Michael Cavadino and James Dignan, *The Penal System: An Introduction* (2nd edn, London: Sage Publications, 1997).

5   See James Dignan and Michael Cavadino, 'Towards a Framework for Conceptualising and Evaluating Models of Criminal Justice from a Victim's Perspective', *International Review of Victimology*, 4 (1996): 153-82.

6   American Friends Service Committee (1971), *Struggle for Justice: A Report on Crime and Punishment in America*, (New York: Hill and Wang, 1971); Andrew von Hirsch, *Doing Justice: the Choice of Punishments, Report of the Committee for the Study of Incarceration* (New York, Hill and Wang, 1976).

7   Robert Martinson (1974), 'What Works? – Questions and Answers About Prison Reform', *The Public Interest*, 35 (1974), 22-54.

8   M. S. Folkard, D. E. Smith and D. D. Smith, *Intensive Matched Probation and After-Care Treatment, Vol II*, Home Office Research Study No. 36 (London, HMSO, 1976); Stephen Brody, *The Effectiveness of Sentencing*, Home Office Research Study No. 35 (London, HMSO, 1975).

9   Tony Palmer, 'Martinson Revisited', *Journal of Research in Crime and Delinquency*, 12 (1975), 133-152.

10 Robert Martinson, 'New Findings, New Views: A Note of Caution Regarding Sentencing Reform', *Hofstra Law Review*, 7 (1979), 243-58.

11 Douglas Lipton, *The Effectiveness of Treatment for Drug Abusers Under Criminal Justice Supervision*, National Institute of Justice Research Report (US Department of Justice, Washington DC, 1995).

12 See e.g. James McGuire (ed.), *What Works: Reducing Reoffending* (Chichester, John Wiley and Sons, 1995), pp. 5-7.

13 See e.g. Iain Crow, *The Detention Centre Experiment: A Review* (London, NACRO, 1979).

14 See Cavadino and Dignan, op. cit., pp. 291ff.

15 D. Thornton, L. Curran, D. Grayson and V. Holloway, *Tougher Regimes in Detention Centres: Report of an Evaluation by the Young Offender Psychology Unit*, Directorate of Psychological Services, Prison Department, Home Office (London, HMSO, 1984).

16 H.C. Deb 25 March 1982.

17 Anthony Bottoms, 'Reflections on the Renaissance of Dangerousness', *Howard Journal of Criminal Justice*, 16 (1977), 70-96.

18 It is ironic that the figure of 60,000 *was* subsequently reached ten years later, following the reversal of the approach which started at Leeds Castle. More recent projections suggest that the prison population could be as high as 92,600 by 2005, necessitating the building of 20 more prisons at a cost of £2 billion (*Revised Projections of Long Term Trends in the Prison Population to 2005*, Home Office Statistical Bulletin, Issue 2/98, London, Home Office, 1998).

19 Lord Windlesham, *Responses to Crime, Volume 2: Penal Policy in the Making.* (Oxford, Clarendon Press, 1993), p. 239.

20 Cm 424 (London, HMSO, 1988).

21 See Cavadino and Dignan, op. cit., p. 26.

22 Paras. 3.7 and 3.42.

23 Paras. 2.15 and 3.38.

24 Home Office, *Crime, Justice and Protecting the Public: The Government's Proposals for Legislation*, Cm 965. (London, HMSO, 1990).

25 Para. 2.7.

26 Para. 4.3.

27 Para. 7.12.

28 Paras. 4.1 and 2.11.

29 Paras. 1.5-1.6.

30 *R v Queen* (1981), 3 Cr App Rep 245, cited in para. 2.18.

31 *The Observer*, 24 April 1988.

32 David Moxon, Mike Sutton and Carol Hedderman, *Unit Fines: Experiments in Four Courts*, Research and Planning Unit Paper 59 (London, Home Office, 1990).

33 See eg Elizabeth Burney, *Sentencing Young People: What went Wrong with the Criminal Justice Act 1982* (Aldershot, Gower, 1985).

34 Para. 9.9.

35 Iain Crow, Michael Cavadino, James Dignan, Valerie Johnston and Monica Walker, (1996) *Changing Criminal Justice: The Impact of the Criminal Justice Act 1991 in Four Areas of the North of England* (Centre for Criminological and Legal Research, University of Sheffield, 1996).

36 Home Office, *Strengthening Punishment in the Community: A Consultation Document*, Cm 2780 (London, HMSO, 1995), para. 4.4.

37 Speech to the Police Foundation on 10 July 1997, reported in *NACRO Criminal Justice Digest* No. 93, July 1997.

38 *Tackling Offending: An Action Plan* (London, Home Office, 1988).

39 See e.g. Steven Box, *Recession, Crime and Punishment*, (London, Macmillan, 1987); Iain Crow, Paul Richardson, Carol Riddington and Frances Simon, *Unemployment, Crime and Offenders* (London, Routledge, 1989); Council of Europe, *Crime and Economy*, Reports Presented to the 11th Criminological Colloquium, 1994 (Strasbourg, Council of Europe Publishing, 1995).

40 See United Nations Social Defence Research Institute, *Economic Crises and Crime* (Rome, UNSDRI, 1976); Stuart Hall, John Clarke, Chas Critcher, Tony Jefferson and Brian Roberts, *Policing the Crisis* (London, Macmillan, 1978); Stuart Hall, *Drifting into a Law and Order Society* (London, Cobden Trust, 1980).

41 Charles Murray, 'The Ruthless Truth: Prison Works', *The Sunday Times*, 12 January 1997.

42 Elliott Currie, 'Market, Crime and Community', *Theoretical Criminology*, 1 (1997), 147-172, at pp. 147 and 167.

43 Elliott Currie, *Is America Really Winning the War on Crime and Should Britain Follow Its Example?* NACRO 30th Anniversary Lecture (London, NACRO, 1996).

44 Jack Straw, quoted in *Prison Report* No. 41, Winter 1997, p. 3.

45 James Q Wilson and George L Kelling, 'Broken Windows', *Atlantic Monthly*, 249 (1982): 29-38. Interestingly, however, Kelling has disavowed the phrase 'zero tolerance' on the grounds that 'it connotes robotic policing' rather than the intelligent use of policing discretion which he advocates. (Rod Morgan,

review of George L Kelling and Catherine M Coles, *Fixing Broken Windows: Restoring Order and Reducing Crime in Our Communities*, New York, Free Press, 1996, in [1997] *Criminal Law Review*, 699-700) .

46 See Anthony E Bottoms and Paul Wiles, 'Environmental Criminology', in Mike Maguire, Rod Morgan and Robert Reiner (eds.), *The Oxford Handbook of Criminology*, 2nd edn. (Oxford, Oxford University Press, 1997), 305-59 at pp. 345-6.

47 William J. Bratton, 'Crime is Down in New York: Blame the Police', in William J. Bratton, Norman Dennis, Ray Mallon, John Orr and Charles Pollard, *Zero Tolerance: Policing a Free Society* (London, Institute of Economic Affairs Health and Welfare Unit, 1997), 29-42.

48 Examples include Los Angeles and San Diego: see Martin Kettle, 'Mr Crime Buster Cleans Up', *The Guardian*, 5 November 1997; Charles Pollard, 'Zero Tolerance: Short-Term Fix, Long-term Liability', in Bratton *et al*, op. cit., pp 43-60.

49 See further *Chapter 2*, under the heading 'The Ineffectiveness of Strategy A'.

50 See above, note 45.

51 Lord Scarman, *The Scarman Report* (Harmondsworth, Penguin, 1986).

52 *The Guardian*, 2 December 1997.

53 Peter Jordan, 'Effective Policing Strategies for Reducing Crime', in Peter Goldblatt and Chris Lewis (eds.), *Reducing Offending: An Assessment of Research Evidence on Ways of Dealing With Offending Behaviour*, Home Office Research Study No. 187 (London, Home Office, 1998): 63-81, pp. 72-3.

54 Douglas Hurd, 'Cooling the Emotions', *Guardian Society*, 18 March 1998.

55 Andrew Ashworth, 'Sentenced by the Media?', *Criminal Justice Matters*, 29 (1997), 14-15.

56 Michel Foucault, *Discipline and Punish: The Birth of the Prison* (London, Allen Lane, 1977).

CHAPTER 2

Back to Basics

I want to be seen as a just and effective Home Secretary who is concerned with people's rights, particularly those who do not have as much power or as great a voice as they should have in society. Jack Straw MP, *The Guardian*, 15 September 1997.

This chapter is about first principles. What can we justifiably and rationally ask the criminal justice system to do? What should its aims be, and what limitations should we accept or impose on those aims? And what, in consequence, should the shape of criminal justice policy look like?

We shall explore these first principles in the context of the three general types of criminal justice strategy we outlined briefly in *Chapter 1*. These are 'ideal-type' strategies. By 'ideal' we mean conceptually pure rather than perfectly desirable: these are three distinct, abstract ideas of how a strategy might look. In practice, no government has ever or would ever follow any one of these in a pure and undiluted form. But they represent discernible and distinguishable threads in criminal justice policy, and each could form the basis of a coherent (if not in every case acceptable or successful) governmental strategy for criminal justice.

STRATEGY A—THE PUNITIVE 'LAW AND ORDER' APPROACH

Our three 'ideal-type' strategies are broadly based on the three rival 'working credos' which Andrew Rutherford has identified as being held by different practitioners in the criminal justice system.[1] Strategy A corresponds to Rutherford's 'Credo One', which he says involves 'a powerfully held distaste and moral condemnation of offenders and the belief that as few fetters as possible be placed upon the authorities in the pursuit of criminals who, when caught, should be dealt with in ways that are punitive and degrading'.[2] In other words, this is a highly punitive credo embodying what might be termed 'law and order ideology'[3] or 'populist punitiveness':[4] the attitude that offenders (and even unconvicted suspects and defendants) should be dealt with as harshly as possible.

A governmental strategy based on this attitude would involve making criminal justice 'tougher' at every stage and in every respect: increasing the powers of the police, reducing safeguards for suspects, clamping down on the use of cautioning as opposed to prosecution of detected offenders, encouraging more pre-trial remands in custody, seeking to ensure that sentences were harsher, with more and longer prison sentences, making non-custodial penalties more punitive and restrictive and conditions within prisons more austere. Strategy A has little or no time for the notion that positive attempts should be made to reform or rehabilitate offenders, except by means of 'individual deterrence': punishing them so severely that they reform out of fear of further hard treatment. Other kinds of reformative training or treatment are seen as excessively 'soft'.

The politics of criminal justice are periodically dominated by the rhetoric of 'law and order', usually with very real practical consequences in encouraging harsher treatment of offenders and alleged offenders. In 1979 the Conservative Party came to power with a manifesto in which 'toughness' on law and order was prominent. In power, however, their criminal justice policies for a long time conformed less closely to Strategy A than a casual observer might have expected. This was especially true after 1987 when the Conservative government pursued what we call in this book 'the Hurd approach': policies influenced greatly by Strategy B and (as we shall argue, to a lesser extent) Strategy C. As we saw in *Chapter 1*, however, the Hurd approach was ignominiously jettisoned in the period 1992-1997 in favour of a much more punitive, 'Strategy A' set of policies, which came to be strongly personally associated with Michael Howard (Home Secretary 1993-1997).

But Strategy A was not born when Michael Howard became Home Secretary, nor did it die when he left office. The rhetoric of both major parties when discussing criminal justice has been dominated for some years by talk of 'toughness', especially since 1992 when Tony Blair became Labour's Shadow Home Secretary and unveiled the slogan 'tough on crime, tough on the causes of crime'.[5] The notion of '*zero tolerance*' of crime and anti-social behaviour, espoused by the Labour leadership, also has at least rhetorical overtones of Strategy A. The impression that Labour has mostly sought to convey since 1992 has been that a Labour government would be at least as 'tough' as the Conservatives.

What, many would ask, is wrong with Strategy A? It is certainly a popular approach. Most members of the public, if asked, would proffer the view that criminals are treated too leniently[6] and that—especially given alarmingly high and rising crime rates—tougher measures are entirely justified, both in principle, because criminals deserve harsher punishment, and for practical reasons, in order to protect law-abiding members of the public.

There are at least two good answers to this question, the first practical and the second principled. The practical answer is that Strategy A is bound to be disastrous. It cannot possibly succeed in controlling crime, and its failure will be catastrophically expensive both in terms of financial resources and human suffering. The principled answer is that Strategy A is morally unacceptable.

The ineffectiveness of Strategy A

Strategy A thinking is largely based on the common sense intuition that tougher treatment would effectively reduce the crime rate, a belief most famously and potently expressed in recent years by Michael Howard at the 1993 Conservative Party Conference when he stated: '*Prison works*. It ensures that we are protected from murderers, muggers and rapists—and it makes many who are tempted to commit crime think twice.' Common sense does indeed suggest that, if criminals were punished more severely, and especially if more of them were imprisoned or kept in prison longer, then crime would be significantly reduced both because offenders would be '*incapacitated*'—physically prevented—from committing crimes by their incarceration, and because more potential offenders would be *deterred* from crime through fear of punishment. Members of the general public, certain politicians and even some academic commentators (although rarely expert criminologists) regularly declare their beliefs that punishment is bound to be effective as both a deterrent and a means of incapacitation.

But examination of the evidence demonstrates that, counter-intuitive though it may be, this simply is not the case. This is not to say that no one is ever deterred from crime by the thought of punishment or that imprisonment has no 'incapacitation effect' at all. But all the evidence is that both deterrence and incapacitation are such *ineffective* mechanisms for controlling crime that even a massive and incredibly costly increase in punishment levels would be unlikely to achieve a noticeable reduction in the rate of offending. It has been authoritatively calculated that for the 'incapacitation effect' to reduce crime by one per cent it would be necessary to increase the prison population by around 25 per cent.[7] As for deterrence, it is a criminological truism that to improve deterrence what is needed is to increase the perceived risk of *being caught*; increased punishments generally have no measurable effect on deterrence.[8]

This is borne out by statistics showing little or no correlation between the levels of punishment meted out in a country and that country's crime rate, whether the comparison is between different countries at the same time or the same country at different times.[9] Occasionally it happens—as on the law of averages it occasionally will—that a country experiences a decreased recorded crime rate coincident with or following an increase in the level of punishment, and this may encourage Strategy A enthusiasts to make extravagant claims about the effectiveness of punishment. For example, in September 1995 Michael Howard claimed that the fall in recorded crime over the previous two years was evidence of the success of his 'prison works' policies (*Guardian*, 28 September 1995). The lie was retrospectively given to this claim by the news that, although 1994 and 1995 experienced a fall of eight per cent in the official figures of crimes *recorded by the police*, the level of crime as measured (almost certainly more accurately) by the British Crime Survey[10] rose by two per cent. This was despite—or as we would put it, irrespective of—a 15 per cent rise in the average prison population over the same two years. Moreover, similar reductions in recorded crime occurred between 1993 and 1995 in other European countries, notably Greece (-8%) and Switzerland (-7%), at a time when both countries had *reduced* their prison populations, by 11 and 27 per cent respectively.[11]

Similarly, the massive 400 per cent increase in the United States prison population between the mid-1970s and the present day[12] partly coincided with a significant decrease in recorded crime following 1980, again giving rise to claims that the one led to the other.[13] Although the 'incapacitation effect' of such a wholesale exercise in mass incarceration might have made a modest (if enormously costly) contribution to the reduction in crime, most criminologists remain of the opinion that the fall can most plausibly be attributed to other factors. For the vast bulk of empirical evidence suggests that the simple truth is this: *levels of punishment have very little effect on the incidence of crime*, whose rises and falls are overwhelmingly attributable to other factors. These other factors include demographic variables (crime increases when the population contains a higher number and proportion of the young males who constitute the most crime-prone age group); economic trends (an improving economy usually ameliorates the rate of crime against property, which accounts for the vast bulk of recorded crime);[14] and changing patterns of drug use, with crack cocaine being apparently significantly more criminogenic than heroin.[15] (The United States has been particularly fortunate as regards all these trends in recent years.)

The conclusion that increased punishment can have little part to play in 'fighting crime' is an unpopular and, for many people, a counter-intuitive one. This is hardly surprising. From a very early age we are all repeatedly exposed to a particular story about crime and punishment, which with minor variations forms the basis of the vast majority of crime fiction, 'true crime' stories, and crime journalism. This story goes as follows: Among all the good people in the world (like you and me) there are a few bad people who do all the bad things. As long as they are at large, we are all in danger. Once they are unmasked, caught and punished by being locked away, everything is all right and the problem is permanently solved. We therefore think of the appropriate response to crime as punishment, specifically incarceration, which works because they are no longer free to do the bad things (incapacitation).

This story has a strong hold on our imaginations, but it is only a story. It ignores the blurred lines that exist between 'law-abiding people', occasional offenders and persistent offenders, and fails to take account of the ways in which many people drift into and out of crime, or grow out of it, at different stages in their lives. It falsely stereotypes all offenders as highly dangerous characters who need to be permanently locked away. It ignores the fact that at any one time the vast majority of offenders and ex-offenders are actually at large, and that this would remain the case even if we had a prison population ten times its present size. (Bear in mind that about one British male in three will receive a criminal conviction by the age of 30—although only seven per cent will receive a custodial sentence the way we do things at present[16]—and that many of the rest will have committed crimes without reaching the conviction stage.) And it ignores the fact that even out of those offenders we do imprison, only a tiny fraction of one per cent will stay inside for ever. If we face these facts, then it becomes clear that what we might call the ultimate Strategy A dream—to lock up all offenders for good and throw away the key—can only ever be a fantasy. A potent fantasy nonetheless.

In pure economic terms, the cost of Strategy A is bound to be enormous. The results of the law-and-order environment of recent years are already proving highly expensive. The average revenue cost of keeping an inmate in prison is currently £24,266 per year,[17] and in April 1998 there were 26,000 more prisoners than there were in December 1992. This rise and the projected future rise in the prison population led the previous Conservative government to plan the building of even more new prisons, plans adopted by the incoming Labour administration in 1997. This comes on top of the largest prison building programme of the century, in which 21 new prisons costing £1.2 billion were built between 1980 and 1995. It is an awful lot of public money to spend to bring about what can *at best* only be a small reduction in crime.

So Strategy A is, to say the least, impractical, expensive and ineffective. Trying to pursue it gives rise to other problems as well, not least within the prisons. A strategy which produces overcrowded, understaffed prisons with austere conditions full of prisoners serving longer sentences with no recognition of their rights is asking for trouble in the form of riots and disturbances. Nor is the problem only a question of economic and material resources. As Lord Woolf rightly identified in his formidable report[18] on the riots at Strangeways and other prisons in 1990, prisoners riot out of a sense of injustice over the way they are treated. Further pursuit of Strategy A would inflame this sense of injustice and make more and worse disturbances a near-inevitability. Unrest among prison staff, with ensuing escalating industrial action, would also be a likely consequence. The strategy's disregard for human rights could hardly fail to exacerbate the crucial and widespread 'crisis of legitimacy' which is the source of so many of the problems of the criminal justice system.[19]

And, in case politicians need any further warning about the pitfalls of Strategy A, they may remind themselves that pursuing it is no guarantee of political popularity. Michael Howard was the most Strategy A Home Secretary in recent history, and also the most unpopular. The Conservative government was perceived by the public as being ineffective on crime despite its much-vaunted 'toughness'. Mr Howard's term at the Home Office ended with a landslide defeat for the Conservatives after a General Election campaign in which he seemed to be deliberately sidelined, and in the ensuing election for a new Conservative leader he came fifth out of five candidates. A cautionary tale indeed.

The immorality of Strategy A

These are all, of course, practical arguments. Many people support Strategy A less for practical reasons than for reasons which could be called moral: they think it is right that offenders should suffer, whether or not this reduces crime. Is this a defensible view?

This is not a work of moral philosophy and we shall merely state our own position (as expounded elsewhere)[20] briefly. We do not abjure the use of punishment. To reject 'zero tolerance' it is not necessary to espouse total tolerance, and we do not. We believe that punishment is justifiable if it effectively and efficiently limits the incidence of crime *and also* is 'deserved' in the sense that the punishment serves as an appropriate social condemnation of the wrong which the offender has done. This means, among other things, that the punishment should not be disproportionate to the 'just deserts' of the offender and the seriousness of the offence. Disproportionately severe (or 'undeserved') punishment is an infringement of the offender's human rights because it represents excessive moral condemnation of the offender. On the other hand, punishment which is ineffective also infringes rights because it is a futile and gratuitous infliction of suffering on a human being to no good purpose.

Yet this is exactly what is advocated by the 'moral justification' for Strategy A which we formulated above. This 'pure retributivist' view that offenders should suffer purely because they are felt to deserve it— should be made to suffer *whatever the consequences* of making them suffer—is not only unfounded, but is a profoundly immoral stance. At bottom, it is morally no better than vengeance or (non-consensual) sadism: it is the infliction of hurt and harm simply because we like to see certain people suffer. In fact it is even worse than hurting people for the sake of it; it is making people suffer, even if it makes us all worse off as a result. Which makes it highly irrational as well as immoral.

We have a sufficiently high opinion of most British people to believe that they do not adhere to this 'pure retributivist' position. Most people's attitudes may be at least tinged with retributivism, but they generally favour increased punishment because they think it is needed to reduce crime. If they understood the ineffectiveness of Strategy A, they would also acknowledge its wrongness.

Punishment that is deserved, effective and not excessive is justifiable and right. But Strategy A aims to punish far in excess of this.

STRATEGY B—MANAGERIALISM

Rutherford describes his 'Credo Two' as one whose prevailing concern is 'to dispose of the tasks at hand as smoothly and efficiently as possible. The tenor is one of smooth management rather than of a moral mission'.[21] Credo Two emphasises economisation of resources by maximizing 'throughput' and efficiency generally. Translating this credo into a governmental strategy yields an approach which can be summed up by the word 'managerialism':[22] administrative and bureaucratic mechanisms are applied to criminal justice in an attempt to make the system as smooth-running and cost-effective as possible. Whereas Strategy A embodies hostility to offenders and suspects and a desire to see them suffer, and Strategy C embodies sympathy towards them, the managerialist Strategy B displays a bureaucratic indifference towards them as human beings. Whatever is most resource-efficient is favoured, whether this entails greater harshness or leniency.[23]

Applying managerialism to criminal justice entails auditing and monitoring the system and its component parts and seeking to rationalise it by techniques such as inter-agency work, restructuring of institutions and practitioners' roles and rewards, use of performance indicators and centrally-issued guidance and standards, devolved cash-limited budgets, performance-related pay and so on. It means trying to ensure that what is done in response to crime is as cost-effective as possible, including the rigorous evaluation and application of crime prevention techniques outside the criminal justice system—an *evidence-based* approach. Unlike Strategy A, Strategy B would favour 'softer' and/or reformative measures for offenders, *provided* they were effective enough to represent value for money. What matters is 'what works', and how much it costs. (This should logically mean that more lenient measures—for example, non-custodial treatment programmes—should be preferred even if they were *no more effective* than punitive responses such as custody, provided they were cheaper and therefore more cost-effective.) If a government which believed in Strategy B was also convinced that the private sector of industry is the repository of all wisdom about efficient management, it would doubtless also seek to privatise as much of criminal justice as possible.

One manifestation of managerialism is the 'systems management' approach to criminal justice, an orientation which seeks to monitor and analyse the workings of the criminal justice system as a whole and intervene to shape its workings by means such as inter-agency cooperation and strategic collective pursuit of agreed goals and targets. Systems management perhaps had its greatest successes in the English juvenile justice system in the 1980s, when its adherents brought about a significant reduction in juvenile custody by developing and popularising techniques to divert young offenders out of the formal criminal justice system (for example, by encouraging cautioning as an alternative to prosecution) or from custody at the sentencing stage (by promoting community measures such as intermediate treatment as alternatives to custody). [24]

Governments have taken, encouraged, or at least mooted measures of all these kinds within the criminal justice system in the recent past. Perhaps this was most noticeable when Kenneth Clarke was the Conservative Home Secretary (1992-1993), loudly declaring his belief in the virtues of modern management, and appointing Derek Lewis (a commercial TV executive who had never previously entered a prison) as Director General of the Prison Service. But the 'Hurd approach' which was followed from 1987 until late 1992/early 1993 can also be seen as predominantly managerialist. The 'Leeds Castle moment' of September 1987 was a defining point at which managers within the Home Office convinced government politicians of the pre-eminent need to *manage* both the crime problem and the criminal justice system; and in particular to limit the prison population. Thereafter the Conservative government significantly toned down its Strategy A law and order rhetoric and pursued a mixture of policies and themes including crime prevention, privatisation, amelioration of prison conditions and diversion of offenders from prosecution via increased cautioning and from custody via increased use of non-custodial penalties—an approach which was to be pursued until an electorally embarrassed government dramatically ditched it in favour of a return to Strategy A in 1992/93.

Central to the 'Hurd approach' was the new framework for sentencing contained in the Criminal Justice Act 1991. This Act was by no means an unalloyed embodiment of Strategy B. Its emphasis on the punitive, freedom-restricting elements of court disposals whether custodial or non-custodial 'punishment in the community' linked it to the rhetoric of Strategy A, while its general espousal of the notion of the 'just deserts' philosophy of sentencing meant that it contained a significant Strategy C element. However, we see its main orientation as being managerialist.[25] Its main aim, in the context of developing government policy at the turn of the decade, was the pragmatic one of reducing the prison population. It attempted to achieve this pragmatic goal by laying down nationwide standards for guiding the discretion of decisionmakers (a classic managerialist technique), the standards in this case being legislative provisions and the decisionmakers being judges and magistrates. Viewed in this light, the key provision of the Act was the 'gatekeeping' measure contained in section 1, which prohibited custodial sentences in most cases unless the current offence was 'so serious that only such a sentence can be justified for the offence'.

And, viewed in this managerialist light, the 1991 Act was a failure, if not initially (for the prison population did indeed decrease in the few months following the Act's implementation) then in the longer run. It failed to achieve its goal for a combination of reasons. The judicial decisionmakers proved to be intransigent and unwilling to be guided by the original spirit of the new rules, which (in an attempt to pacify the judiciary) had been framed sufficiently vaguely to enable them to act against their spirit. Probably even more importantly, the government itself explicitly rejected its erstwhile goal and from 1993 encouraged *greater* use of custody. In the prevailing climate sentencers needed little encouragement.

Strategy B is anathema to many who favour Strategy A and would consequently seek to maximise punishment however inefficient and costly this might be. It is often also criticised, sometimes in very absolutist terms, by advocates of the humanitarian Strategy C. Andrew Rutherford, for example, has suggested that threats to human rights are 'more likely to come from the pressures that favour the pragmatic and expedient stance to criminal justice than from the crude assertions of Credo One [Strategy A]'.[26] For such critics, Strategy B is seen as dehumanising in its indifferent bureaucratic attitude to individuals (offenders and victims alike), with the result that rights can be ignored or trampled upon in an unprincipled manner if this is the easy, expedient or cost-effective course of action. Rutherford cites as examples the longstanding reluctance of the Home Office to accept that prisoners have any basic rights, and an instance where a governor, doctors and a prison service director knowingly turned a blind eye to staff brutality against prisoners in the interests of easing the job of management.

In our opinion these criticisms, while valid as a response to the 'ideal-type' Strategy B sketched out so far, fail to acknowledge some important virtues of the managerialist approach. Notions such as 'efficiency' are, after all, *instrumentalist*—about means rather than ends or ultimate values. Critics of managerialism often assume, either that it is necessarily *amoral*, containing an ethical void at the centre where moral values should be, or that its morality is implicitly the philosophy of *utilitarianism*. If either were true then the critics would be right, and managerialism would be unacceptable. There would be no moral or political virtue in a strategy which, as efficiently and cost-effectively as possible, served the interests of politicians or functionaries—and this would, in effect, be the upshot of an amoral version of Strategy B. We would also reject a utilitarian version aimed at efficiently producing the 'greatest happiness of the greatest number'; while this might be all very well for the majority of the population, it implies that the rights of minorities and individuals can be ruthlessly sacrificed in the interests of that majority. A good illustration of this utilitarian approach, which suitably horrified one of Rutherford's interviewees, was Lord Denning's opinion in 1980 that the case of the Birmingham Six should not be reopened because it might expose an 'appalling vista' of malpractice which would decrease public confidence in the police—thus valuing the satisfaction of the general public above the rights of innocent people wrongly convicted.

But managerialism, being instrumentalist, is capable of serving any number of goals or moral values. It could, for example, be used to pursue punitive Strategy A aims—and we shall come across this kind of 'punitive managerialism' in *Chapter 4*. It can also be put to work in the service of human rights or other liberal or humanitarian goals. Nicola Lacey makes a powerful point about the Criminal Justice Act 1991 when she attributes its failure to the government's predominantly managerial attitude to it and the 'failure to argue for the Act on the basis of values— the values of a less extensive prison system, of fairness to poorer defendants, of avoiding the socially divisive effects of an ever-growing criminal justice system'. Yet she rightly points out that, whatever one's values, there can be an important rôle for managerialism when trying to put values into effect by means of the state and its agencies: 'Government and its satellites and agencies are involved in the provision of services, and efficiency in this delivery is not an irrelevance from either a political or a humanitarian point of view.'[27] If we are concerned about human rights, then we should want the state to protect rights effectively and efficiently. There is nothing to be said for wasting public resources which could be used to enhance and promote human rights on measures which do not work, whether those measures are supposed to be punitive, deterrent or even reparative or reformative. What works, and how well it works, should be of concern to all.

We have already mentioned an outstanding example of what looks very much like Strategy B employed for humanitarian ends. This is the 'systems management' approach to youth justice which was developed and deployed to particularly great effect in England in the 1980s, and whose adherents continue to do their best in the more discouraging climate of today. Systems management uses many techniques (and indeed much of the jargon) associated with managerialism: inter-agency cooperation, targeting, monitoring, systems analysis etc. Yet all of this is in the pursuit of the humane goal of reducing the numbers of young people in custody. And—at least for a time, prior to the government's lurch towards Strategy A in the 1990s—it worked. By contrast, systems managers demonstrated that the sincere but less rigorously monitored efforts of many caring practitioners had previously had the effect of *increasing* the numbers in custody and care.[28] A good heart is indeed not enough; good organization and management are also vital.

This is not to say we subscribe wholesale to all the fashionable nostrums which comprise 'modern management techniques'; indeed we suspect that many of them if properly evaluated would prove to be counter-productive precisely because of the utilitarian and insensitive management strategies they are often associated with. For example, some systems of performance-related rewards for individuals can make the organization as a whole less efficient by diminishing staff morale, solidarity and cooperation within the corporate body. The managerialism of Strategy B is only acceptable—and, we suspect, can only succeed even on its own terms—if it is used as a means of pursuing Strategy C.

STRATEGY C—HUMAN RIGHTS

Rutherford's 'Credo Three' is almost the diametrical opposite of Credo One. It embodies 'empathy with suspects and offenders and the victims of crime, optimism that constructive work can be done with offenders, adherence to the rule of law so as to restrict state powers, and an insistence on open and accountable procedures.'[29] Human rights—of victims as well as offenders—are central to this credo, which seeks to minimise punishment and ensure fairness and due process within the criminal justice system. This approach should be espoused because it is inherently morally right; but it also has the advantage that an injection of genuine justice into the criminal justice system should have the effect of alleviating the crippling 'crisis of legitimacy'—the pervading sense of injustice—which lies at the root of so many of the system's problems.[30]

A corresponding governmental strategy would seek to reduce levels of punishment, and most importantly the number and length of custodial sentences. It would involve vigilant scrutiny of the threats to individual liberty posed by police powers and put in place effective due process safeguards against the occurrence and continuance of miscarriages of justice. It would ensure humane and just treatment of prisoners and other penal subjects. It would place human rights—of suspects, offenders, victims and (often overlooked) the personnel of the criminal justice system—at the centre of criminal justice policy.

It would be unfair to say that governments have never tried to further the cause of human rights within criminal justice. The 'Hurd approach' of 1987-1992 contained substantial elements of Strategy C, including a legislative framework for sentencing based on the philosophy of 'just deserts' (discussed shortly), attempts to limit the number of custodial sentences, and a programme to ameliorate conditions within prisons following the recommendations of Lord Justice Woolf's report[31] published in 1991. Positive developments in this respect have included significant improvements in most prisoners' ability to communicate with the outside world, action to end the long-running scandal of 'slopping out' and the creation of the Prisons Ombudsman. But Strategy C has never been central to governmental criminal justice policy. When pursued at all, it has always been combined with Strategies A and B in such a manner as to negate any notion that human rights and moral legitimacy are truly at the heart of the government's approach. At best it has provided a legitimating gloss to a pragmatic and philosophically incoherent package of measures.

There are different and competing views about exactly what rights human beings have and about the implications this should have for a Strategy C approach to criminal justice. Rutherford's Credo Three encompasses some significantly varying schools of penological thought, notably advocates of *reform* (or rehabilitation), '*just deserts*' and *restorative justice*; schools with quite different ideas about what humanitarianism entails. We shall say a word about each.

The humane approach to criminal justice is probably still associated in most people's minds with the wish to *reform* offenders—to provide them with positive training or treatment (usually, if not necessarily accurately, envisaged as being invariably 'softer' than punitive measures) which it is hoped will encourage them to behave better in future. The reformative orientation famously suffered a severe blow in the 1970s with what is called 'the collapse of the rehabilitative ideal' and the rise to prominence in official and much unofficial thinking of the notion that *'nothing works'* to reform offenders. Although the heyday of blithe 'rehabilitative optimism' in the 1960s is unlikely to return, there is nevertheless growing interest in the idea that *'something works'*, and that research is uncovering promising methods and techniques which, if applied systematically and well, can make a real difference to the likelihood of offenders reoffending. For ourselves, we are less than totally convinced by some of the bolder recent claims of reformative efficacy, but there are indeed hopeful signs that some kinds of treatment programme may really work with some offenders.[32]

Another version of Strategy C—and the one which we particularly favour—goes under the name *restorative justice*. This is the movement which seeks to respond to crime with positive measures whereby offenders make reparation for the harm they have done and both offenders and victims are reconciled with the community as a whole.[33] Restorative justice encompasses measures such as mediation, whereby offenders communicate with the victims of their crimes (as long as the victims are willing to participate) and an attempt is made to reach agreement on what reparation the offender should make. Restoration is seen as upholding the rights of both offenders and victims, whether or not it also has the desirable effect of making the offender less likely to commit crimes in the future.

A third variation of Strategy C is the *'just deserts'*[34] school of thought. This approach is sceptical about reforming offenders, and is highly conscious that enforced 'treatment' can be as oppressive as anything that is overtly labelled as punishment—indeed, can be more oppressive if the rhetoric of reform is used to legitimate intrusive treatments which are completely out of proportion to the seriousness of the offence. (As in the proverbial example of the child who is removed from home indefinitely on the grounds that this is what the child 'needs', having only stolen a chocolate bar.)[35] Consequently, this approach demands that all compulsory measures applied to offenders should be justified as *deserved punishment*, punishment which should be strictly proportional to the seriousness of the offence. A thoroughgoing application of this doctrine would probably rule out not only most attempts to reform offenders, but also many components of the 'restorative justice' approach. For example, those restorative projects which seek to foster mediated agreements between offenders and victims about exactly what and how much reparation the offender should perform for the victim are unlikely always to lead to strictly proportional results.

Our own view is that this is over-purist, and that a government pursuing Strategy C should favour a limited 'just deserts' doctrine which permits enthusiastic encouragement of both promising attempts to pursue reform of offenders and moves towards restorative justice, within a general framework of (limited and flexible) proportionality. This is not the place to argue the philosophy underlying this 'eclectic' version of Strategy C, although we have done so elsewhere.[36] One practical advantage of this eclecticism—which should commend itself to government and criminal justice managers—is that it allows a wide range of practices, and of pilot projects which can be duly monitored and evaluated for effectiveness in both reformative and restorative justice, and could give rise to a wide range of differing non-custodial options most or all of which are likely to be cheaper than custody.

THE COMMUNITARIAN PERSPECTIVE

The 'New Labour' government—especially in the persons of Prime Minister Tony Blair and Home Secretary Jack Straw—has shown itself to be attracted towards the philosophy of 'communitarianism'.[37] What is communitarianism, and what is its relationship to the strategies we have mapped out (in particular Strategy C)?

Communitarianism is a philosophy which can be seen as a third way between extreme collectivism and extreme individualism. It recognises that humans are intrinsically social beings who live and can only flourish within human communities: that there is indeed (contrary to Margaret Thatcher's famous dictum) such a thing as society, and that the communal well-being of society must be cherished and fostered. Individuals not only have rights owed to them by society and the state; they also have important responsibilities to uphold the common good and not merely pursue their own personal selfish interests. With all this we are entirely in agreement; indeed, in our own advocacy of restorative justice we have elsewhere stated our preference for a 'communitarian' version which seeks to involve the wider community in the process of restoration and not view it simply as a privatised business between individual victims and individual offenders.[38]

We would enter a caveat, however.[39] Communitarianism comes in different forms, ranging along a continuum between more liberal and more authoritarian versions of the doctrine. The more authoritarian forms accord the 'community' rights equal or even superior to those of all the human individuals who comprise it, and stray towards the effective rejection of individual rights in favour of the claims of the community. This is tantamount to a collectivism or utilitarianism whose moral unacceptability we have already noted. The danger is that the concept of 'community' can lend a spurious legitimacy to all kinds of illiberal attitudes and policies if it is taken to mean that the (assumed) wishes or prejudices of the majority of the population must always be allowed to take precedence over the rights and interests of (doubtless unpopular) minority groups or individuals.

Related to this liberal/authoritarian dimension is a slightly different distinction, between *inclusionary* and *exclusionary* approaches to society and its individual citizens. This distinction has been well summarised by David Faulkner, formerly a senior civil servant at the Home Office and one of the principal architects of the reform package centred around the Criminal Justice Act 1991, as follows:[40]

> The "exclusive" view emphasises personal freedom and individual responsibility but is inclined to disregard the influence of situations and circumstances. It distinguishes between a deserving majority who are self-reliant and law-abiding and entitled to benefit themselves and those around them without interference from others, and an undeserving, feckless, welfare-dependent and potentially criminal minority — or under-class — from whom they need to be protected . . . The contrasting "inclusive" view . . . recognises the capacity and will of individuals to change — to improve if they are given guidance, help and encouragement; to be damaged if they are abused or humiliated. It emphasises respect for human dignity and personal identity, and a sense of public duty and social responsibility. It looks more towards putting things right for the future than to allocating blame and awarding punishment, although the latter may sometimes be part of the former.

The exclusionary mind-set can be allied to a form of 'communitarianism' which cares only for 'people like us', the relatively comfortable and non-deviant majority of the community, and demands that everyone abides by their norms and culture. Those who do not are scapegoated—blamed for all the evils which befall society—written off and effectively excluded from the community, either physically by placing them behind prison walls or more subtly by denying them any opportunity to participate in the life of mainstream society. Society does not have to bend, compromise or help the deviant, who is kept under control by the threat of force and by the fact of exclusion itself. An inclusionary communitarianism, on the other hand, would seek to maintain the deviant within the community of citizenship, certainly applying such sanctions as are necessary to protect other citizens, but at the same time seeking to engage with deviants as moral agents, attempting to help, correct and reintegrate them into the wider community.

Within the field of criminology, this kind of inclusionary communitarianism is expressed by John Braithwaite's theory of 'reintegrative shaming'.[41] Braithwaite argues that successful societal responses to crime are those which bring about the *reintegrative shaming* of the offender. Offenders should be dealt with in a manner that shames them before other members of their community. But the shaming should not be of a 'stigmatising' nature which will tend to exclude them from being accepted members of the community; it should be of a kind which serves to reintegrate them within it, by getting them to accept that they have done wrong while encouraging others to readmit them to society. In principle, measures associated with restorative justice ought to be particularly suitable vehicles for the pursuit of reintegrative shaming, for the performance of reparation shames the offender symbolically while seeking to set matters right between the offender, the victim and the community.[42]

The implications of inclusionary communitarianism for the problem of crime go wider than this. If the philosophy were to be applied effectively outside the criminal justice system as well as inside, to fields of social policy such as housing and employment policy, there are good reasons to believe that among its other benefits it could have an important 'social crime prevention' effect. If Braithwaite's analysis is accurate, a society in which all citizens are genuinely valued and treated accordingly will be a more cohesive society (albeit a pluralistic one which accepts a variety of cultures and subcultures), a 'society at ease with itself'. As such, it is likely to suffer less from problems such as crime, which have their roots in social dislocation, fragmentation, insecurity and alienation.[43]

But there is a danger that 'communitarianism', if it takes an exclusionary and authoritarian form, could be used as a façade for illiberal populism. The logical result for criminal justice would be Strategy A. We fear that we detect echoes of this in (for example) the present government's early enthusiasm for the slogan of 'zero tolerance' and some of the policies associated with that slogan. We hope and believe, however, that the general philosophy of New Labour is more consonant with a liberal and inclusionary version of communitarianism—as evidenced, for example, by the Labour government's early establishment of a Social Exclusion Unit to combat the problems of excluded sections of the population. This kind of communitarianism would seek not only to reassure the majority of law-abiding citizens that the problem of crime is being effectively addressed, but also to treat deviant citizens fairly and humanely and try to rehabilitate them and restore them to membership of a healed and inclusive community. This requires a central respect for the human rights of every individual citizen, and an important place for all three strands of Strategy C—justice, reform and (especially) restoration—which we identified above.

CONCLUSIONS: WHAT DO WE WANT FROM CRIMINAL JUSTICE POLICY?

We saw earlier that—unpopular and counter-intuitive though this conclusion may be—varying levels of punishment can have little part to play in 'fighting crime'. This is not to say, however, that nothing can be done about crime, let alone that there is no need to reform criminal justice policy. We advocate a complete rejection of the destructive punitive fantasy embodied in Strategy A and the pursuit of a judicious and principled amalgam of Strategies B and C. Human rights—those of victims, offenders and even criminal justice practitioners—must be respected as a central hub of government policy as we move towards the new century. In pursuit of this essentially moral purpose it is necessary to be practical, efficient and effective, taking steps to discover what measures work and putting them into practice.

We can distil this preferred strategy into a series of general recommendations:

1. *We should cease to look to severity of punishment to control crime*

It is of course the main objective of criminal justice to control crime, which needs to be prevented, deterred and denounced. Punishment is necessary, and custodial punishment is necessary for some (most obviously, for those who are for the moment too dangerous to release). But beyond a certain point—and we are already far, far beyond it—increasing the severity of punishment is, as we have seen, an extremely ineffective and wasteful method of crime control. We are engaging in overkill. We should instead adopt a principle of '*parsimony*',[44] seeking to keep punishment—and especially custodial punishment—to a minimum, not only because it is uneconomic (a Strategy B reason) but because it is inhumane and wrong to punish more than is necessary (a Strategy C reason). For both these reasons, the government should aim to reduce our current severely inflated levels of punishment—and especially of imprisonment—significantly.

This is not soppy idealism. On the contrary, it is *penological realism* to recognise that the criminal justice system can on its own do relatively little to control crime, and that if it punished less it would be doing its job more efficiently.

2. *In seeking to reduce crime, we should look primarily to measures of crime prevention outside the criminal justice system*

The evaluation and application of crime prevention techniques are regrettably still in their early days, having been relatively neglected by governments until now, but there is already abundant evidence that certain types of crime prevention scheme can effectively reduce crime far more efficiently and cheaply than punishment typically does.[45] There is scope to go much further in the pursuit of crime prevention. In this, as with other areas of policy, government and criminal justice managers should employ (as Strategy B would suggest) scientific research methods to establish 'what works' and to apply the lessons learnt, as part of a rational 'evidence-based' policy.

In addition to employing this kind of approach to crime prevention in its more narrow sense, government would do well (for other reasons as well) to pursue general policies to foster 'social inclusion' rather than exclusion, for this seems likely to prove the best 'crime prevention' of all.

3. *Sanctions for those who offend should wherever possible take place within a framework of restorative justice, seeking to repair the relations between offenders, victims and the community*
This is also in line with the philosophy of 'inclusionary communitarianism' we discussed earlier.

4. *Where punishments are used, they should not be disproportionate to the seriousness of offences; but there should be sufficient flexibility to allow for mitigation, reform and reparation*
Respect for human rights requires that punishments are not disproportionate; but we should also seek to rehabilitate offenders and get them to make amends for the wrong they have done to victims and to the community. Again, it is only rational to pursue an 'evidence-based' approach, carrying out research and monitoring of reformative and restorative projects to develop measures which work effectively.

5. *Government should seek to work in partnership with criminal justice agencies and foster inter-agency cooperation*
Inter-agency cooperation is usually thought of as part of a 'systems management' or Strategy B approach—and none the worse for that, holding out as it does the promise of more effective and efficient operation of the criminal justice system as a whole if its component parts can be encouraged to work together in pursuit of jointly agreed goals. But inter-agency work also has a human rights, Strategy C aspect. Practitioners within the criminal justice system also need to be consulted and treated with respect; a partnership approach should lend legitimacy to the government's strategy which may also assist in operationalising policies more successfully. In recent years, the relationship between government and many criminal justice practitioners has been at a disturbingly low point, with high levels of dissatisfaction among practitioners about the current workings of the system and the changes

to it which government has repeatedly imposed with what has been perceived as inadequate consultation with those who have to implement those changes.[46] A more gentle and cooperative approach towards those who work in the system as well as to those who are on its receiving end would be welcome for both practical and principled reasons.

LOVE ME TENDER, LOVE ME TOUGH: A POSTSCRIPT ON BEING TOUGH

Our new society will have the same values as ever. It should be a compassionate society, but it is compassion with a hard edge. (Tony Blair, speech to Labour Conference, 30 September 1997)

We will be tough on crime and tough on the causes of crime. (Labour Party Manifesto, 1997)

On taking power in the summer of 1997, the new Labour government found that the penal system was in a far worse and more rapidly deteriorating state than they had imagined. The prison population continued to rocket upwards at a much faster rate than had been officially predicted even in April of that year. The government's response in July 1997 was not to take immediate steps to reduce the prison population but to allocate an extra £43 million of public money to the prison service in 1997 and 1998 to accommodate the rising numbers,[47] while in June 1997 Home Secretary Jack Straw had also gone back on previous Labour policy by announcing that more 'private prisons' would be built. Mr Straw's justification for these moves included the consideration that he had promised to be tough on crime and consequently felt constrained not to take actions which might be seen as being soft on crime.[48]

In our opinion there is nothing wrong with being tough, as long as it is the right sort of 'toughness'—which this isn't. We should distinguish between being *hard-hearted* and being *hard-headed*. To be hard-hearted is not to care about the suffering of offenders or even victims of crime, and indeed to positively favour the infliction of suffering on the former. But it is both possible and right to be 'tender-hearted' in this sense while at the same time being hard-*headed* about how we can effectively deal with crime and being willing to impose penalties on offenders when these are justified. The moral and practical bankruptcy of Strategy A (as pursued by Michael Howard) stems from the fact that it gets these two completely the wrong way round, being at the same time hard-hearted and soft-headed. In its eagerness to provide severe punishment it ignores the evidence of its ineffectiveness as well as failing to care sufficiently about either offenders or the welfare of victims.

Apart from Strategy A, there are three other logical combinations of these two dimensions (as shown diagrammatically in *Figure 2.1*), giving a total of four different positions on 'law and order'. What might be caricatured as a 'woolly liberal' approach to crime and punishment would combine soft-heartedness with (alas) soft-headedness: the benign but naive prison officer Mr Barrowclough in the 1970s television comedy *Porridge* portrays this stereotype well. In the diagonally opposite cell, a ruthless amalgam of Strategies A and B would be both hard-hearted and hard-headed, seeking to punish to as great an extent as was pragmatically viable: we would call this 'punitive managerialism'. On the other hand, our recommended blend of Strategies B and C provides what we regard as the ideal combination of 'tender-heartedness' and 'hard-headedness'.

	HARD-HEADED	SOFT-HEADED
HARD-HEARTED	STRATEGY A combined with STRATEGY B (punitive managerialism)	STRATEGY A (M Howard)
TENDER-HEARTED	STRATEGY B combined with STRATEGY C (Our preference)	'Woolly liberal' (Mr Barrowclough)

Figure 2.1 Four positions on law and order

It may be worth a brief consideration of the meaning of the word 'tough' in the prominent New Labour slogan (first coined by Tony Blair when Shadow Home Secretary in 1992) 'tough on crime, tough on the causes of crime'. 'Tough on the causes of crime' can only mean 'tough-*headed*': the determined pursuit of policies on the economy, employment, housing and the family which seem likely to reduce the incidence of crime. This 'social crime prevention' approach can only be applauded, at least in general terms, especially if it takes the form of fostering 'social inclusion'. 'Tough on crime' is more ambiguous. No doubt for deliberate electoral reasons, the phrase carries overtones of being 'tough' on *criminals*—of being hard-hearted towards offenders as well as being hard-headed about crime reduction. But, despite New Labour's espousal of a variety of specific measures (such as semi-mandatory penalties for repeat offenders, discussed in *Chapter 3*) which do indeed represent harsher punishment for offenders, and despite what must have been severe temptation to do so, Labour has never amended its slogan to 'tough on criminals', nor has it espoused Michael Howard's claim that 'prison works'. Indeed, prior to the 1997 General Election, the Conservatives attempted to make political capital out of this very point, with Michael Howard telling the 1995 Tory Conference: 'You can't be tough on crime unless you're tough on the criminals.'

Although we can hardly deny that New Labour's attitude to law and order has so far proved to be significantly more hard-hearted than we would like, the general philosophy of 'compassion with a hard edge' which Tony Blair has commended to the country should fit best with the tough-minded but tender-hearted position we advocate. This is still a 'tough on crime' policy—and should be politically saleable as such by a principled and self-confident government—but it is toughness of the right sort.

ENDNOTES: *Chapter 2*

1 Andrew Rutherford, *Criminal Justice and the Pursuit of Decency* (Oxford, Oxford University Press, 1993; reprinted Winchester, Waterside Press, 1994).

2 ibid., p. 11.

3 Michael Cavadino and James Dignan, *The Penal System: An Introduction*, 2nd edn (London, Sage Publications, 1997).

4 Anthony Bottoms, 'The Philosophy and Politics of Punishment and Sentencing', in Chris Clarkson and Rod Morgan (eds), *The Politics of Sentencing Reform* (Oxford, Clarendon Press, 1995).

5 Mr Blair first used this phrase in a radio debate with the then Home Secretary Kenneth Clarke in 1992, and used it repeatedly thereafter. It was prominent in the Labour Party's General Election manifesto for 1997, *New Labour: Because Britain Deserves Better*.

6 Note, however, that research has repeatedly demonstrated that such opinion poll responses are based on misconceived notions about typical levels of punishments. Members of the public receive distorted images (for example, from outraged media reports of genuine or alleged instances of over-lenient sentences) and as a result think punishments are generally too soft. Their own suggested punishments, however, are in line with those actually passed by the courts. See e.g. Michael Hough and Julian Roberts, *Attitudes to*

Punishment: Findings from the British Crime Survey, Home Office Research Study No 179 (London, Home Office, 1988).

[7] Roger Tarling, *Analysing Offending: Data, Models and Interpretations*. (London, HMSO, 1993): 154.

[8] See further Cavadino and Dignan, op. cit., pp. 33-39.

[9] See e.g. Warren Young, 'Influences Upon the Use of Imprisonment: A Review of the Literature', *Howard Journal of Criminal Justice*, 25 (1986): 125-36, pp 126-7.

[10] Catriona Mirrlees-Black, Pat Mayhew and Andrew Percy, *The 1996 British Crime Survey, England and Wales*, Home Office Statistical Bulletin 19/96. The BCS measures crime by interviewing a large national sample of the population to discover what crimes they have been victims of, whether or not they have reported these to the police or the police have officially recorded them. The 1996 BCS estimated that only 41 per cent of the crimes it counted in 1995 were reported to the police and only 50 per cent of those reported were recorded.

[11] The relevant statistics can be found in *NACRO Digest*, October 1995 and February 1997 and the *Prison Statistics England and Wales 1995*, Cm 3335 (London, HMSO, 1996). The case of Greece was pointed out in a letter published in *The Guardian* of 4 April 1997 by David Downes.

[12] In 1974 there were 218,205 prisoners in state and federal prisons in the US; on 30 June 1995 there were 1,104,074. To this must be added around a half million more inmates in local jails (483,717 on 30 June 1994, up from 141,588 in 1972). By 1998, a total of 1,800,000 people were incarcerated in the US.

[13] See for example the article by American 'right-wing guru' Charles Murray, 'The Ruthless Truth: Prison Works', *Sunday Times*, 12 January 1997. The fact that, according to this argument, the reduction in crime did not kick in until *six years* after punishment levels started increasing should put us on guard, especially given the brevity of many offenders' 'criminal careers'. Also embarrassing for proponents of the 'prison works' theory is the *rise* in recorded crime in the US in the late 1980s.

[14] See Simon Field, *Trends in Crime and their Interpretation: A Study of Recorded Crime in Post War England and Wales*, Home Office Research Study No. 119 (London, HMSO, 1990).

[15] Howard Parker and Tim Bottomley, *Crack Cocaine and Drugs-Crime Careers* (London, Home Office, 1996).

[16] *Criminal Statistics, England and Wales 1994*, Cm 3010 (London, HMSO, 1995), ch. 9. By age 40, fully 40 per cent of males have a criminal record for a non-motoring offence (Hough and Julian Roberts, op. cit., p. 11.)

[17] *Prison Service Annual Report and Accounts April 1996-March 1997* (London, The Stationery Office, 1997).

[18] Lord Woolf and Judge Stephen Tumim, *Prison Disturbances April 1990*, Cm 1456 (London, HMSO, 1991).

[19] Cavadino and Dignan, op. cit., especially chs. 1 and 11.

[20] See ibid., ch. 2 and Michael Cavadino, *The Law of Gravity: Offence Seriousness and Criminal Justice* (Sheffield: Joint Unit for Social Services Research), ch. 2

for summaries of penal philosophy and fuller statements of our preferred 'human rights' position.

[21] Rutherford, op. cit., p. 13.

[22] See Bottoms, op. cit; Cavadino and Dignan, op. cit., p. 37.

[23] We speak here in very general terms. As we shall see in *Chapter 4,* there are various versions of 'managerialism': we distinguish there between 'technocratic', 'consumerist', 'systemic' and 'punitive' managerialisms, concepts which refer to managerialism used as a means towards a variety of ends. 'Punitive managerialism', for example, denotes the deployment of managerial techniques in the service of Strategy A.

[24] See Cavadino and Dignan, op. cit., pp. 254-61, and *Chapter 7* below.

[25] Cf. the analysis of Nicola Lacey, 'Government as Manager, Citizen as Consumer: The Case of the Criminal Justice Act 1991' *Modern Law Review*, 57 (1994), 534-554.

[26] Rutherford, op. cit., p. 18.

[27] Nicola Lacey, op. cit., pp. 552-3.

[28] David Thorpe, David Smith, Chris Green and John Paley, *Out of Care: The Community Support of Juvenile Offenders* (London, George Allen and Unwin, 1980), chs. 1 and 4.

[29] Rutherford, op. cit., p. 18.

[30] Cavadino and Dignan, op. cit., especially chs. 1 and 11.

[31] op. cit.

[32] See further Cavadino and Dignan, op. cit., pp. 36-7.

[33] See James Dignan and Michael Cavadino, 'Towards a Framework for Conceptualising and Evaluating Models of Criminal Justice from a Victim's Perspective', *International Review of Victimology*, 4 (1996): 153-82. Another term that is sometimes used in this context is 'relational justice': see, e.g. Jonathan Burnside and Nicola Baker, *Relational Justice: Repairing the Breach* (Winchester, Waterside Press, 1994). For the purposes of the present discussion the two terms can be treated as synonymous. The same can be said of the terms 'positive justice' (Philip Priestley, 'The Victim Connection and Penal Reform', Bromsgrove, Speech to Margaret Fry Centenary Proceedings, unpublished) and 'communitarian justice' (see e.g. David Moore and Terry O'Connell, 'Family Conferencing in Wagga Wagga: a Communitarian Model of Justice' in Christine Alder and Joy Wundersitz (eds.), *Family Conferencing and Juvenile Justice: the Way Forward or Misplaced Optimism?* Canberra, Australian Institute of Criminology, 1994).

[34] Cavadino and Dignan, op. cit., pp. 49-51.

[35] This is not just a fanciful hypothetical example; such things do happen in systems dominated by welfarism and the notion of reform. The victims of such systems include the comedy actor Neil Morrissey (of 'Men Behaving Badly') and his brothers who were sent away indefinitely to separate children's homes in the early 1970s when Neil was ten because of their relatively petty property crimes (*The Guardian*, 11 July 1998). The juvenile justice legislation in force at the time was the supposedly liberal and enlightened Children and Young Person Act 1969.

[36] See further Michael Cavadino and James Dignan 'Reparation, Retribution and Rights', *International Review of Victimology*, 4 (1997), 233-53.

[37] See e.g. Amitai Etzioni, *The Spirit of Community: Rights, Responsibilities and the Communitarian Agenda* (London, Fontana Press, 1995). Tony Blair is said to have been particularly influenced by the Scottish theologian John Macmurray (see e.g. his *Persons in Relation*, London, Faber, 1961). See also Gordon Hughes, 'Communitarianism and Law and Order', *Critical Social Policy*, 16 (1996): 17-41; Bill Jordan and Jon Arnold, 'Democracy and Criminal Justice', *Critical Social Policy*, 44/45 (1995): 170-82; Steven Driver and Luke Martell, 'New Labour's Communitarianisms', *Critical Social Policy*, 17 (1997), 27-46.

[38] Dignan and Cavadino, op. cit.

[39] See further Michael Cavadino, 'A Vindication of the Rights of Psychiatric Patients', *Journal of Law and Society*, 24 (1997): 235-51.

[40] David Faulkner, *Darkness and Light: Justice, Crime and Management for Today* (London, Howard League, 1996), 5-6.

[41] John Braithwaite, *Crime, Shame and Reintegration* (Cambridge, Cambridge University Press, 1989).

[42] See James Dignan, 'Reintegration Through Reparation: A Way Forward for Restorative Justice?', in Anthony Duff, Sandra Marshall, Rebecca Dobash and Russell Dobash (eds.), *Penal Theory and Penal Practice: Tradition and Innovation in Criminal Justice* (Manchester, Manchester University Press, 1994), 231-244.

[43] See also James Dignan, 'Restorative Crime Prevention in Theory and Practice', *Prison Service Journal* 123 (1999), 2-5. Cf. the arguments of Paul Ormerod ('Stopping Crime Spreading', *New Economy*, 4, 1997: 83-88). Ormerod notes that societies with relatively low crime rates such as 'Britain in the 1930s and many rural areas in the Third World today are examples of societies which possess strong community relationships. In turn, these both foster a sense of belonging and provide . . . the setting in which informal social sanctions against aggression and crime can operate effectively.'

[44] See Cavadino and Dignan, op. cit., pp. 35, 54.

[45] See e.g. Ken Pease, 'Crime Prevention' in Mike Maguire, Rod Morgan and Robert Reiner (eds), *The Oxford Handbook of Criminology*, 2nd edn. (Oxford, Clarendon Press, 1997), 963-95. It has been estimated that the money spent on the right kind of crime prevention programme can prevent burglaries costing victim and state 3.67 times as much. But it costs at least £1 to prevent 36p worth of burglary by imprisoning burglars (Helen Edwards of NACRO, quoted in *New Law Journal*, 5 September 1997, p.1266). Cf. the calculation in Peter Goldblatt and Chris Lewis (eds.), *Reducing Offending: An Assessment of Research Evidence on Ways of Dealing with Offending Behaviour*, Home Office Research Study No. 187 (London, Home Office, 1998), 135. This report estimated that spending £38 million on burglary prevention for the ten per cent of households most at risk would cut burglary by 5.5 per cent and recorded crime by 0.6 per cent, saving £95 million. By contrast, to achieve

the same crime reduction through increases in the prison population would cost £380 million—ten times as much—per year.

46 Iain Crow, Anne Celnick, Clare Palmer and Paul Wiles, *Attitudes to Criminal Justice: The Results of the South Yorkshire Study* (University of Sheffield, 1995).

47 A further £70 million was allocated to the Prison Service in February 1998, and a massive extra £660 milliion in July 1998 following the government's Comprehensive Spending Review.

48 Interview with Jack Straw MP, *Inside*, BBC2, 2 November 1997.

CHAPTER 3

Sentencing Strategies for a New Century?

Sentencing plays a crucial role in determining the size of the prison population, which is chiefly influenced by the rate at which the courts (and particularly the Crown Court) impose custodial sentences, the average lengths of those custodial sentences, and the number of offenders coming before the courts.[1] All but the last item are factors for which the sentencing decisions of the courts are directly responsible. Moreover, sentencing decisions are also the source of considerable injustice (both perceived and real) on account of the enormous disparities that regularly come to light in both the *rate* of custody and the *average lengths* of prison sentences that are imposed by courts in different parts of the country.[2]

In this chapter we will mainly concentrate on sentencing policy, though we will also comment briefly on policies regulating the procedure for determining when an offender should be released since these are also closely bound up with the sentencing process, not least in respect of their impact on prison numbers. We will begin by reviewing sentencing strategies that have been tried in the past and also possible alternative approaches, before assessing the prospects for the emergence of a more rational and constructive sentencing policy.

LAISSEZ FAIRE: LESS FAIR, LESS EFFECTIVE AND LESS EFFICIENT: THE SENTENCING POLICY VACUUM PRIOR TO 1979

For much of the post-war period preceding the 1979 general election, sentencing policy was largely characterised by a *laissez faire* approach. As in most other common law jurisdictions at the time, successive British governments had in effect conceded to the judiciary responsibility not only for the sentencing of individual offenders but also, if only by default, for determining sentencing policy at a more strategic level. This 'hands-off' approach on the part of elected politicians represented a tacit acceptance of the rather sweeping gloss that British judges had traditionally given to the age-old doctrine of judicial independence, which manifested itself in a judicial dislike of any restrictions at all on their sentencing discretion.[3]

Paradoxically, however, the effect of this uncharacteristic self-denying ordinance on the part of the legislature was to preclude the formulation of *any* sentencing policy, at least in the sense of articulating a coherent set of principles intended to guide the decision-making process of individual sentencers. For one thing, there was no greater consensus among senior members of the judiciary than among politicians of the day or the public at large as to what coherent rationale for the punishment of offenders might replace the once-paramount 'treatment ethic' (see *Chapter 1*). This lack of judicial consensus was reflected most strikingly in a Court of Appeal judgment[4] which explicitly endorsed each of the four traditional main aims of sentencing (retribution, deterrence, prevention and reform) despite their apparent incompatibility.

Even if there had been a greater degree of consensus, however, the English judiciary were neither constitutionally entitled nor functionally equipped to assume a more general policy-making role. Indeed, there was no institutional forum—apart from the Court of Appeal—in which general sentencing policies might be articulated by the senior judiciary. Nor, probably, were they temperamentally inclined to assume such a role. For even at its most innovative, the closest the Court of Appeal came to issuing general policy pronouncements was in developing the concept of 'guideline judgments', which attempted to provide more detailed and systematic guidance for sentencers by suggesting what the appropriate penalty might be in a variety of circumstances instead of just confining itself to the particular facts of the case. But not even these judgments could claim to provide comprehensive guidance, since their scope was still constrained to a considerable extent by the facts and circumstances of the cases in which they were articulated. And even if they had worked as intended, they would almost certainly have inflated general sentencing levels, since the (largely informal) 'sentencing tariff' that is applied by the Court of Appeal is higher than that in the Crown Court (which in turn is higher than the one used by magistrates).[5]

The absence of a coherent sentencing policy had a number of unfortunate consequences which were likely to render such an approach unacceptable to proponents of each of the three main strategies we are considering in this book, albeit for very different reasons. One highly predictable effect of the sentencing policy vacuum that persisted during the 1970s and beyond was that the decision-making process itself was both highly discretionary in nature and relatively unconstrained by either external (legislative) controls or internal (judicial) forms of self-regulation. In the absence of any judicial consensus regarding the main aims of punishment during the 1970s and 1980s, it is not surprising that successive investigations[6] reported high levels of disparity in the way offenders were dealt with by courts in different parts of the country. This in turn raised concerns among civil libertarians and others, who invoked neo-retributive arguments based on the increasingly influential 'just deserts' philosophy in arguing that 'like cases should be treated alike'. The growing perception that contemporary sentencing practices were *unfair* in their widely differing impact on 'like' offenders was further fuelled by research findings[7] which suggested that sentencing patterns might also reflect an ethnic disparity in the way offenders of different races are dealt with by the criminal justice system. These moral and political concerns formed the basis of a coherent 'Strategy C' critique against the *laissez faire* approach of the 1970s.

From a rather different perspective, *laissez faire* was also found wanting by Strategy A proponents, some of whom came to believe that a more consistently tough 'law and order' approach would be preferable to the inconsistent, perhaps even amateurish decision-making process favoured by sentencers. To those of a more punitive persuasion, which included many newly elected Conservative MPs in the 1979 Parliament, some sentencing decisions appeared irresponsibly lenient—particularly in respect of more serious or persistent offenders. In the immediate aftermath of the 1979 General Election, however, the prominence that had been given to 'law and order' issues in the run-up to the campaign was mainly reflected in the dramatic increase in public expenditure on prisons and the police which was sustained for most of the next decade. In the field of sentencing reform, law and order impulses were for the moment restricted to the revival of the 'short sharp shock' approach for young offenders' detention centres. However, this flirtation with a more punitive approach for young offenders was at the same time counter-balanced by a variety of other sentencing reforms (for example the shortening of detention centre sentences, and the introduction of criteria for the imprisonment of young offenders) which stemmed from several very different ideological stand-points. At this early stage in the long period of Conservative rule the hey-day for Strategy A was still to come.

Meanwhile, a far more serious problem which stemmed directly from the *laissez faire* approach to sentencing policy was that it left policy-makers and penal practitioners alike at the mercy of tendencies which resulted directly from the day-to-day decisions of sentencers, but over which they had no direct control and only limited indirect influence. The most pressing and problematic of these tendencies was the seemingly inexorable increase in the prison population. This in turn contributed to the growing problem of prison overcrowding and placed further demands on limited penological resources, thereby exacerbating the overall sense of crisis in the penal system which was to culminate in the Strangeways prison riot of April 1990. The most serious failing of the *laissez faire* approach was thus its *inefficiency* in the face of mounting penal problems during the 1970s and 1980s. The overall strategy for the prison population during the 1970s had been based on a 'standstill policy',[8] the main aim of which was to try to maintain a ceiling on prison numbers by curbing further growth in the system while refusing to countenance the need for sentencing reform.

Instead, the methods which were resorted to included the expansion of non-custodial options, which sentencers were persuaded and exhorted to use wherever possible in place of custody. And, when this 'strategy of encouragement'[9] proved insufficient, other mechanisms were resorted to, over which the government did have more direct control. The most important of these mechanisms were the executive processes of remission and parole which enabled adjustments to be made in the length of time spent in prison, thereby acting as a valuable safety valve to relieve some of the pressure being caused by excessive use of custody on the part of sentencers. Numerous changes were made to these early release mechanisms during the 1970s,[10] whenever upward pressure on prison numbers threatened to overwhelm the system. However, the early 1980s marked the end of an era after an attempt by Home Secretary William Whitelaw to extend the scope of parole still further was ignominiously defeated by a combination of judicial hostility and opposition from grass-roots Conservatives at that party's annual conference in 1981.

The abandonment of the erstwhile standstill policy on prison numbers was heralded by the launch of an extensive prison building programme in March 1982, though attempts to *limit the rise* in the prison population continued to be made discreetly behind the scenes for the next few years. During this period the government attempted to balance an increasingly tough rhetorical stance on law and order including harsher treatment for more serious offenders with moves to promote a more parsimonious use of custody for less serious offenders. This *'bifurcatory'* approach (see *Chapter 1*) also relied on changes to the parole system (notably by Home Secretary Leon Brittan in 1983), rather than abandoning the *laissez faire* sentencing policy that had been inherited by the Conservative government in 1979. Following the 1987 General Election, however, it was finally acknowledged that this approach was unsustainable, and that the increasingly intractable resource and managerial problems confronting the penal system could only be tackled by accepting the need for a fundamental reform of the sentencing process itself.

MANAGING THE REFORM OF SENTENCING POLICY: STRATEGIES B AND C AND THE CRIMINAL JUSTICE ACT 1991

Managerialism and the 1991 reforms: The influence of Strategy B

Ever since 1979, successive Conservative administrations had pursued the holy grail of promoting greater 'efficiency' in the management of public sector enterprises with almost missionary zeal. During the following decade, virtually all the remaining public services were exposed to this new form of managerial orthodoxy, which previously had been associated only with private enterprises operating in the market place. These managerial reforms of the 1980s were inspired by the three doctrines of 'efficiency', 'effectiveness' and 'economy' and, viewed in this light, the traditional *laissez faire* approach to sentencing policy came increasingly to be seen as an anomalous heresy.

From a managerialist perspective, the sentencing process (and particularly the inappropriate use of imprisonment) was increasingly coming to be perceived by criminal justice policy-makers during the 1980s as ineffective. This was reflected in the new mood of realism which imbued both the 1988 Green Paper *Punishment, Custody and the Community*, and also the 1990 White Paper *Crime, Justice and Protecting the Public*[11] (see *Chapter 1*). Both documents appeared to acknowledge the uncomfortable truth that the effect of punishment is strictly limited, and thus offers little prospect of even containing, let alone reducing or eliminating the problem of crime. And both warned that the use of imprisonment, in particular, could even be counter-productive.

By the late 1980s, policy-makers were also becoming increasingly anxious about the rapidly escalating costs to which the sentencing process gives rise, both in terms of direct public expenditure and also in the demands it places on the finite, and increasingly limited resource of prison accommodation. Moreover, the sentencing decisions of the court contributed indirectly to the ever more serious managerial problems facing those running the prison system in particular, but also other agencies such as the probation service.[12]

Not surprisingly, therefore, managerial considerations of this kind played an important part in the genesis of the sentencing reforms contained in the Criminal Justice Act 1991. Indeed, the whole sentencing reform programme is premised on an acceptance of the need to formulate a strategic policy in an area of decision-making where none had existed previously. Managerialism is also reflected to some extent in the content of the reform programme although here its influence is rather less direct.[13] The provisions of the 1991 Act are mostly consistent with a rather weak form of managerialism which demands *procedural* rationality in the making of decisions rather than substantive rationality in the decisions which are made. Thus, the Act requires sentencers to adopt a coherent and systematic process of reasoning (based on the principle of proportionality), provides guidance on the kind of information that should or should not be taken into account,[14] and there is an insistence on the giving of reasons in the interests of greater openness and accountability.[15] The intention here appears to have been to subject the courts themselves, and sentencers in particular, to some of the procedural requirements (of accountability, transparency, and conformity with clearly articulated decision-making criteria) that the courts themselves regularly impose on other public bodies.[16]

In addition to these procedural requirements, however, managerialist concerns can also be detected in some of the substantive provisions of the reform programme. For one of the main aims of the 1991 Criminal Justice Act was that of bringing about a reduction in the proportionate use of custody, particularly in the case of minor property offenders. In managerialist terms, this can be seen as a first tentative step towards the establishment of a more rational process for determining the specific categories of convicted offenders in respect of which the scarce public resource of imprisonment should be allocated.[17] Taken to its logical conclusion, this approach could offer the prospect of developing some form of 'gearing mechanism' requiring the seemingly insatiable judicial demand for scarce prison resources to take account of the limited supply of prison places. The English sentencing reforms of 1991 patently fell a long way short of this 'strong' managerialist approach. Nevertheless they were based on an explicit repudiation of the excessively broad interpretation of the doctrine of judicial independence that had traditionally been insisted on by the judiciary; and this symbolic but limited reassertion of responsibility for sentencing policy on the part of the legislature is also consistent with a (relatively weak) managerialist agenda. Elsewhere in the 1991 Criminal Justice Act, managerialist tendencies of a rather different kind can be detected, though these lie beyond the scope of this chapter.[18]

Just deserts and the 1991 reforms: The influence of Strategy C

Although the impetus for the 1991 sentencing reforms was largely fuelled by managerial concerns, their content owed more to the principle of proportionality which was derived from the *'just deserts'* approach to sentencing. The philosophy of desert leads to the conclusion that offenders have certain rights, and so is in itself more redolent of Strategy C than of the instrumentalist Strategy B. Desert theory is crucially linked to the concept of fairness,[19] and this is true in two distinct but complementary senses. First, desert theory is related to the notion of *procedural fairness*, which stipulates that 'like cases be treated (and sentenced) alike'.[20] Secondly, desert is also linked with the notion of *substantive fairness* which stipulates that people should be treated (and sentenced) in accordance with what they deserve.

Of the two, the concept of procedural fairness is normally considered to be the less contentious, since consistency is usually thought to be a prerequisite of justice.[21] In comparison, the concept of substantive fairness is highly controversial since this involves establishing an appropriate relationship between the severity of punishment and the seriousness of the offence for which it is imposed (sometimes referred to as the 'principle of commensurability'). The problem here, as even some of its most ardent supporters[22] concede, is that there is no commonly accepted yardstick nor any credible external calculus for determining what level of punishment is commensurate in relation to any given offence. Consequently, the notion of just deserts is itself a vigorously contested concept which has had a highly variable impact on the overall level of sentencing in the numerous jurisdictions in which it has held sway.

Some of its earliest and most vigorous advocates[23] have invoked the principle of just deserts in an attempt to both promote consistency and at the same time *reduce* the overall level of punishment (an approach that is based on the 'parsimony principle').[24] Many of these advocates of the parsimony principle saw it as a way of countering what they felt to be the excessively punitive and inconsistent outcomes that were associated with the indeterminate sentences favoured by adherents of the treatment model. However, the principle has also frequently been invoked by those on the political right—for example in many jurisdictions in the United States during the 1970s and 1980s—to argue for consistently harsher determinate sentences. This more punitive variant of the just deserts model clearly has much more in common with the 'law and order' mentality associated with Strategy A rather than the more liberal and humanitarian impulses underlying Strategy C.

In spite of this uncertainty over what it entails (or maybe because of it), the just deserts model has become increasingly influential in recent years, and has significantly influenced sentencing policy in jurisdictions as diverse as Scandinavia and the United States. Its influence can also clearly be seen in the English sentencing reforms which culminated in the Criminal Justice Act of 1991. Indeed, at least in its original form, the Act could be described as a 'just deserts' statute.[25] This is partly an acknowledgement of the extent to which the White Paper which preceded it was heavily imbued with 'just deserts' thinking and terminology,[26] and although the Act itself did not embody the justice model unswervingly, it did nevertheless espouse the 'just deserts' principle as the primary aim of sentencing. Thus, while the White Paper spoke of the need for punishment to be 'in proportion to the seriousness of the crime',[27] the Act sought to enshrine this 'proportionality principle' by stipulating that custody should only be imposed for offences that are *'so serious that only such a sentence can be justified for the offence'*.[28]

Similarly, in respect of the imposition of 'community sentences'—those non-custodial penalties which entail significant restrictions on the offender's liberty—the Act prescribed (in section 6) that they too should be reserved for offences which are 'serious enough' to warrant such a sentence.[29]

In this way, the 1991 Act sought to prioritise the 'just deserts' principle of proportionality as the primary aim of sentencing, in place of the more traditional 'pick-and-choose' or 'supermarket' approach that had prevailed during the *laissez faire* era. Moreover, when determining the length or severity of punishment to award, the Act[30] provided that this should also be commensurate (or proportional) with the seriousness of the offence. The Act thus sought to secure compliance with the principle of procedural fairness, by establishing a more coherent and consistent framework for the decision-making process. And in terms of substantive fairness, the Act was intended, *inter alia*, to discourage the use of imprisonment in respect of less serious (even if persistent) property offenders, with a view to reducing the prison population. In this respect, at least, it was consistent with the liberal, rights-based version of the just deserts model. However, this 'Strategy C' component of the 1991 reforms was compromised in part by the inclusion of more punitive and populist law and order elements that are more redolent of Strategy A.

This was particularly true in relation to the treatment of more serious violent and sexual offenders, for whom the Act authorised harsher custodial sentences in order to protect the public, even where the level of punishment would be disproportionate to the seriousness of the offence. In respect of offenders such as these, the sentencing aim of incapacitation was allowed to override the principle of proportionality, thus giving a further twist to the bifurcatory spiral that had already been evident in pre-reform days. Moreover, the Act also sought in various ways to toughen the punitive impact of community penalties,[31] even though these were intended to apply to less serious offenders whose crimes were not thought to merit a custodial sentence. Although the just deserts-based variant of Strategy C thus featured prominently in the 1991 Criminal Act, its overall strategy was therefore something of a hybrid—which we have termed 'punitive bifurcation'—since it also incorporated strong elements of managerialist Strategy B thinking, and even a generous measure of 'law and order-style' Strategy A provisions. This is the context in which we need to assess the success or failure of the Act. In doing so, we will attempt to address two sets of questions: first, the extent to which it succeeded in achieving certain of its key penological aims; and secondly the extent to which it advanced or retarded the cause of progressive sentencing reform. Although this is not a straightforward exercise—given the ideological mix on which it was based, and the inevitable tensions and compromises to which these give rise—there are grounds for concluding that, in certain respects at least, it could be judged to have been a qualified (if highly transient) penological success story, while at another level it undoubtedly ranks as an unqualified managerial and political (and long-term penological) disaster.

VERDICTS ON THE 1991 ACT

A qualified short-term penological success
Three key penological aims of the Criminal Justice Act 1991 (intended effects on the penal system) were:

(1) to reduce the use of custody, (particularly for less serious property offenders) by requiring the amount of punishment to be determined by the seriousness of the offence;
(2) to boost the use of community sentences; and
(3) to reduce the extent to which the severity of punishment is based on previous convictions.[32]

With regard to the use of custody, there were some promising early signs of success since the prison population registered a sharp decrease during the period immediately following the implementation of the Act on 1 October 1992. The numbers in prison had ranged between 46,600 and 47,700 during the first half of 1992; by the end of December the figure was 40,606. Moreover, the proportionate use of immediate custody for indictable offences also fell significantly, from 16 per cent in the period January-September 1992 to 12 per cent in the final quarter of 1992.[33] The falls occurred in both magistrates' courts and Crown Courts, and affected all age groups. A special data collection exercise conducted by the Home Office in the summer of 1992 and early 1993 recorded a fall in the proportionate use of immediate custody, particularly among offenders with a substantial number of previous convictions.[34] The study also showed that in the ten Crown Court centres surveyed, the proportionate use of custody in the case of 'property' offences fell by four per cent, compared with an increase of two per cent in respect of 'violent' offences and eight per cent for 'other' offences.

As regards the second aim of reducing the extent to which the severity of punishment is based on the number of previous convictions, David Thomas[35] has correctly made the point that the only strategy which would be likely to significantly reduce the use of custody for adults is one which restricts or prohibits the imprisonment of recidivists who repeatedly commit relatively minor offences. The 1991 Act sought to do this by stipulating 'an offence shall not be regarded as more serious . . . by reason of any previous conviction of the offender'.[36] There is some evidence[37] that this provision did have the desired effect in the short term, but once the controversial provision was amended in 1993 (as part of the government's penal U-turn towards Strategy A) magistrates and judges took this to mean they were free to revert to using previous convictions as an aggravating factor just as they always had before, despite legal authorities ruling against this practice.[38]

When it comes to boosting the use of community sentences, once again there is evidence[39] that their usage did increase to some extent following implementation of the Act, though this seems to have been largely at the expense of the suspended sentence whose use was drastically curtailed by the 1991 Act,[40] rather than as a substitute for immediate custody. Moreover, there is little evidence that the Act succeeded in enhancing the credibility of community penalties in the eyes of sentencers.

In addition to the three main aims which we have just been considering, the 1991 Act also incorporated some bifurcatory tendencies, and the Home Office's special data collection exercise showed clear signs that it might also be having an effect on sentencing practice during the period immediately after its implementation,[41] at least in the Crown Court. Here, the average length of custodial sentences imposed on 'violent' offenders increased (by three months to 31 months) irrespective of the number of previous convictions, whereas the average length imposed on 'property' offenders decreased (by two months to 12 months), though here the fall was more apparent for those with substantial numbers of previous convictions (21 or more). Moreover, the survey also showed increases in both the proportion of male offenders sentenced in the Crown Court to *short terms of imprisonment* (up to four months) for all offence groups; and in the proportion sentenced to *terms of imprisonment longer than four years* (for all offence groups except robbery and drug offences).[42] All these figures are consistent with a shift towards a more pronounced bifurcatory approach, based on the perceived seriousness of the offence. So, whatever one's views of the rightness or wisdom of the policy of bifurcation, the Act can be said to have reinforced this tendency in sentencing.

An unqualified managerial and political (and long-term penological) disaster

But what of the longer term picture? First let us examine the performance of the Act in relation to its principal underlying objective: to tackle the many long-term problems associated with the *laissez faire* era by undertaking a fundamental and lasting reform of the entire sentencing decision-making process. When judged against this admittedly demanding standard, the Act must rank as a dismal failure even if we disregard the political turmoil which embroiled it shortly after its implementation. And this is a verdict which exposes the shortcomings of the managerialist approach upon which the whole programme of reform was based. One of its main aims was to fill the penological void which had characterised the sentencing system since the demise of the rehabilitative ideal by articulating a coherent set of principles. These were intended to promote a more consistent approach on the part of sentencers, and also a more parsimonious approach with regard to the use of custody. As we have seen, however, the overall coherence of the new sentencing framework was seriously undermined by first giving primacy to the principle of proportionality based on offence seriousness, and then subordinating this principle to the aim of incapacitation in cases involving sexual or violent offences. This was unlikely to aid the cause of consistency in sentencing. Moreover, the bifurcatory strategy on which it was based ran the risk that any reduction in the *number* of prison sentences passed might be offset by the increased *length* of those sentences which were imposed for violent and sexual offences.

A second main aim of the reform process was to reduce the proportionate use of custody in respect of less serious property offenders, and so ease some of the growing pressure on the prison system which resulted from the seemingly inexorable increase in the prison population. This involved a radical repudiation of the 'hands off' approach which the doctrine of judicial independence had come to embody, and a reassertion of Parliamentary responsibility for policy-making in this increasingly sensitive and controversial arena. Remarkably, however, no attempt was made either to define the key concept of offence 'seriousness' on which the whole proportionality principle was based; or to constrain the discretion of sentencers in the way they interpreted it by relating the concept to particular offence categories. Instead, it was left entirely to the sentencers themselves to determine whether a given offence was sufficiently serious in their eyes to merit a custodial sentence.

Given their hostility to the perceived interference with their hallowed notion of their own independence, it was hardly surprising that the Act quickly proved vulnerable to the classic techniques of destructive interpretation at the hands of a resentful judiciary who are past masters at exploiting technical deficiencies in badly drafted legislation. Whether the episode is attributed to a failure of political nerve, as some have claimed,[43] or to more mundane technical incompetence, it highlights the extent to which the government's assertions of managerial competence were belied by its actions. Nor are these isolated examples, since the Act has also been criticised[44] for the obscurity of the language used, particularly when indicating how previous convictions should be dealt with.

However, these managerial deficiencies were to prove even more destructive in the increasingly highly charged political atmosphere which began to prevail shortly after the implementation of the 1991 Act. This was characterised not only by the extraordinary *volte face* by the Conservative government itself, which we describe in the next section, but also by the public relations disaster over the introduction of unit fines (see *Chapter 6*), and by growing media unease over the problem of youth crime and certain key aspects of the 1991 reforms themselves. In this increasingly febrile climate, judicial resentment and resistance helped to fuel a backlash in which the judiciary have even been accused[45] of transgressing the boundary between judicial independence and judicial anarchy.

Three clear examples of this judicial backlash may be cited. The first relates to the brazen way in which the Court of Appeal effectively rewrote the key concept of offence seriousness by stipulating that this could also be related to the need for a *deterrent* response, and not simply to the degree of retribution that is thought to be warranted.[46] This reading of the term was flagrantly at odds with the just deserts philosophy underlying both the 1990 White Paper and the Act itself, and sent a clear early warning that, far from being an ill-fitting straitjacket as senior members of the judiciary had claimed,[47] they themselves viewed the Act as a pattern-book from which they could select and adapt the garment they felt most comfortable with.

The second example illustrates the judicial sleight of hand with which the ostensibly objective standard of 'seriousness' was converted into a much more intuitive test, based on the perceptions of 'right-thinking members of the public'.[48] This was one which judges clearly felt much more comfortable with, in their self-appointed role as sole custodians and oracles of the Delphic thoughts and attitudes of 'informed' public opinion. The plasticity of the criterion of 'seriousness' in the hands of the judges was vividly demonstrated in the case of *Keogh*,[49] in which a one month prison sentence was upheld on an offender who had pleaded guilty to obtaining by deception a car alarm valued at £35. Invoking the 'right-thinking member of the public' test, the

Court of Appeal referred to the prevailing climate of opinion in 1993 in support of its conclusion that 'only a custodial sentence could be justified for the offence'.

The third example of a judicial backlash following the implementation of the 1991 Act relates to the cavalier treatment which the judges gave to the requirement to give reasons when passing a custodial sentence. Here, the Court of Appeal effectively ruled that a sentencer's failure to give any legally adequate reasons of the kind required by the Act when sentencing to custody did nothing to invalidate the sentence.[50] In plainer language, the effect of this act of judicial levitation meant that the provision had no legal effect whatsoever, which was presumably not the intention of those who had drafted the legislation.

Quite apart from the change in the party political climate following the 1991 reforms, therefore, they also failed at a less partisan political level. This was because the judiciary did not hesitate to use their own considerable discretionary power to devastating effect. In doing so they could be said to have both abused and betrayed the confidence which those who drafted the 1991 Act had reposed in them; perhaps naïvely, and possibly on the basis of misplaced deference to their renowned sensibilities on the subject of their own independence. However, this flexing of their political muscles was to prove a short term and ultimately Pyrrhic victory, since these sensibilities were soon to be brusquely sacrificed on the altar of resurgent law and order dogmatism. This culminated in the overthrow of the whole reformist strategy in the curiously changed political climate following the 1992 general election. But the judiciary themselves could also prove to have been weakened in the long run by these acts of political bravado, which have cast serious doubt on the extent to which they may be relied upon as responsible partners in any future managerial or humanitarian programme of sentencing reform.

And what of the long-term effects of the 1991 Act on the penal system? There was a mixed result as regards the use of the middle-ranking 'community sentences', whose usage had increased after the Act was introduced, but from late 1993 onwards levelled off and actually declined in the Crown Court.[51] The aim of downgrading the role of previous convictions in sentencing was, as we have seen, abandoned by legislative amendments in 1993 (along with the unit fine system discussed in *Chapter 6*). And the aim of reducing the use of custody? Well, the initial trend away from custodial sentencing following the implementation of the Act proved to be all too short-lived. Between 1992 and 1996, the custody rate at the Crown Court nationally rose from 44 to 60 per cent while the average length of sentences for adults increased from 21.0 to 23.4 months.[52] Even in the magistrates' courts the custody rate doubled from five to 11 per cent for males aged 21 and over, though here average sentence lengths did not rise. By 1997, the Lord Chief Justice himself was heard to lament that judges were pushing up the prison population to record levels by 'sending more defendants to prison for longer periods than at any time in the last 40 years'.[53] And indeed the prison population—which initially dropped from around 47,000 in early 1992 to 40,606 in December of that year—had risen spectacularly thereafter as a consequence of the harsher sentencing, reaching 66,800 by April 1998. Hence, the longer term verdict on the penological effects of the Criminal Justice Act 1991 can only be damning. But the fault did not so much lie with the provisions of the Act or the merits of the reforms it contained—although its provisions certainly were not well or tightly drafted enough to ensure the desired effects—but with an almost tidal wave of law and order revivalism which the weak defences of the Act could do little to withstand.

LAW AND ORDER REVIVALISM: THE REBIRTH OF STRATEGY A

In the event, the real death knell of the 1991 reforms was not sounded by the judicial backlash to which we referred above (damaging though it undoubtedly was); nor by the legislative backtracking which began in 1993, almost immediately after the Act had been implemented. Some hasty changes were indeed made to the 1991 Act following the chorus of complaints it unleashed from some sectors of the media and the judiciary. They included, most notably, the precipitate abolition of the entire system of unit fines that had been introduced at enormous expense only months earlier (see *Chapter 6*). In addition, further hastily prepared amendments to the Criminal Justice Act 1993 also watered down still further the obscurely worded restriction on the extent to which sentencers could take previous convictions into account when passing sentence.[54] However, none of these changes altered the overall sentencing framework, and the legislative substance of the 1991 reforms remained substantially intact in spite of this legislative sniping and the more sustained barrage of hostile judicial interventions which they endured. Instead, it was the dramatic shift in political rhetoric which accompanied these changes that effectively signalled the end of the reform programme. It also heralded the start of what has been called the 'law and order counter-reformation'[55] which in turn resulted in a marked increase in the use of custody for both remand and sentenced offenders, starting in 1993.

For most of its adherents, Strategy A is based on a wholly exaggerated belief in the power of punishment to secure compliance with the law, and thereby reduce the level of crime. Hence, its adherents are apt to view the criminal law, and the sanctions which uphold it, as a 'quick fix' solution to a wide range of social ills. Its revival was unmistakably proclaimed in Michael Howard's 'prison works' speech to the Conservative Party conference in 1993. This was followed up by changes in the scope of the criminal law, starting with the Criminal Justice and Public Order Act of 1994 which, among other things, toughened the law against trespassers, squatters and other marginal groups such as hunt saboteurs and new age travellers. The enforcement of the criminal law also became more repressive, with restrictions on bail and cautioning (and also the suspect's right of silence), as did the penal system itself. Thus, the 1994 Act ushered in a new custodial penalty in the form of the secure training order for persistent young offenders, increased the maximum terms of detention for children and young persons and removed the presumption in favour of bail in the case of anyone charged with certain serious offences against the person if they had pervious convictions for similar offences.[56]

However, Strategy A reached its apotheosis (in England and Wales) in the Crime (Sentences) Act 1997, which was passed in the dying days of the Conservative administration, just before the General Election of May 1 in the same year.[57] The Act contained two main sets of provisions which bear the hallmark of Strategy A: those relating to the introduction of mandatory and minimum sentences; and those relating to the system of early release.

The sentencing provisions of the 1997 Act were based on the 'three strikes and you're out' principle which is to be found in many US jurisdictions. There, such sentences are explicitly intended to have an incapacitative effect by ensuring that certain repeat offenders are automatically jailed for life after being convicted of a third offence. Although the precise form they take differs from state to state, in some of the more extreme versions (such as California) it is possible for an offender to be imprisoned for life after stealing a slice of pizza.[58] In England, section 2 of the Crime (Sentences) Act of 1997 requires the imposition of a life sentence after an offender is convicted of a *second* serious violent or sexual offence, unless there are exceptional circumstances. This particular provision was brought into effect by the incoming Labour government from 1 October 1997.

Section 3 of the Act requires the imposition of a minimum sentence of at least seven years imprisonment on an offender who is convicted for a third time of a class A drug trafficking offence, unless the court considers this to be 'unjust in all the circumstances'. This provision was also brought into effect from 1 October 1997. The third and final sentencing provision contained in the 1997 Act (section 4) would oblige a court to impose a minimum sentence of at least three years on an offender who is convicted for a third time in respect of the offence of domestic burglary, again unless the court considers this to be 'unjust in all the circumstances'. The exception, which provides for a degree of judicial discretion to be exercised where injustice might result,[59] was only secured as a result of an eleventh hour amendment supported by an all-party alliance in the House of Lords in the run-up to the general election. The effect of the amendment was to convert the mandatory minimum sentence favoured by Michael Howard[60] into a slightly less restrictive presumptive minimum sentence. Unlike the other two presumptive sentence provisions, this measure had not yet been brought into force at the time of writing but plans to implement it 'soon' had been announced (*Guardian*, 13 January 1999).

The early release provisions of the 1997 Act were also based on a widespread American practice, which has been dubbed the 'truth in sentencing' principle.[61] This is a proposition which requires a prisoner to serve all, or almost all (usually between 80-85 per cent) of the full sentence handed down by the court, irrespective of the prisoner's behaviour in custody—which might otherwise have been expected to earn a much more substantial reduction in the effective length of the sentence served by qualifying the inmate for early release. In the United States, the adoption of so-called 'truth in sentencing' legislation has been prompted largely in response to growing dissatisfaction with indeterminate sentencing policies. These were criticised partly on the grounds of inconsistency and partly because they were felt by right-wing political and penological advocates of a 'just deserts' approach to be insufficiently punitive. In other words, the trend has been fuelled, in part, by a mixture of Strategy A and Strategy C concerns.

Truth in sentencing measures are said to have the following aims: to increase the proportion of time spent in custody; to promote clarity and consistency among sentencers and to relate the sentence handed down in court to the sentence that is actually served.[62] If successful, it is believed that such an approach will help to restore public (and judicial) confidence in the sentencing process. It has even been claimed that it may contribute to a reduction in the crime rate (as a result of the incapacitatory effect of longer sentences of imprisonment) and—less plausibly still—that it could even generate cost savings since the expense of long-term incarceration is said to be out-weighed by reductions in the cost incurred by both victims and society as a result of the preventive effects of the policy. Finally, truth in sentencing has also been advocated, albeit less commonly, as a way of relating sentencing decisions to a more rational use of available prison space, and to promote an awareness on the part of the judiciary of the economic impact of their sentencing decisions. This managerialist concern suggests that support for truth in sentencing policies might also be seen—albeit perhaps a little far-fetchedly—as compatible with a Strategy B approach.

In England and Wales, the Crime (Sentences) Act of 1997 provided for the abolition of the existing system of early release and supervision, even though this system had only been established as recently as 1992. For, in addition to its sentencing reforms the 1991 Criminal Justice Act had also undertaken a fundamental reform of the old system of remission and parole, replacing them with a new system of early release. This was largely prompted by concerns that the steady succession of pragmatic changes to these original early release mechanisms over the preceding two decades had antagonised the judiciary by widening the differential between the nominal or 'headline' sentence which is imposed by the court, and the actual or 'effective' term that is actually served once the various early release mechanisms had been brought into play.[63]

Accordingly, under the 1991 Criminal Justice Act a new system of early release was introduced, which was intended to restore some meaning to the nominal sentence originally imposed by the court.[64] It did so by introducing the principle that all prisoners who qualified for early release would still remain liable to be recalled to prison to serve the unexpired portion of the sentence if a new offence was committed before the end of the original term. Subject to that qualification, prisoners who were sentenced to custodial sentences of less than 12 months would normally expect to be released (without supervision) after serving one-half of their sentence. Prisoners who were sentenced to 12 months or more, but less than four years also qualified for automatic release at the half way stage, but had to undergo a compulsory period of supervision in addition. Prisoners serving determinate sentences of longer than four years were only eligible for discretionary release (which was subject to the same conditions regarding liability to supervision and to recall in the event of a fresh offence) at the half way stage of their sentence, but would normally (subject to good behaviour) be released on the same basis after serving two-thirds of their sentence.

In an about-turn that was every bit as dramatic as the abolition of the unit fine (see *Chapter 6*), the Crime (Sentences) Act of 1997 sought to dismantle the entire system of early release provisions that had been painstakingly put together (by members of the same governing party) in the 1991 Criminal Justice Act. The new provisions were said to be inspired by the principle of 'honesty in sentencing', though the Anglicisation of the term does little to disguise its American provenance. Michael Howard, as Home Secretary, staked out the 'law and order' credentials of this new 'Strategy A' approach in characteristically forthright terms when announcing the proposed changes at the Conservative Party conference in October 1995. He told them that, with the sole exception that

> model prisoners should get a little time off for good behaviour . . . everyone else should serve their sentences in full . . . five years should mean five years. It's time to get *honesty back into sentencing*. . . . No more automatic release, no more release regardless of behaviour, and no more half time sentences for full time crimes. (Italics added)

Under the Crime (Sentences) Act 1997, prisoners who were sentenced to terms of imprisonment of up to three years would have earned a discount of up to one-sixth, only, for good behaviour and co-operation (section 11). Longer term prisoners (those sentenced to over three years) would be eligible to apply to the Parole Board for release, but not until they had served five-sixths of their sentence, and then only if the Board was satisfied that they no longer presented a danger to the public (section 12). Finally, the Act also provided for additional days to be awarded against prisoners who are guilty of disciplinary offences, and deducted from any early release days they may have earned (section 14). Not only would these provisions have had a catastrophic effect on prison numbers (one estimate being a staggering 24,000 extra prisoners),[65] they would also have forfeited the benefits to be gained from the compulsory supervision of paroled prisoners during their 'licence period'. In the event, none of these early release provisions were brought into force by the incoming Labour government and all of them were ultimately repealed by the Crime and Disorder Act 1998—in contrast to the sentencing reforms contained in the 1997 Act, some of which, as we have seen, have been implemented.

Compared with the Criminal Justice Act 1991, the 'law and order' changes associated with the 1997 Act represented a far more radical and sustained assault on the notion of judicial independence. This was particularly true of the sentencing provisions and indeed, as originally worded, judges would not even have been granted the vestige of discretion which was eventually afforded them by virtue of the 'unjust in all the circumstances' exception. Not surprisingly, therefore, the proposals unleashed a ferocious judicial revolt, which was led by the Lord Chief Justice Lord Bingham and supported by an impressive array of past and present senior judges including Master of the Rolls Lord Woolf, and former law lords such as Lord Ackner.[66] In addition to their predictable complaints about the erosion of the principle of judicial discretion, they also complained, more cogently, about the injustice that would inevitably result from the imposition of mandatory sentences regardless of any extenuating circumstances. By forcing them to treat unlike cases alike, judges would indeed be obliged to acts as agents of injustice. This time round however—in contrast with their successful skirmishings which greeted the Criminal Justice Act and contributed to its emasculation—they were relatively powerless in the face of a government that appeared determined to ride rough-shod over their constitutional sensibilities.

Indeed, the one concession which belatedly restored their discretion to depart from the presumptive sentence when it would be in the interests of justice to do so would almost certainly not have been granted but for the leverage that was afforded by the Conservative government's overriding desire to secure the passage of the Bill in the last few days before the May 1997 General Election brought the Parliamentary session to a close. Without this exception, the clear and unequivocal wording of the original clause would have left much less room for judicial manoeuvring by exploiting ambiguities in the language used.

As for the lessons that can be learned from the attempts at sentencing reform over the past decade, three main conclusions may be drawn. First, it is possible for even flawed legislative action to reduce the use of imprisonment by the courts when it is firmly backed by governmental exhortation. But second, it is equally possible for governmental 'law and order' rhetoric alone to effectively 'talk up' the use of imprisonment (by relying on the willing complicity of sentencers) even without any change in the legislative position. And third, it is also possible to push through much more restrictive changes in sentencing policy even when these are unpopular with the judiciary, provided the government is single-minded enough to do so and chooses its legislative language with care.

WHITHER STRATEGY A: THE DOOMSDAY SCENARIO?

One noticeable but bewildering recent tendency has been for British penal policy-makers to seek their inspiration from the United States which contains some of the least sophisticated (and arguably least successful)[67] penal jurisdictions in the world, instead of taking heed from some of the more enlightened approaches that have been developed elsewhere, for example in parts of Western Europe. This is particularly true of the 'three strikes and you're out' and 'truth in sentencing' provisions which, as we have seen, directly influenced the shape and content of the 1997 reforms that were destined to serve as the Conservative government's 'law and order swan song'. Although there are significant differences in certain respects between the British provisions and their American precursors (and even though there are also differences as between the various states themselves), there are also sufficient similarities between them for the latter to be viewed as a 'natural experiment' in which a number of claims that have been advanced on behalf of the 'law and order' lobby might be put to the test. By examining the effects that have been associated with these measures it might also be possible to gain some insight into the probable outcomes if British penal policy continues to be influenced by Strategy A thinking.

The boldest claim that has been advanced in relation to the United States' heavy reliance on the use of imprisonment, particularly in the form of mandatory sentences and 'truth in sentencing' measures is that they result in real and measurable reductions in the overall levels of crime by virtue of their incapacitative and deterrent effects. Although such claims appear intuitively plausible, they are not borne out by the recent evidence from the United States.[68] For example, supporters of mandatory minimum sentences and 'three strikes and you're out' provisions have cited a recent 13 per cent decline in the recorded homicide rates for California since the introduction of 'three strikes' legislation in 1994 as evidence of the policy's effectiveness.[69] However, homicide rates have declined nationally in the United States by about 16 per cent since 1991, and there appears to be no clear correlation between the degree of punitiveness exhibited by a state and its recorded rate of serious crime.[70] For example, some states, such as New York, which has seen the biggest recent reductions in the rate of serious crimes have been less punitive than some other states (such as Arizona and Virginia), where homicide rates have increased dramatically despite the fact that they have relatively high rates of incarceration. Moreover, Texas, which has earned the dubious reputation for achieving the highest incarceration rate of any Western democracy,[71] has only seen a decrease in the crime rate of 19 per cent between 1989 and 1993, which is broadly in line with the national average though the overall crime rate is still one of the highest in the whole of the United States. And, going back to California, a recent study there could find no impact on crime rates attributable to 'three strikes and out' sentences.[72]

Perhaps this dearth of supporting evidence is one explanation for the British government's failure to substantiate the bold prediction contained in the 'Protecting the Public' White Paper[73] that the deterrent effect of its new sentencing proposals would reduce the need for prison places by 20 per cent. Exaggerated claims of this kind are simply not borne out by the wealth of American experience and appear disingenuous at best.

Recent American and Australian experience also provides sobering evidence of the enormous cost that is likely to be incurred as a result of pursuing Strategy A policies in relation to sentencing and early release.

By the end of 1994 the state of Texas alone had 653,907 adults who were under some form of punitive social control, which is equivalent to 4.7 per cent of the adult population in Texas.[74] In financial terms alone, the cost of sustaining this rate of incarceration is a staggering $2.25 billion per year,[75] which represents a doubling in the proportion of total spending that is consumed by the corrections industry from three to six per cent since 1990. Similarly, it has been estimated that the introduction of 'three strikes' legislation in California will help to fuel an increase in the prison population from 125,000 in 1994 to 211,000 in 1999, which will require the construction of 20 extra prisons by the year 2000 at an additional cost of $5.7 billion per year.[76]

Even more disturbing than these financial costs, however, are the social costs and opportunity costs that are inevitably associated with Strategy A policies of this kind.[77] As Elliott Currie has pointed out, the recent dramatic rise in correctional spending in the United States has been accompanied by an almost equally radical reduction in most other kinds of publicly funded social spending, particularly in relation to education, health and mental health care and recreational facilities.

> As a result the prison [has become] . . . in some respects the chief agency for dealing with the social problems of the most disadvantaged people in America. Between 1980 and 1993 total federal spending on employment and training programmes was cut nearly in half. Federal spending on correctional activities meanwhile increased by 521 per cent. (Make no mistake, this shift was influenced very heavily by the increasingly prominent argument that prison works to reduce crime, and that jobs and job training do not.).[78]

This assessment is also in line with an analysis of the Californian 'three strikes' measures and their impact on crime rates, the criminal justice system and its budgetary implications, which was conducted by the RAND Corporation.[79] The study concluded that in order 'to support implementation of the law, total spending for higher education and other services[80] would have to fall by more than 40 per cent over the next eight years'.

Care needs to be taken when assessing the implications of penal measures that are adopted in one criminal justice system based on the experiences in another very different one. Nevertheless, even taking this caveat into account, the implications for English sentencing policy if the Strategy A measures which were contained in the Crime (Sentences) Act had been adopted in full are profoundly disturbing. Indeed, it is no exaggeration to say that they run the risk of 'testing to destruction' the thesis that crime can be successfully dealt with by punishment alone. Consequently, the dropping of the early release provisions and the watering down of the mandatory sentencing measures by the incoming

Labour government following the 1997 general election are to be welcomed, though even this partial turn-around falls a long way short of a total repudiation of Strategy A. The anticipated impact on the prison population as a result of Labour's implementation of the mandatory sentencing provisions of the Crime (Sentences) Act 1997 in respect of repeat violent and sexual offenders and drug traffickers is fairly modest—150 extra places by the end of financial year 1999/2000 according to Home Office projections[81]—compared with the effect of implementing the 'repeat burglar' provisions (likely to add several thousand to prison numbers). Thus, the new government's failure so far to implement this particular sentence represents not so much an abandonment of Strategy A in this respect as a tempering of it in the interests of prudent (Strategy B) managerial considerations.

ALTERNATIVE STRATEGIES FOR SENTENCING REFORM

Strategy B revisited
In this section we consider some alternative strategies for reform before concluding with an assessment of the prospects for reform after the 1997 change of government in England and Wales. Although, as we saw earlier, a previous attempt to reform English sentencing policy in line with a predominantly Strategy B approach failed disastrously when it was attempted in 1991, other jurisdictions have enjoyed more success in developing a broadly similar strategy. Here we will consider just one example of a combined 'truth in sentencing' and sentencing reform programme which was adopted in North Carolina.[82] The need for such a programme was prompted by successful litigation on the part of inmates, who persuaded the courts that overcrowded conditions or confinement represented 'cruel and unusual punishment', contrary to the Eighth Amendment to the United States Constitution. This resulted in the imposition of a cap on prison numbers by the North Carolina Department of Corrections, which in turn led to earlier parole being granted and a significant reduction in the effective length of sentences (sometimes to as little as 18 per cent of the nominal or 'headline' sentence pronounced by the sentencing court) being served by prisoners.

As has happened elsewhere, this pragmatic response resulted in an outcry from the public. However, instead of resorting to a general toughening of existing sentencing policy along Strategy A lines, the North Carolina legislature undertook a fundamental review of sentencing policy in the context of the entire correctional system, with a view to achieving a better balance between the demand for custodial places on the part of the judiciary and the supply that was actually available to them. In order to secure this balance, the legislature established a Sentencing and Policy Advisory Commission. This kind of body had previously been instituted in several other jurisdictions, but what was distinctive about this particular variant was that the Commission was given clear resource priorities according to which sentencing reform was to be linked to prison capacity. In accountancy terms, the Commission was instructed to devise a fiscally responsible formula which would 'balance the books' by calibrating sentencing policy in accordance with available custodial accommodation.

Guided by the Sentencing Commission, the legislature of North Carolina enacted new 'structured sentencing' laws on 1 October 1994. This implemented a form of 'truth in sentencing' policy in which parole was abolished and offenders were required to serve the full minimum term imposed by the judge, and up to 20 per cent longer than that if they failed to behave, work, or participate in the required programme. But the new laws also sought to ensure that more low-risk offenders were channelled into community sanctions, in order to free up sufficient prison space to accommodate the violent and repeat offenders for whom these longer spells in prison were intended. This was achieved by developing a 'guideline' approach[83] which prescribes a range of presumptive penalties, based on the seriousness of the offence and also the extent and gravity of the offender's previous history. One important element in the strategy was an extension in the range and number of community programmes[84] available in the case of lower risk offenders. Another key component in the strategy consisted of its reliance on sophisticated prison population projections which were derived by a forecasting advisory sub-committee based on a computer simulation model.

Based on the structured sentencing policy, the prison population was projected to increase relatively modestly (in comparison with many other American states) from 29,000 in 1985 to over 35,000 by early 1998, and prison population and capacity were projected to be in balance until the year 2004.[85] A prison building programme was inaugurated to accommodate this increase, and at the same time the rest of the prison estate was being re-structured in order to reflect the changing composition of the prison population. Finally, changes were also introduced in relation to both staff training, and also the prison regime itself, in order to make available more productive work which pays a competitive wage.

Despite its success in achieving its (relatively modest) objectives, we ourselves would not advocate this strategy, even though it represents a more rational and constructive approach than is to be found in many other state jurisdictions within the United States and also compares favourably with the Conservative government's attempt at pursuing a Strategy A approach in the Crime (Sentences) Act of 1997. One of the main objections to it is that it represents an instrumentalist rather than a principled approach to sentencing reform—what we have called 'punitive managerialism' (see *Chapters* 2 and 4). Thus, while it makes sense to ensure that the demand for prison places is more effectively geared to the supply that is known to be available, the approach is still compatible with a high degree of punitive overkill, since it is still dependent on political judgements relating to the optimum size of the prison estate. So politicians of a more punitive disposition could choose to combine such an approach with a massive prison building programme, the only merit of which would be the aim of avoiding prison overcrowding.

A second objection to the North Carolina approach is that it further institutionalises, and indeed reinforces, the policy of bifurcation (see *Chapter* 1) which is itself open to a number of serious objections.[86] For both these reasons, we would prefer a programme for sentencing reform whose overall goals are inspired by Strategy C, while relying on some of the techniques that are associated with Strategy B in order to ensure their successful implementation.

A Strategy C approach to sentencing reform

As we said in *Chapter* 2 in relation to our Strategy C approach to criminal justice generally, our approach to sentencing is not one of näive idealism. On the contrary, we would contend, one of the main problems which has blighted virtually all sentencing reform initiatives to date that we are aware of is the wholly unrealistic expectations on which they are normally based. The principle of 'penological realism' which we put forward as one touchstone for any principled programme of sentencing reform is founded on an appreciation of the extremely limited role which sentencing policy can reasonably expect to play in influencing crime rates.

There are many reasons for rejecting as naive what Andrew Ashworth has aptly described[87] as the 'hydraulic' theory of sentencing, which postulates that 'if sentences go up, crimes go down, and vice versa'. One of these reasons is the so-called 'attrition rate' of crimes:[88] of all offences committed, only two per cent result in a sentence of any sort. Consequently, the typically optimistic expectation of most offenders that they will 'get away with it' has strong empirical backing, which in turn means that only the most extreme penalties—which one would imagine to be both financially and politically unacceptable—would be likely to have any impact on the recorded crime rate. It is not only unrealistic, therefore, but also politically dishonest (and, we would suggest, in the long term self-defeating) for those promoting sentencing reform to raise people's expectations that this in itself will bring about a reduction in crime levels. And yet this is the premise on which most sentencing reforms have been based, even before recent lurches towards Strategy A.

In terms of sentencing policy, one clear inference to be drawn from this appreciation is that *we currently punish offenders far too severely* and, in particular, we make grossly excessive use of custody. Whichever variant of Strategy C is adopted, therefore, we believe that it should be guided by the 'principle of parsimony' we referred to in *Chapter 2*. The minimum requirement for any sentencing reform programme should be that it will effectively curtail the use of custody on anything like the present scale. Using imprisonment to excess is ineffective, often counter-productive and wastes precious resources. There is far more to be gained by devising constructive social policies that place far greater emphasis on the prevention of crime than by persisting with ineffectual attempts to combat crime by increasing the punishment which occurs after an offence has been committed.

One clear lesson that may be learned from recent attempts at sentencing reform, is the need to adopt a coherent and consistent approach, and to render this explicit in any legislative proposals that might be put forward. Although seriously deficient in most other respects, the Crime (Sentences) Act 1997 did at least nail its Strategy A credentials unambiguously to the mast, whereas the ambiguous approach that was adopted by the Criminal Justice Act 1991 rendered it particularly vulnerable to judicial obfuscations and (sometimes wilful) misinterpretation. It follows that any sentencing reform that is based on the parsimony principle should clearly and unambiguously prohibit the use of custody for designated categories of offences and offenders. (In our opinion, these non-imprisonable categories should include all but the most serious and recalcitrant non-violent offenders.)[89] The principle could also be used to bring about significant reductions in the length of custodial sentences for all offenders except those who have already committed a serious offence involving violence and in respect of whom there is clear evidence that they pose a severe and lasting risk to the physical safety of others.

When it comes to implementing such a strategy, the managerialist approach which was adopted by the North Carolina legislature (see above) offers some helpful guidance as to how these aims might be realised. They include the establishment of a Sentencing Council to set standards and guidelines for sentencers, which might help to insulate the decision-making process from at least some of the more obvious forms of manipulation on the part of politicians; the articulation of clear objectives which the Council would be expected to adhere to; and the use of techniques to predict sentencing patterns allied to effective monitoring processes in order to anticipate and measure the effect of the proposed changes.

The case in support of a Sentencing Council has been set out with admirable clarity by Andrew Ashworth,[90] who sees its crucial function in terms of providing a much-needed 'transmission mechanism' which would enable the general statutory sentencing framework to be translated into a corpus of consistent and coherent practical guidance for the different levels of courts which are responsible for passing sentence. This is a task for which the Court of Appeal, as we saw earlier, is not well suited. One of its main deficiencies is its lack of sensitivity to two crucial sets of constraints. The first relates to the pragmatic (Strategy B) requirement to seek a more effective way of synchronising judicial demand for prison capacity with the supply that is currently available. The second relates to the longer-term (Strategies B and C) requirement that both the supply and demand for custodial penalties should be the product of a rational, coherent and just sentencing strategy rather than its driving force. To extend Ashworth's mechanical metaphor, what is required is not just a decent 'transmission mechanism' but also an effective 'steering mechanism' and a clear 'route planner' which points clearly and unambiguously in a 'reductionist' direction, overtly aiming to bring down the prison population.

Securing a reduction in the overall use of custody by the courts is one important aim of sentencing reform, but by no means the only one. Among the other possible aims encompassed by Strategy C, our preference would be to offer support for current attempts to promote restorative justice initiatives in sentencing, provided that these developments are sensitive to the human rights of both victims and offenders. We also view the principles of procedural fairness and consistency which underpin the 'just deserts' approach as a desirable ancillary aim, but one which will require considerable adaptation if, as we would hope, the system increasingly comes to be shaped by restorative justice principles in the future. Finally, we are broadly sympathetic to the humanitarian aims that have inspired attempts to reform offenders by penal measures, although we remain somewhat sceptical about some of the more enthusiastic claims for effectiveness that are sometimes made on behalf of this approach, and are mindful of the capacity for injustice that may be caused if the zeal for reform on the part of some exponents and sentencers is not strongly tempered by principles of parsimony and justice.

NEW LABOUR, NEW PENAL POLICY? THE PROSPECTS FOR SENTENCING REFORM

While in opposition, the Labour Party claimed that the criminal justice system was in a state of crisis, and in particular that the sentencing system was not working: the 'transmission mechanism' between Parliament, Home Office and judiciary was ineffective and inadequate.[91] In 1990 the Party had come out in support of creating a Sentencing Council.[92] In both its analysis of the problem and the remedies it prescribed for dealing with it, the 'Old Labour' Party essentially subscribed to a version of Strategy C. However, the main problem it diagnosed in the sentencing system was a lack of consistency, and the main role it envisaged for the Sentencing Council was to iron out 'unacceptable discrepancies'[93] in sentencing. This is consistent with a 'just deserts' approach to sentencing reform but falls far short of what is required if the more serious problems of prison overcrowding and punitive overkill are to be addressed.

Subsequently, however—before the 1997 general election—Shadow Home Secretary Jack Straw presented a policy paper to the Parliamentary Labour Party entitled *Honesty, Consistency and Progression in Sentencing*,[94] which contained indications that the 'New Labour' Party was changing its tune about sentencing. As both the word 'progression' in the document's title and its detailed contents make clear, the New Labour critique against the sentencing framework set out in the Criminal Justice Act 1991 reflected a partial strategic realignment. The Strategy C concern for greater consistency which had been championed by Old Labour was accompanied by a Strategy A concern—in keeping with the 'tough on crime' rhetoric espoused by New Labour—about a lack of progression 'up the tariff' towards ever harsher sentences for repeat offenders. On the issue of promoting *consistency* in sentencing, the policy document also appeared to backtrack on the very idea of a Sentencing Council, even one with such a modest aim as the promotion of greater consistency. While taking care not to rule out a Sentencing Council altogether, the paper spoke of the need to look carefully at 'how the existing machinery could be made to work better, and be made more accountable to Parliament and the public'.[95] It saw a need to give a formal, proactive role to the Court of Appeal Criminal Division to consult on, and then deliver, a system of sentencing guidelines for all offences. As an alternative to a Sentencing Council, the document envisaged an enhanced role for the Judicial Studies Board, whose remit might be extended to include the provision of considered advice to the Court of Appeal on sentencing matters.[96]

One of the incoming Labour government's first forays into the field of penal reform was on the third question of *'honesty'* in sentencing. The Labour policy here marked a significant departure from the Conservatives' approach which, as we saw, would have virtually eliminated the possibility of any early release by substituting the concept of 'real time custodial sentencing', in which 'what you get is what you serve'. Labour's approach was rather to ensure 'transparency': when an offender is imprisoned, the actual meaning of the prison sentence should be made clear at the time sentence is pronounced. Lord Bingham, the Lord Chief Justice, had originally proposed such a measure in the House of Lords debates on the Crime (Sentences) Act, as an alternative to the Conservative government's 'honesty in sentencing provisions'. The incoming Labour government supported this suggestion, and in January 1998 the Lord Chief Justice issued a Practice Direction[97] instructing judges and magistrates to announce the full effects of each sentence they impose, including the minimum time to be served with parole (indicating the length of time that might have already been spent in custody on remand), the minimum length of time spent in custody if parole is not granted, the maximum term possible and the earliest release date.

These changes were intended to combat deep public cynicism among the public towards the courts, following research[98] which showed that one reason for the apparently more punitive attitudes on the part of the public stems from a profound ignorance about the punitiveness of the courts, particularly regarding the extent to which they actually make use of custodial sentences in practice. Public attitudes are likely to be of crucial importance in any attempt to reform the sentencing system, and for this reason alone the new provision for 'transparency' should be seen as a (limited) step in the right direction. If, as seems to be the case, the lack of confidence which people have in the criminal justice system is largely to be explained by their misperceptions and (understandable) ignorance as to how the system operates,[99] it makes much more sense to tackle this by a programme of elucidation and education rather than by vainly attempting to make sentencing policy even more punitive in order to reflect this false image. But much more could be done to lead public opinion and those in the media who help to shape it in the opposite direction, by stating clearly and unequivocally the case for more constructive and progressive reform.

How the actual content of sentences should be arrived at (rather than how they should be presented) was a matter dealt with in the Labour government's Crime and Disorder Act 1998. This legislation differed somewhat from the 1996 *Honesty, Consistency and Progression in Sentencing* policy document, which had cast doubt on the desirability of creating a new body like a Sentencing Council. It was also based on a broader and more interesting mixture of all three Strategies. Under section 80 of the Crime and Disorder Act 1998, the role of the Court of Appeal is extended by giving it the duty to consider whether to frame a set of sentencing guidelines to cover a whole category of cases whenever it hears a sentencing appeal. When it does create or revise guidelines, the Court is required to have regard to the following four principles:

(a) the need to promote consistency in sentencing;

(b) the sentences imposed by courts in England and Wales for offences of the relevant category;

(c) the cost of different sentences and their relative effects in preventing re-offending; and

(d) the need to promote public confidence in the criminal justice system.

Section 81 of the Act creates a 'Sentencing Advisory Panel', which on inspection quite closely resembles the Sentencing Council favoured by Andrew Ashworth and ourselves. Its role under the Act is two-fold. First, in relation to guidelines which the Court of Appeal proposes to frame or revise, it will carry out consultations with a variety of bodies, formulate its own views and communicate them to the Court of Appeal. And secondly it may—either on its own initiative or as directed by the Home Secretary—propose that the Court of Appeal should frame or revise guidelines for a particular category of offence. In either case, the Court of Appeal must 'have regard to' the views of the Sentencing Advisory Panel as well as to the four principles set out above. The Panel also has the job of providing the Court of Appeal with information relating to present levels of sentencing, and—significantly—the *costs* of different sentences and their relative *effectiveness* in preventing re-offending.

Proponents of a Sentencing Council may be disappointed that the Act leaves the Court of Appeal rather than the panel with the power to frame the guidelines, after all we have said about the unsuitability of the Court to perform this task. However, the legislation leaves open the possibility that, in practice, the Panel could be the body which *drafts* guidelines (when it 'formulates its own views' and 'communicates them to the Court'), which the Court could then issue with little or no amendment if happy with them. This may depend on the attitude taken by the Court itself; if it proves to be as jealous of its own power as English judges have historically been it may well prefer to hold a much tighter rein over the process than this.

In terms of the three strategies that we have been considering, the superficial impression given by these provisions is of an eclectic mixture of strategies. This invites the criticism that the government has not yet made up its mind which to pursue or, worse still, is unaware of the tensions and even the potential for conflict between them. Thus, among the factors to which the Court of Appeal is required to have regard, there is still a hint of Strategy A surrounding the 'need to promote public confidence in the criminal justice system', although this is much more muted than, for example, the specific references to the need for 'progression' up the tariff to harsher sentences for repeat offenders contained in Labour's 1996 policy document to which we have referred above.

The Strategy C concern for consistency in sentencing also remains a strong theme in the Crime and Disorder Act. Not only is the Court of Appeal directed to have regard to the need for consistency, but the duty imposed on the Sentencing Advisory Panel to furnish the Court with information concerning the sentences that are imposed by courts for the relevant category of offence could be regarded as an attempt to provide a 'transmission mechanism' between different levels of court, thus helping the Court of Appeal to discharge its own duty on a more informed (and thus potentially more effective) basis. In the Parliamentary debates preceding the enactment of the measure, the role of the panel was described as being 'to provide informed, well-researched and objective advice to the Court of Appeal. It must be independent, but it must be capable of reflecting the view of a wide range of interested parties and of acting as a conduit for those views to the Court of Appeal'.[100] And of course, the reference to the 'cost of different sentences and their relative effectiveness in preventing re-offending' clearly incorporates elements of a managerialist, Strategy B agenda. At the end of the day, however, the Act leaves the Court of Appeal free to decide for itself what relative weight to place on the Strategy A, B and C components of its remit. It must 'have regard' to all three, but it can still pick and choose its own priorities.

One way of looking at the sentencing reforms contained in the Crime and Disorder Act is as an attempt at a principled compromise between the demands of public opinion, consistency and cost-effectiveness. But it could also be seen as a subtle and politically astute attempt to finesse a difficult policy dilemma. On the one hand, it has to be recognised that political expectations of 'tough' punishments for offenders have been raised, not least by the 'tough on crime' rhetoric of the Labour Party itself in recent years: hence the insistence on the need to promote public confidence. But at the same time there is a clear need, as we have seen, to undertake a radical yet realistic reform of sentencing policy (one that is hopefully to be informed by the principle of 'penological realism').

It is too early as yet to pass judgment on whether the Crime and Disorder Act will succeed in squaring this difficult circle, but the developments do represent a considerable advance on the earlier hybrid proposal which involved a more proactive role for the Court of Appeal combined with an enhanced role for the Judicial Studies Board. Indeed, the requirement to have regard not only to the need for consistency but also to the costs and relative effectiveness of different sentencing measures in preventing re-offending could conceivably evolve into a somewhat different kind of 'transmission mechanism', the 'ratios' of which might well come to be geared to a reductionist, and not simply a managerialist, agenda. Much will depend on the composition of the Sentencing Advisory Panel[101] and the people and organizations with whom it is directed to consult, the way it interprets its brief, and the research it commissions in order to furnish the Court of Appeal with the information it needs in framing or revising its guidelines. Much will also depend on the attitude of the Court itself. However, the potential is there for the course of sentencing reform to strike off in a new and much more promising direction, even though we strongly suspect that it will require a much firmer hand on the 'policy tiller' before the final destination is reached.

ENDNOTES: *Chapter 3*

1   See Philip White and Iqbal Powar, *Revised Projections of Long Term Trends in the Prison Population to 2005*, Home Office Statistical Bulletin 2/98 (London, Home Office, 1998), especially para. 4; also Michael Cavadino and James Dignan, *The Penal System: An Introduction* (2nd edn, London, Sage, 1997): 94-99. Early release procedures act as an additional influence on the effective lengths of prison sentences and hence the prison population.

2   For example, West Mercia's Crown Court currently imprisons 74 per cent of the offenders it sentences compared with 39 per cent in Gloucestershire, while the average length of a Kent Crown Court prison sentence is 27.9 months compared with 16.7 months in Staffordshire. (Cited in Penal Affairs Consortium, *The Prison System: Some Current Trends*, London, 1997: 9n). Similar figures (for both magistrates' courts and in the Crown Court in 1994) can be found in Jack Straw, *Honesty, Consistency and Progression in Sentencing*, Paper for the Parliamentary Labour Party Home Affairs Committee: Appendices 1 and 2.

3   See Cavadino and Dignan, op. cit., pp. 87-8.

4   *R v Sargeant* (1974), 60 Cr App R 74.

5   See Cavadino and Dignan, op. cit., p. 97.

6   See for details Cavadino and Dignan, op. cit., p. 94.

7   See Barbara Hudson, *Justice Through Punishment* (London, Macmillan

Education, 1987): ch. 4, and also her *Penal Policy and Social Justice* (Basingstoke and London, Macmillan, 1993): ch. 2. These early concerns were reinforced by more recent studies investigating the significance of racial and ethnic characteristics in sentencing decisions, e.g. Roger Hood, *Race and Sentencing* (Oxford, Oxford University Press, 1992) and Tony Jefferson and Monica Walker, 'Ethnic Minorities in the Criminal Justice System' [1992] *Criminal Law Review* 83-95.

8 Andrew Rutherford, *Prisons and the Process of Justice*, (Oxford, Oxford University Press, 1986): 54ff.

9 See Cavadino and Dignan, op. cit., ch. 8.

10 See Cavadino and Dignan, op. cit., ch. 7 for details.

11 Home Office, *Punishment, Custody and the Community*, Cm 424; *Crime, Justice and Protecting the Public: The Government's Proposals for Legislation*, Cm 965 (London, HMSO, 1988 and 1990).

12 See Cavadino and Dignan, op. cit., pp. 94ff.

13 For differing but complementary assessments of the influence and impact of managerialist thinking on the 1991 sentencing reform process see Anthony Bottoms, 'The Philosophy and Politics of Punishment and Sentencing' in Chris Clarkson and Rod Morgan (eds.), *The Politics of Sentencing Reform* (Oxford, Clarendon Press, 1995): 17-49; and Nicola Lacey, 'Government as Manager, Citizen as Consumer: The Case of the Criminal Justice Act 1991' *Modern Law Review*, 57 (1994), 534-54.

14 For example, the insistence that the imposition of custody or community sentences should be based principally on the seriousness of the current offence (sections 1(2)(a) and 6(1) Criminal Justice Act 1991).

15 At least in respect of the custody decision (section 1(4) of the 1991 Act), though not where other restrictions on liberty are imposed.

16 Nicola Lacey, (op. cit., p.544) relates these measures to a variety of other managerial reforms associated with the post-1990 Conservative administration led by John Major—notably the *Citizen's Charter*—which are intended to benefit the public as a 'customer' of public services. In somewhat similar vein, Bottoms (op. cit., pp.24ff) draws a distinction between three separate forms of managerialism, one of which he refers to as 'consumerist' managerialism, of the kind described by Lacey. The others include 'systemic' managerialism, which has to do with the efficient control of internal system processes, and 'actuarial' managerialism, which is more concerned with the development of techniques for identifying and managing unruly groups, as opposed to individuals.

17 See Bottoms, op. cit., p. 30.

18 See Lacey, op. cit., for details. Briefly, they include the imposition of cash limits for both magistrates' courts and probation services; provision for the extension of 'contracting out' or privatisation in relation to prison and court escort services (see also *Chapter 5*, below); and the introduction of duties to publish more information about the operation of the criminal justice system. The latter was aimed partly at enabling criminal justice decision-makers to become more aware of the financial implications of their decisions, and was

also intended to facilitate monitoring of the degree of compliance with equal opportunities legislation.

[19] Bottoms, op. cit., p. 22.

[20] This is sometimes referred to as the 'parity principle'; see e.g. Andrew von Hirsch, *Past or Future Crimes* (Manchester: Manchester University Press, 1986); and his *Censure and Sanctions* (Oxford, Oxford University Press, 1993).

[21] There can be some apparent tension between the principle of like cases being treated alike and the practice of restorative justice which usually involves a process of dialogue between victim and offender over the outcome. The tension only exists, however, if the only relevant 'likeness' is taken to be the gravity of the offence. See Michael Cavadino and James Dignan, 'Reparation, Retribution and Rights', *International Review of Victimology*, 4 (1997): 233-53.

[22] Notably von Hirsch (see note 20 above).

[23] See e.g. American Friends Service Committee, *Struggle for Justice*, (New York, Hill and Wang, 1971); and von Hirsch (see note 20 above).

[24] See Cavadino and Dignan, op. cit. at note 1, pp.35, 49-51; Canadian Sentencing Commission, *Sentencing Reform: A Canadian Approach*, Report of the Canadian Sentencing Commission (Canada, Ministry of Supply and Services, 1987); Sir Mark Carlisle, *The Parole System in England and Wales: Report of the Review Committee*, Cm 532 (London, HMSO, 1988).

[25] See John Patten, 'Making the Punishment Fit the Frame', *The Guardian*, 20 February 1991.

[26] Though the effect was somewhat marred by the unfortunate spelling error which gave rise throughout to the more appetising, if less accurate, rendition of 'just desserts': Home Office (1990), op. cit., note 11, *passim*.

[27] ibid., para. 2.2.

[28] Criminal Justice Act 1991, section 1(2)(a).

[29] ibid., section 6(1).

[30] ibid., sections 2(2)(a) and 6(2)(b).

[31] Under the policy of 'punishment in the community': see *Chapters 1* and *4*.

[32] A fourth main aim was to put a stop to and reverse the steep decline in the use of the fine over the previous decade. This is an issue we will address in *Chapter 6;* but to cut a longish story short, the results here were similar. The Act was a penological success for a short period, but its political failure led to its abandonment by the government and a resumption in the decline of the fine.

[33] Home Office, *Criminal Statistics, England and Wales 1992*, Cm 2410 (London, HMSO, 1993), para. 7.11.

[34] *Monitoring of the Criminal Justice Act 1991 – Data from a Special Data Collection Exercise*, Home Office Statistical Bulletin 25/93 (London, Home Office, 1993).

[35] David Thomas, 'Sentencing Reform: England and Wales', in Clarkson and Morgan, op. cit., ch. 5, p.135.

[36] Section 29(1). However, courts were still allowed (by section 28(1)) to regard a previous *good* record as a mitigating factor.

[37] See Iain Crow, Michael Cavadino, James Dignan, Valerie Johnston and Monica Walker, *Changing Criminal Justice: The Impact of the Criminal Justice*

Act 1991 in Four Areas in the North of England, (Sheffield, University of Sheffield, 1996) and Home Office Statistical Bulletin 25/93 (op. cit.).

[38] *R* v *Queen* (1981), 3 Cr App R (S) 245.

[39] See above, note 37.

[40] Section 5 of the 1991 Act forbade the use of the suspended sentence unless the case exhibited 'exceptional circumstances', with the result that use of the sentence dropped dramatically from over six per cent of all sentences in 1991 to below 1 per cent, and has remained at this low level since.

[41] Home Office Statistical Bulletin 25/93, op. cit. The survey examined the effect on sentencing during the period from the implementation of the 1991 Act in October 1992 up to February 1993.

[42] The largest increase in the proportion of offenders sentenced to four years or more related to sex offences (up from 14 to 36 per cent).

[43] For example, Lacey (op. cit., p. 547) attributes it to the irreconcilable pressures that built up as the government sought to achieve a pragmatic (and managerialist) solution to the pressing yet contradictory demands which its own hard-line law and order instincts had generated; a task which was compounded by the desperate attempt not to appear to have 'gone soft' on crime.

[44] See e.g. Andrew Ashworth, *Sentencing and Criminal Justice*, (2nd edn, London, Butterworths, 1995), ch. 3; Lacey, op. cit.; Cavadino and Dignan, op. cit. at note 1, ch. 4.

[45] Lacey, op. cit., p.554.

[46] In the case of *R* v *Cunningham* (1993) 14 Cr App R (S) 444.

[47] For example Lord Taylor, as reported in a leader in *The Times*, 23 October 1993.

[48] This was the formulation which Lord Taylor himself suggested should be applied in *R v Cox* (1993), 14 Cr App R (S) 479 at p.481. The fact that this formula had been suggested in a decision *(R v Bradbourn* (1985), 7 Cr App R (S) 180) which predated the 1991 Act again suggests a judicial preference for cosy homespun judicial garments rather than the more sartorially elegant but tighter fitting legislative variety.

[49] *R* v *Keogh* [1993], *Criminal Law Review* 895.

[50] In the case of *R* v *Baverstock* [1993], 2 All ER 32.

[51] Claire Flood-Page and Alan Mackie, *Sentencing Practice: An Examination of Decisions in Magistrates' Courts and the Crown Court in the Mid-1990s*, Home Office Research Study No. 180 (London, Home Office, 1998), ch. 2.

[52] White and Powar, op. cit., para. 4.

[53] Lord Bingham of Cornhill, speaking to the Police Foundation on 10 July 1997, reported in *NACRO Criminal Justice Digest* No. 93, July 1997.

[54] Contained in section 29 of the 1991 Act; see note 36 above. Another change involved the abolition of the judicially unpopular 'two offence' rule which had restricted courts to taking into account only two current offences when assessing the seriousness of the offender's conduct for the purpose of determining whether a custodial sentence was merited.

[55] Cavadino and Dignan, op. cit., note 1, pp.5, 103, 296ff.

56 It also provided for further expansion of the prison system and greater support for private sector involvement in virtually all aspects of its operation; see Cavadino and Dignan, op. cit., note 1, ch. 6, for details.

57 This Act received the Royal Assent on 21 March 1997 and, although none of its provisions had been implemented by the time of the election, a number of them were subsequently brought into force by the incoming Labour Home Secretary, Jack Straw.

58 See Cavadino and Dignan, op. cit., note 1, p. 39.

59 For a discussion of the degree of discretion permitted under the exception, see David Thomas, 'The Crime (Sentences) Act 1997' [1998], *Criminal Law Review* 83-92 at pp. 87-8.

60 And initially supported by the Labour Party as the Bill was progressing through the Commons.

61 Versions of this principle are also to be found in other jurisdictions, e.g. Canada's Sentencing Commission report (op. cit.) on sentencing and parole, which referred to the concept of 'real time sentencing'; in which 'what you get is what you serve'; the Australian states of New South Wales which enacted the Sentencing Act (NSW) in 1989 and also Victoria which enacted the Sentencing Act 1991 (Vic). In the United States itself, a survey carried out for the National Criminal Justice Association in 1995 reported that approximately half of the states had implemented a truth in sentencing system, while a number of others had legislation pending. See Prison Reform Trust, *Truth in Sentencing* (London, Prison Reform Trust, 1996) for details of the Australian and American experiences with truth in sentencing measures.

62 See Prison Reform Trust, op. cit., p. 1.

63 See Cavadino and Dignan, op. cit., note 1, ch. 7 for details relating both to the history of early release provisions in England and Wales, and also the early release provisions themselves, both before and after the 1991 reforms.

64 As advocated by the Carlisle Report (op. cit.), which in turn had been influenced by the 'real-time' sentencing approach that had been advocated in the Canadian Sentencing Commission report (op. cit.).

65 Penal Affairs Consortium, *Sentencing and Early Release: The Home Secretary's Proposals* (London, Penal Affairs Consortium, 1995).

66 They also provoked a storm of trenchant criticism from academic commentators. See e.g. Thomas, op. cit., note 59, who stated in stark terms that 'The Crime (Sentences) Act 1997 represents a low point in the development of English sentencing legislation. It is difficult to think of any legislation in the field of criminal justice enacted during the present century which has so little to do with the improvement of the administration of justice.' (p. 83.)

67 The fact that the United States has managed to quadruple its prison population over the last 20 years without significantly affecting either the overall level of crime (see *Chapter 2*) or the level of people's fears about crime serves to underline Duncan Campbell's observation that 'looking to America for penal guidance is like giving an arsonist the keys to an oil tanker'

('Prisons of the Soul', *The Guardian*, 28 February 1995).

[68] For a review of some of the more recent evidence, see Ralph Henham, 'Anglo-American Approaches to Cumulative Sentencing and the Implications for UK Sentencing Policy', *The Howard Journal of Criminal Justice*, 36 (1997), 263-283.

[69] Prison Reform Trust, *Mandatory Minimum Sentences: The American Experience* (London, Prison Reform Trust, 1996), 4.

[70] Elliott Currie, *Is America Really Winning the War on Crime and Should Britain Follow its Example?* (London, NACRO, 1996), 13.

[71] At 636 offenders incarcerated per 100,000 population (Prison Reform Trust, *Texas: Testing the Case for Incarceration*, London, Prison Reform Trust, 1997), compared with a figure for England and Wales of around 120 currently, itself a very high figure by Western European standards.

[72] Lisa Stolzenberg and Stewart J. D'Alessio, '"Three Strikes and You're Out". The Impact of California's New Mandatory Sentencing Law on Serious Crime Rates', *Crime and Delinquency*, 43 (1997), 457-69.

[73] Home Office, *Protecting the Public: the Government's Strategy on Crime in England and Wales*, Cm 3190 (London, HMSO, 1996).

[74] Prison Reform Trust, op. cit., note 71. This includes those who are held in custody in local jails, those detained in state and Federal prisons and also those under some form of community-based supervision, such as probation or parole.

[75] This includes spending on the entire correctional system, but imprisonment consumes by far the biggest share of the budget.

[76] See Henham, op. cit., p. 272.

[77] There are also, of course, objections to the Strategy A approach on moral grounds. These include the immorality of inflicting excessive and unnecessary suffering, the unfairness of disproportionate penalties such as life for stealing a pizza, and the risk of 'three strikes' laws operating in a racially discriminatory manner (see *Chapter 2* above; Henham, op. cit., p. 275; Prison Reform Trust, *The Florida Sentencing System: A Double-Edged Sword*, London, Prison Reform Trust, 1997, 5).

[78] Currie, op. cit., p. 7.

[79] Peter Greenwood, C P Rydell, Allan Abrahamse, J P Caulkins, J Chiesa, K E Model and S P Klein, *"Three Strikes and You're Out": Estimated Benefits and Costs of California's New Mandatory Sentencing Law*. (Report No. MR-509-RC, Santa Monica, RAND, 1995).

[80] Defined as pollution control, park and other natural resource management, workplace safety assurance and insurance industry regulation.

[81] See White and Powar, op. cit., para. 15.

[82] See Prison Reform Trust, *Balancing Sentencing Policy with Resources: Structured Sentencing in North Carolina* (London, Prison Reform Trust, 1997).

[83] Guideline systems can take various forms. The North Carolina system used numerical guidelines, sometimes called a 'matrix' or 'grid' (they resemble road mileage charts): see Cavadino and Dignan, op. cit., note 1, 105; also Ashworth, op. cit., pp.339-40. Other varieties like those issued by the Court

of Appeal, use a less mathematical and more discursive approach.

84 These included day reporting centres, intensive probation programmes, intensive drug rehabilitation facilities and residential housing programmes.

85 Prison Reform Trust, op. cit., note 81, para. 21.

86 See Cavadino and Dignan, op. cit., note 1, pp. 23, 101 and 293-5.

87 Andrew Ashworth, 'Reflections on the Role of the Sentencing Scholar', in Clarkson and Morgan, op. cit., p. 253.

88 Gordon C. Barclay, with Cynthia Tavares and Andrew Prout (eds.), *Digest 3: Information on the Criminal Justice System in England and Wales* (London, Home Office Research and Statistics Department, 1995), 25.

89 We are not alone in urging that imprisonment is almost never an appropriate penalty for property offenders, however often they repeat their offences, and should only be used for people on remand in the most exceptional circumstances. Even the former Director General of HM Prison Service, Derek Lewis, has taken a similar line (*The Guardian*, 9 April 1997).

90 op. cit., note 44, pp. 342ff.

91 Straw, op. cit., para. 24.

92 Labour Party, *A Safer Britain: Labour's White Paper on Criminal Justice* (London, The Labour Party, 1990).

93 Shadow Home Secretary Roy Hattersley, speaking in the debates on the 1991 Criminal Justice Bill (H. C. Deb. vol. 181, 20 November 1990, col. 155).

94 Straw, op. cit., paras. 56-66.

95 Straw, op. cit., para. 56.

96 ibid., para. 61.

97 See *New Law Journal*, 6 February 1998, p. 158.

98 Michael Hough and Julian Roberts, *Attitudes to Punishment: Findings from the British Crime Survey*, Home Office Research Study No. 179 (London, Home Office, 1988); see also Michael Hough, 'People Talking About Punishment'. *Howard Journal of Criminal Justice*, 35 (1996), 191-214; Andrew Ashworth and Michael Hough, 'Sentencing and the Climate of Opinion' [1996], *Criminal Law Review* 776-787.

99 Although the particular issue of the relationship between the sentence announced by the judge and the time actually served by the prisoner does not seem to be one on which the public suffer from any great misconception: see Hough and Roberts, op. cit., p. 16.

100 Home Office Minister Alun Michael, Session 1997-8, Standing Committee B, Thursday 2 June 1998 (part 1).

101 The Panel met for the first time on 1 July 1999 under the chairmanship of Professor Martin Wasik. The ten other members included academics, sentencers (both magistrates and a Crown Court judge), those with knowledge of the criminal justice system (including prisons and the Probation Service) and independent members (one management consultant, a County Education Officer and a Professor in Ethnic Health).

CHAPTER 4

Punishment and the Community

In *Chapter 3* we looked at developments in sentencing policy and assessed the prospects for reform of the sentencing system. In the next three chapters we examine various outcomes of the sentencing process, beginning with a range of punishments that have come to be known as 'community sentences'. Under the Criminal Justice Act 1991, the term community sentences was applied to a specific, limited range of non-custodial measures that involve some form of supervision or compulsory activity in the community. They include probation, community service orders, combination orders, supervision orders, attendance centre orders and curfews. Collectively, these measures occupy a distinctive, middle-range place within the 1991 sentencing framework. Other forms of 'punishment in the community' (but which are not technically 'community sentences' in the terms of the 1991 Act) include financial penalties—which are the subject of *Chapter 6*—and 'nominal' or 'warning' penalties such as the absolute and conditional discharge.[1] These financial and warning penalties form the lowest category of sentence within the 1991 framework. The penalty of imprisonment—the highest category of sentence—is dealt with in *Chapter 5*.

CONTEXT AND CONCEPTS

The concepts of 'punishment' and the 'community' are both deeply problematic, albeit for different reasons. A major problem with the concept of punishment is that—in the words of Lord Bingham which we cited in *Chapter 1*—'in the public mind . . . custody is generally seen as the only truly retributive or punitive sentence. Anyone who commits a crime of any seriousness and is not sentenced to custody is generally perceived to have got away with it.'[2] This despite the realities that custody is far from being the most frequently imposed sanction available to the courts,[3] is easily the most expensive, and is also by far the most troublesome. This enduring penological paradox represents the biggest challenge for those seeking to promote community-based alternatives of any kind to imprisonment.

If the notion of punishment suffers from an excessively restrictive interpretation due to its association with incarceration, the concept of 'community' suffers from almost the opposite problem, and has even been described (somewhat prudishly) as one of the most promiscuous words in contemporary political usage.[4] The term has three connotations that are particularly relevant in the context of community based penalties. The first (which is also the most familiar) is based on a distinction between prison-based and non-custodial sanctions, in which the notion of 'community' is exceedingly tenuous and refers at most to the locale in which punishment is administered (namely, its non-custodial setting, as opposed to an actual community), while seeking to exploit the positive connotations (of inclusiveness, support and identity) that are associated with the term.[5]

The second connotation of the term 'community' relates to the notion of '*local* community', and is based on a distinction between centralised and decentralised arrangements for the delivery of different types of sanctions. If non-custodial sanctions are to have a genuinely 'community' flavour in this sense, there has to be a willingness to delegate some measure of autonomy to local probation areas or to encourage partnerships between probation services and non-statutory bodies such as voluntary or charitable organizations and private corporations. The 'communities' who might be involved in delivering the sanctions can again be conceived of in different ways: either as purely geographical entities or as interest groups (for example ethnic minorities, female victims of violence etc.) who are represented in a pluralist forum of some kind.

Arguably, neither of these connotations has much affinity with 'real' communities in which people inhabit a shared spatial, occupational or social milieu. But in principle, and increasingly also in practice, communities in this 'real' sense could be expected to assume responsibility for the resolution of criminal disputes and even the application of community-based sanctions such as reparation. This third aspect of the 'community' concept—the community as a decision-making forum made up of people who really do 'live together'—is closely related to the philosophy of communitarianism which we outlined in *Chapter 2*, to which we shall return later in this chapter when proposing our own agenda for reforming punishment in the community.

All three connotations of the term 'community' are relevant in any account of the way punishment in the community has evolved in the past, or might evolve in the future. The first almost came to acquire the status of a 'master definition' during the long years when the Conservatives were in power. The second understanding—community as a geographical or 'interest group' entity—is germane to the 'local' roots of the probation service, while the third sense of the term—real communities with power to make decisions—is gaining increasing prominence as a result of the growing interest in the notion of restorative justice. It is worth noting that both these latter connotations imply a preference for 'individualised' as opposed to 'standardised' outcomes to a given dispute or conflict, including even the resolution of a criminal offence. Consequently, they appear to run counter to the 'rationalising' impulses that are associated with each of the three strategies we outlined in *Chapter 1*. This is most obvious in the case of Strategy B, whose 'managerialist rationality' is based on efficiency and tends to lead to standardised penalties. But it is also the case that Strategy A entails a 'punitive rationality', based on the desire to make offenders suffer, which leads to standard sentences such as 'three strikes and you're out'. Similarly, a 'just deserts'-based variant of Strategy C evinces an 'equitable rationality' based on consistency and proportionality of punishment, which will also seek to standardise outcomes. Communitarianism, on the other hand—whether allied to a humane Strategy C, as we would wish, or even to a punitive Strategy A—would seem to favour a more flexible, individualised system which permits the community to respond in an appropriate manner to the particular offender, in the light of the specific relationships between this offender and this community.

THE LIFE CYCLE OF COMMUNITY PUNISHMENTS TO DATE

The birth of community punishment: A false dawn for Strategy C?

The origins and subsequent development of community-based punishment are inextricably linked with the history of probation which we review briefly below. Before the end of the nineteenth century there were no non-custodial sentences in regular use apart from the fine, and even this frequently resulted in imprisonment in the absence of any provision for paying by instalments. The sole alternative (apart from the death penalty) involved a form of conditional release, based on the common law doctrine of recognisance, which involved an undertaking[6] to 'be of good behaviour'. For impecunious offenders, this procedure offered the only way of mitigating the punitive sentencing policies of the day, the severity of which was matched only by the exceedingly harsh regimes awaiting those who were sentenced to custody.

By the middle of the nineteenth century this legal procedure was being invoked by philanthropic members of the community such as members of the Church of England Temperance Society who sought to persuade the courts to conditionally release into their supervision offenders whose crimes appeared to be drink-related, with a view to reforming them by 'saving their souls'.[7] The founding of the Police Court Missionaries in 1876 and the gradual extension of their 'missions' from the Central London Police Courts to other petty sessional divisions[8] provided magistrates with an alternative method of dealing with offenders and can be seen as a prelude to the evolution of the modern probation service. Even in the 1870s and 1880s the scope it afforded for avoiding the costly use of custody proved attractive to the government,[9] which extended the statutory basis for the taking of recognizances from juveniles to petty adult offenders in order to encourage this development.[10]

Gradually the evangelising religious ethos of the early Police Court Missionaries gave way to the more secularised 'social welfare' philosophy which came to characterise the probation service throughout its formative years. And in place of its original 'soul saving' mission, the role of the service came to be defined much more prosaically in the Probation of Offenders Act of 1907 as a duty to 'advise, assist and befriend' those offenders placed under their supervision. But despite this secularisation, the probation service was to retain its attachment to a Strategy C type of rehabilitative, welfare-oriented and non-punitive philosophy until at least the final quarter of the twentieth century. Ultimately, however, this humanitarian and proselytising zeal proved incapable of withstanding the challenges posed by the collapse of the rehabilitative ideal and the growing political appeal of rival creeds such as the managerialist Strategy B and the 'law and order' stance associated with Strategy A.

Community punishment comes of age: *Laissez faire* and the permissive era

By the end of the 1960s, the probation service had evolved from a locally-based, amateur, 'grass roots' mission to a nation-wide, professional, secular, social work service to the courts—though this is not to deny the existence of a 'controlling' and 'coercive' element that also dated back to the origins of the service. By this stage, its responsibilities were not restricted to the supervision of offenders in the community but extended also to advising and assisting the courts in their sentencing decisions by providing them with social inquiry reports[11] on offenders. In addition, they were also responsible for the welfare of prisoners, and for supervising many inmates after release—quite apart from their involvement in civil matters such as assisting with matrimonial problems and issues relating to child care.

This era of expansionism was reflected also in the size of the profession, which increased five-fold, from 1,006 probation officers of all grades in 1950, to 5,033 by 1976,[12] though the rate of growth slowed down considerably thereafter and more recently went into reverse (peaking at 7,776 in 1994 but declining to 7,171 in 1997).[13] In organizational terms, however, the probation service still reflected its localised origins, since it was (and remains to this day) area-based,[14] each area having a chief probation officer who is responsible for the direction and delivery of the service in that area. Moreover, until well into the 1980s each probation area still enjoyed considerable autonomy to develop its own policies and practice. However, this *laissez faire* approach was to prove unsustainable in the face of growing internal and external pressures on the service.

One index of the changing status of the profession and its ability to withstand external pressure relates to the source of its funding and the gradual transfer of responsibility from local to central government. It was only in 1948 that the proportion of central government funding reached the level of 50 per cent. In 1971, however, it was raised to 80 per cent, with the remainder coming from local authorities. This change in the source of funding by itself would probably have undermined the autonomy enjoyed by the service in the longer term (if only on the principle of 'he who pays the piper calls the tune'), but other developments were to pose an even more immediate threat. The two most potent forces for change were the growth of managerialism (Strategy B) and the sustained assault on probation's traditional welfare philosophy from the increasingly dominant 'law and order' ethic associated with Strategy A.[15] Although these developments are clearly inter-related, and to some extent contemporaneous, for the sake of analytical clarity we will deal with them sequentially in the following two sections.

Handling maturity: Strategy B and the Managerial Revolution

The concept of managerialism encompasses a number of distinct themes which, at various times, have played a decisive role in shaping the development of the probation service. The first main theme is that of '*administrative control*' which is one of the characteristic features of all bureaucratic organizations and involves the subjection of professional skills or working practices to management ideals in pursuit of goals that are identified by the organization itself. Far from posing a threat to the autonomy of an organization, this particular form of managerialism can provide a strategy for preserving and even enhancing the organization's control over its own destiny and its capacity for independent action. This was certainly true of the probation service at least during its formative years and throughout much of the *laissez faire* era.

However, when imposed from without, managerialism can also be used as an *instrument of control and subordination*, and this potential was exploited to the full by successive Conservative governments during the period from the mid 1980s up until their period of power was brought to an end by the General Election of May 1997. This was an era of almost unprecedented centralisation of power and control over the direction of public policy and, in the case of the probation service, represented an unrelenting attempt to harness the work, ethos and management of the service to the policy objectives defined by the government. A number of different policy objectives can be identified, which may be thought of as sub-themes that are encompassed under the broad heading of managerialism. These have been variously described, but we will refer to them as '*technocratic managerialism*', '*consumerist managerialism*',[16] '*systemic managerialism*', and '*punitive managerialism*'. Before exploring these different strands, however, we will briefly narrate the beginning of the managerial revolution within the probation service. This was initially prompted by central government, but also involved an attempt by the service itself to develop forms of administrative control that would enable it to meet the challenges posed by its rapid growth and its quest for a professional identity.

The first stirrings of the 'managerial revolution' within the probation service can be traced back to the mid-1920s which is when the foundations were laid for an administrative framework for the probation service.[17] Under the Criminal Justice Act 1925 and the Criminal Justice Amendment Act 1926 petty sessional divisions (the catchment areas for magistrates' courts) were designated as probation areas and were all obliged for the first time to employ at least one probation officer. Local probation committees were set up to appoint probation officers, pay them and oversee their work. In a separate but related development, a hierarchical career structure for the probation service was gradually established following the publication by the Home Office of the 1926 Probation Rules which differentiated between principal probation officers and others.

The next steps were taken by the probation service itself, which gradually 'professionalised'—transforming itself into a professional and bureaucratic organization in its continuing quest for enhanced career status. This was achieved in part by re-aligning the philosophical basis of the service and also its working practices from the 'missionary ideals' of its progenitors towards a more diagnostic and therapeutic approach to working with offenders, based on the adoption of American-style social casework techniques.[18] During the 1960s and 1970s, this quest was assisted by the proliferation of additional duties and responsibilities which were assigned to the service, including the welfare of prison inmates, and their post-release supervision and after-care, plus the administration of new non-custodial punishments such as community service orders. The effect of all this was to integrate the role of the service more closely with the rest of the penal system. Meanwhile, there was also evidence from within the service of a move towards an increasingly hierarchical career structure.[19] This broader remit combined with a more bureaucratic form of organization helped to pave the way for a more pervasive and radical form of managerialism. But this time both the agenda and the pace of reform were to be set by the government, with a view to bringing the probation service under much firmer central control than it had ever experienced in its history.

The election of the Conservatives in 1979 heralded a radical departure for the relations between government and probation service, not so much on account of the government's strident law and order rhetoric, but by virtue of its commitment to a much more insidious form of centrally-directed managerialism that was fundamentally incompatible with the probation service's long tradition of local autonomy. The managerial revolution which was unleashed by the Conservative government took a number of different forms. The first involved the zealous application of various managerial techniques and philosophies that were borrowed from the private sector in order to raise standards of service and promote greater accountability while operating within tightly constrained cash limits. This has come to be referred to as the 'new public management', and can be thought of as a form of *technocratic managerialism'* in which high priority is given to the setting of performance indicators, quantifiable output measures and collective targets with a view to delivering the 'Three Es' of 'economy', 'efficiency' and 'effectiveness'.

The first manifestation of this new orthodoxy in relation to the probation service took the form of a Statement of National Objectives and Priorities (SNOP). This was issued by the Home Office in 1984 as part of the government's Financial Management Initiative,[20] and clearly signalled that the old *laissez faire* approach to probation policy was about to be replaced by a much more assertive form of centralised control. SNOP urged local probation committees and chief officers to ensure that probation resources were managed 'efficiently and effectively' in pursuit of clear objectives with a view to delivering value for money to the taxpayer.

An explicit aim of the statement was to promote a degree of uniformity and consistency on the part of individual probation services. The process marked the beginning of a change of ethos within the service which placed greater emphasis on the need for accountability by devising area and team objectives, action plans and the like while downgrading the traditional commitment to professional autonomy on the part of individual case workers. Moreover, the SNOP initiative represented only the first shot in an intensifying barrage of measures which were designed to increase the degree of central oversight and control of local service provision. They included use of the Audit Commission, National Audit Office and Her Majesty's Inspectorate of

Probation to maintain the momentum by undertaking periodic reviews to monitor local services against a standard range of 'key performance indicators' designed to measure their quality and effectiveness. The emphasis on prudent resource-management culminated in the adoption of a new funding arrangement in 1992 which was based on the imposition of cash limits according to a national formula determined in Whitehall rather than in response to locally determined needs. (Many local services responded by recruiting their own financial management consultants.) This switch represented another nail in the coffin of local autonomy and a further centralisation of policy-making power.

The form of managerialism we have been focusing on so far lays great stress on the largely abstract and rational values that are associated with bureaucratic organizations of all kinds—efficiency, effectiveness and value-for-money—and appears to value the process of managerialism almost as an end or goal in itself. However, most other forms of managerialism adopt a more instrumentalist approach one of which, as Tony Bottoms has pointed out,[21] is oriented towards the protection of consumers' interests, and not just those of tax payers.

Anne Worrall has suggested[22] that when National Standards for probation services were introduced in 1992 (see below) they contained certain provisions which appeared to be consistent with this form of *'consumerist managerialism'*, and to fit nicely with the rhetoric of the *Citizen's Charter* which was introduced by John Major's government. However, the only example she cites is the requirement that offenders 'should have access to a fair and effective complaints system if they are dissatisfied with the service they receive',[23] and as she herself notes this requirement was redrafted in the later (1995) version of the National Standards to read, '[offenders] should be informed of what is expected of them and the action which will be taken if they fail to comply with the requirements of the standards'.[24] Perhaps it is not surprising, given their views on law and order, that the Conservative government's strong support for managerialism in the context of probation reform should have had other, more strategic, objectives in mind than the protection of consumers' interests, if the relevant 'consumers' are offenders.

One of these broader political objectives was to integrate the probation service much more closely into the wider penal system, of which it has always been an important, if somewhat detached, component. But this required much more sweeping changes than were likely to be achieved simply by reforming the internal administrative machinery of the probation service by means of a technocratic form of managerialism. Instead, it called for the aims and agenda of the probation service to be aligned much more closely with those pursued by the rest of the penal system. The name that has been given to this broader strategic approach is '*systemic managerialism*'; and this also manifested itself for the first time in the Statement of National Objectives and Priorities. This statement was not restricted to establishing a mechanism for reforming the internal administration of the probation service but also set out to prioritise the work of the probation service by promoting the aim of providing alternatives to custody above all other aspects of probation work (in line with the government's desire, prior to the 'prison works' era of Michael Howard, to divert offenders from custody), followed by the preparation of social inquiry reports.[25]

However, this required a fundamental realignment of the traditional aims of the probation service which had historically been much more involved in the rehabilitation of relatively low risk, petty offenders. The need for the probation service to focus its attention 'higher up the tariff', by working with more serious offenders who would otherwise be at risk of custody, was spelt out repeatedly and unequivocally in a deluge of policy papers and reviews of the probation service over the following months and years. They included the 1988 Green Paper *Punishment, Custody and the Community*[26] which signalled its clear determination to redefine probation in terms of 'punishment and control' rather than welfare, in line with the 'punitive bifurcation' policy of 'punishment in the community' (see *Chapter 1*). This was reinforced by a request issued the same year that each probation service should publish its own complementary strategy in the form of an action plan, indicating how it intended to target more intensive forms of probation supervision on young adult offenders with a view to reducing the use of custody for this age group.[27]

In 1989 the Audit Commission reviewed the service and concluded that it was not delivering value for money.[28] It also called for the probation service to re-target its activities in the direction of more serious offenders and to develop new skills, emphasising the importance of intensive supervision and more active management of the offender while downplaying the traditional casework skills that had come to be identified as the hall-mark of the profession in its quest for professionalisation. Finally, just in case the probation service had not got the message, a government Green Paper on the reorganization of the probation service[29] reiterated that the primary role of the probation service should be to serve as a criminal justice agency, complementing the work of other agencies such as the police, prisons and, principally, the courts, rather than as a social work agency. Its distinctive contribution was defined in terms of preventing or reducing re-offending by those under supervision, with a view to reducing overall levels of crime.[30] And in the event of a refusal by the probation service to play the part which had been allocated for it within this systemic managerial framework, the 1988 Green Paper had floated the possibility of establishing a new organization to undertake some of the tasks which the probation service was being 'invited' to take on.

A final post-script to this 'systemic realignment' project which the Conservative government was determined to push through relates to the issue of social work training for the probation service. This was repeatedly criticised by the government as being inappropriate for the 'new model' probation service which the government clearly had in mind, and eventually the legal requirement for all new probation officers to hold a Diploma in Social Work was removed by Michael Howard during his period at the Home Office. One of the justifications offered for this move was to encourage recruitment from a 'broader base' including those who were perceived to have relevant experience and skills (such as those from the armed forces), even if they lacked the formal qualifications. Having effectively already removed the probation service's erstwhile (conditional) freedom to determine its own policy, and challenged its identifying ethos and working practices, the removal of its distinctive training base represented a further stage in the transformation of the probation service into a much less autonomous professional body.

However, the government's ambitions for the probation service were not simply confined to securing its integration within the wider penal system and reordering its functional priorities and level of intervention within the tariff of offences. The Conservatives also had equally firm views regarding the *nature* of the intervention they deemed it appropriate for the probation service to be undertaking, and were prepared to use the managerial tools they were fashioning in order to achieve their other objectives for this purpose also. We refer to this aspect of managerialism as '*punitive managerialism*' since it represents the utilisation of managerial techniques in pursuit of broader penological (and political) objectives that are inextricably linked with Strategy A. This is something we will examine more closely in the next section.

Hardening of the arteries: The iron grip of Strategy A

The managerialist reforms we concentrated on in the previous section started in the early 1980s but are mainly associated with the 'Hurd era' of sentencing reform which lasted from 1987 until the 'law and order counter-reformation' began in 1992/1993. Thereafter, as we have seen, criminal justice policy was increasingly driven by Strategy A. In relation to community punishment, however, several aspects of the 'managerial revolution' which we have described already also appear to have been decisively influenced by Strategy A thinking, even before the counter-reformation set in. Indeed, it is possible to identify at least four illustrations of this tendency.

The first of these, mentioned in the previous section, is the frontal assault which the government launched on the probation service's traditional social work philosophy and value-base, which in turn underpinned much of its training curriculum. Virtually all the government's reports and documents on probation at this time rammed home the same message that probation had to revamp its values away from its traditional centring around the 'client'.

The second example of the influence which Strategy A had on the content of the government's managerial reforms is directly related to this rejection of the social work ethic, and involves the redefinition of probation as a form of punishment in its own right. This was accomplished rhetorically (and unambiguously), in Home Office Minister John Patten's address to the Annual Conference of Chief Officers of Probation (ACOP) in September 1988 in which he emphasised that in the government's view, 'all probation-based disposals are already in varying degrees forms of punishment' and said it was 'bizarre' to pretend otherwise. Legislative confirmation followed in the 1991 Criminal Justice Act which converted the probation order into a sentence in its own right for the first time (rather than being imposed 'instead of sentencing' the offender,[31] as had previously been the case). The effect of this was largely symbolic, though it did have one important practical consequence, which was to enable probation for the first time to be combined with other penalties (in respect of a single offence). The ideological import was that probation was a punishment, not an alternative to punishment, that the 'client' was primarily an 'offender', and that probation was to shift its orientation from care for the 'client' towards punishment and control in the service of wider penal aims.

Two other examples of the influence of Strategy A thinking on the content of the 'managerial revolution' relate to matters of substance, not just symbol, and both are profoundly important developments in the evolution of community punishment. The first involved an attempt to 'calibrate' the concept of punishment in terms of a graduated scale in which the unit of measure was based on the degree of restriction it imposed on the liberty of the offender. The idea was originally derived from the writings of the right-wing American criminologist James Q. Wilson[32] and, combined with the principles of proportionality and just deserts, it played an important part in developing the hierarchical sentencing framework which was established by the Criminal Justice Act 1991.[33] The various 'community sentences' were intended to occupy an intermediate position within the hierarchical framework and were aimed at offenders for whom a warning or financial penalty would not be deemed sufficient, and yet custody would be excessive. In order to emphasise the more unified and incrementalist approach which sentencers were being asked to adopt, the government sought to recategorise these non-custodial sentences as 'community penalties' or 'punishment in the community' and to drop the term 'alternatives to custody' which had been commonly used in the past.

The final illustration of the extent to which Strategy A thinking underpinned many of the managerial reforms we were looking at in the previous section relates to the attempt to position the various existing non-custodial penalties within the sentencing hierarchy as part of the 1991 sentencing reforms and, where necessary, to introduce new ones. One of the first attempts at repositioning was directed at community service orders when the first set of national standards was introduced in 1988.[34] The National Standards emphasised the need to ensure that sentencers viewed community penalties such as the CSO with confidence, and suggested that this was most likely to be achieved by seeing to it that the penalty 'makes uniformly stiff demands on offenders'. A similar approach was adopted as National Standards were gradually extended to all aspects of probation service supervision, including new and existing orders, the content of supervision sessions and rules governing enforcement and breach procedures. All of them emphasised that the primary role of community sentences was intended to restrict the liberty of offenders and to make very real mental and physical demands on them—to be punitive rather than rehabilitative—in order to gain and retain credibility in the eyes of sentencers.

The 1991 Criminal Justice Act itself not only gave legislative effect to this 'punitive calculus' which the government had painstakingly put together, but also introduced a number of new community sentences with the aim of enhancing still further the credibility of community punishment in the hope of thereby discouraging the unnecessary use of custody. These included the introduction of curfew orders, a form of house arrest enforceable by electronic monitoring (or 'tagging').[35] Provision was made for this monitoring to be carried out by agencies other than the probation service. Another new community punishment which was more demanding than the curfew order, albeit less intrusive, was the 'combination order'[36] which combines probation supervision with community service. Responsibility for administering this new order was given to the probation service.

The professed aim of all of these measures was to provide demanding non-custodial penalties in order to enable and encourage a much greater proportion of offenders—especially petty persistent property offenders—to be dealt with in the community rather than in prison, reserving the use of custody for only the most serious offences.[37]

This was the strategy which we have termed 'punitive bifurcation' in view of the persistent emphasis on increasing the severity of punishment in the community as well as trying to decrease the use of custody (see *Chapter 1*). The probation service was being expected to play an important part in developing and delivering 'credible' community penalties for the courts. For a while it seemed that a centre-stage role at the heart of a more integrated criminal justice system might provide some compensation for its loss of autonomy (and the introduction of cash limits), even if the script it was being asked to perform was not of its choosing. However, that was before the 'law and order counter reformation'.

Once it became clear that custody was not to be sidelined after all, it was much less likely that probation would continue to receive star billing. And so it turned out. Soon, Michael Howard was reiterating exactly the same criticisms of community punishments as had his predecessors in the Home Office, in spite of the considerable increase in their 'punitive bite' since the 1991 reforms. Thus, in yet another Green Paper (ominously entitled *Strengthening Punishment in the Community*)[38] the government reverted to its earlier complaints that the role of probation was poorly understood. This was attributed in part to inconsistencies in the implementation of orders around the country, particularly in relation to enforcement procedures, with the result that, in the government's view, probation was still widely regarded as a 'soft option'. The Green Paper also provided yet another opportunity to attack the social work ethic with which the probation service was still considered to be indelibly tainted. And shortly after this the government finally removed the requirement for probation officers to hold a social work qualification as a condition of entry into the profession.

The government's proposed solution to the 'problems' it had identified envisaged the introduction of a new integrated 'community sentence' which would subsume within it all the existing orders, enabling sentencers themselves to specify the exact content of the order. However, responses to these proposals (including those of sentencers themselves) were unenthusiastic, and the idea was abandoned. Instead, the White Paper which was published in the run-up to the 1997 General Election set the tone for the ensuing hustings debate by reiterating the government's 'prison works' mantra and insisting that the essential prerequisite for all community-based sentences was to ensure that 'offenders have to undergo physically, mentally or emotionally challenging programmes and are required to conform to a structured regime'.[39]

After nearly 18 years of persistent attempts by successive Conservative governments to reform the nature and function of non-custodial punishment, their stark legacy appeared to have combined the worst of all possible worlds. Thus, having in 1991 scaled up the 'punitive bite' exacted by community penalties in order to enhance their credibility with sentencers and help to secure a reduction in the use of custody, the government was now saying that they were still too soft and needed to be toughened even further. Meanwhile, following the abandonment of the reductionist approach to custody which was associated with Douglas Hurd and the 1991 reforms, the custodial population was now expanding at an ever greater rate. In short, the ratchet-like increase in the overall level of punitiveness seemed to have become a treadmill from which it would be politically difficult if not impossible to escape, at least while public attitudes and expectations continued to be shaped by the increasingly strident law and order rhetoric being disseminated by the two main political parties.

FACING THE FUTURE: SOUL SEARCHING AND ROLE SEARCHING

For many years the probation service had been sustained by a clear sense of purpose. This was derived in part from its commitment to the goal of rehabilitation, supported by its humanitarian value-base and a broadly reformist ethic and agenda. Within a relatively short space of time, all these traditional supports were under sustained attack, leaving the service without a clear *raison d'etre*. The effect was to unleash a lengthy and continuing debate (which is still inconclusive) over its future role and direction. The demise of the rehabilitative ideal during the 1970s served to undermine the 'therapeutic professional' rationale on which the service had staked its claim to enhanced professional status based on its professed occupational competence. This alone would have been sufficient to precipitate a crisis of confidence within the service regarding its ethical justification and future direction. However, the effect was compounded, as we have seen, by the election in 1979 of a government whose increasingly resurgent 'law and order' instincts were to unleash a sustained external assault on the probation service's traditional ethos, philosophy, priorities and working practices.

The initial effect of these internal and external challenges was to rekindle a deep-rooted and long-standing philosophical conflict between the 'welfare' and 'controlling' functions which have always been inherent in the probation order. One response to the soul-searching that has ensued has been to acknowledge the perceived new political realities and to accept the need for a fundamental realignment of the probation service's role and priorities by putting a much greater emphasis on the punishment of offenders and the provision of demanding alternatives to custody. Taken to its logical conclusion, this approach could result in probation becoming a 'community correctional service', as advocated by adherents of Strategy A. Such views are not confined to right-wing politicians but have also been increasingly echoed within the probation service in recent years, particularly among more pragmatically-minded senior management ranks.[40]

Although the reforms associated with the 1991 Criminal Justice Act were accompanied by some 'tough', punitive rhetoric, and were also intended to carve out a new and more disciplinary role for the probation service, they sought at the same time to accomplish a more liberal and pragmatic set of aims consistent with Strategy B: restraining the use of custody while creating a more coherent and principled sentencing policy. If the 1991 reform process had been allowed to continue, it appeared to envisage an expanded and more responsible role for the probation service and (despite the imposition of cash limits) the prospect of better funding for the future. Although it was well received in some quarters, not all were convinced, including many in the probation service—such as the National Association of Probation Officers—who rejected the government's punitive emphasis and lamented the curtailment of the service's traditional role as a social work agency.

Other contributors to the debate have attempted to reformulate and update the probation service's traditional Strategy C values. For a long time one of the most discussed and influential contributions was a 1979 article by Tony Bottoms and Bill McWilliams[41] in which they urged that the 'medical model' (which is based on the concepts of 'diagnosis', 'treatment' and 'cure') should be replaced by the less coercive terminology of 'help', 'shared assessments' and 'task-centred work'. Whatever the merits of this attempt to reconcile the humanitarian impulses of the probation service's 'core values' with the seemingly contradictory demands of the more mainstream criminal justice agencies, it was unable to withstand the much harsher political climate that began to assert itself during the 1980s.[42]

More recent contributions to the debate—typified by Mike Nellis[43]— are also consistent with a Strategy C approach but offer a very different vision for the future, based on the emerging philosophy and practice of 'restorative justice'. As we explained in *Chapter 2*, restorative justice is a movement which seeks to respond to crime in a more constructive way than is achieved through the use of punishment, by seeking to engage with offenders to try to bring home to them the consequences of their actions while at the same time trying to address in a positive way the needs of victims. For the probation service this entails a departure from its traditional preoccupation exclusively with offenders, though it would of course continue to be involved in supervising them and working towards their rehabilitation. However, the service would also provide greater support for victims, in part by expanding the service's involvement in 'restorative justice' programmes including victim/offender mediation programmes and community mediation services.[44] It would also entail a rejection of the traditional generic social work orientation for the probation service and the substitution of a new value base which would be derived in part from the principles of restorative justice. Nellis also advocates a more active role for the probation service in local crime prevention initiatives, and suggests that this shift of focus would enable the service to retain its commitment to 'anti-custodial' values and a reformist stance on social justice issues, based on a recognition that rehabilitation alone offers an insufficient value base for the future. The logic of this approach would result in probation seeking to establish itself as a 'community justice agency' that is dedicated to the pursuit of greater social justice for offenders, victims and the wider community. Nellis believes that only in this way might probation be able to resist being conscripted as yet another punitive institution and retain much of its traditional reformist and humanitarian ethos. The disjuncture between this restorative justice model and the traditional values and practices of the probation service does not seem all that dramatic, and this might enhance the model's prospects of gaining wider acceptance within probation—certainly compared with some of its recent rivals.

Over the past two decades, the probation service has made some limited moves in the direction of restorative justice. For example, it has become increasingly involved in a number of victim/offender mediation programmes and community mediation services. Some of the former have attempted to combine the practices of mediation and reparation with the diversion of offenders from the criminal justice system. Others accept referrals at different stages in the criminal justice process, for example following an adjournment between conviction and sentence, or a deferment of sentence. There has also been some encouragement from government for these developments. We have seen how the government has actively sought to steer the probation service away from a social work model and towards an 'offender-management model'.[45] It has also made the service responsible for undertaking certain kinds of victim inquiry work—for example, reporting to the court on the effect which crimes have had on victims; and contacting victims to seek their views prior to the release of long-term prisoners. Thus probation officers are less exclusively preoccupied with the concerns of offenders now than at any time in the past.

During the Conservatives' period in office, however, the government had been much less enthusiastic about promoting the idea of restorative justice, with or without the involvement of the probation service. There was a brief period during the mid-1980s when the Home Office showed some interest in the development of mediation and reparation schemes and funded four new pilot projects[46] over a two year period, all of which were thoroughly evaluated. Although these early evaluations confirmed other research findings that mediated encounters between victims and offenders can have benefits for those involved, problems were also encountered with several of the early schemes, particularly with regard to the principal aims of the projects and also the extent to which the interests of both offenders and victims could be secured simultaneously.[47] Doubts were also raised regarding the extent to which mediation and reparation schemes could successfully operate within the context of the conventional criminal justice system.

Later research[48] suggested that the difficulties that had been encountered with some of the early schemes were not insuperable, but by then the government had lost interest in the idea of funding the development of victim offender mediation. From then on it was left to the voluntary efforts of individuals and local agencies (including, as we have noted, some probation services) to pioneer the embryonic movement by obtaining funding and securing the necessary managerial and institutional support in the face of scepticism, inertia and (especially) competing demands for funding during a period of unprecedented challenge for the probation service. And despite occasional successes, restorative justice seemed destined to languish on the margins of the criminal justice system, the victim of 'benign neglect' in which, as Tony Marshall has ruefully noted, the emphasis has more often been on the 'neglect' than the 'benign'.[49] This state of affairs continued until the General Election of 1997. In the final two sections we assess the prospects for the future of community punishment following the change of government and comment on the further reforms that might be required in both the short and longer terms in order to tackle some of the problems that we have identified in the course of this chapter.

New Labour: New life for community punishment?

Since the General Election of 1997, the future of community punishment has been the subject of n ixed messages from the incoming Labour government. On the positiv₂ side, some of the more destructive policies introduced by their Conservative predecessors have been reversed, either in whole or in part. Thus, the new Home Secretary, Jack Straw, was swift to reinstate a university-based training programme for the probation service, leading to a Diploma in Probation Studies, which would involve a mixture of university teaching and work-based assessment. But he also made it clear that training for probation officers would no longer be linked to social work education, and reaffirmed that the aim would still be to attract a wider range of recruits to the probation service than in the past.[50]

It is also apparent that the government envisages a much bigger role for the probation service in the future. For example, they will be expected to play an active part in the local youth offending teams which will have wide-ranging responsibilities for dealing with youth crime under the Crime and Disorder Act (see *Chapter 7*). The probation service will also be responsible for administering compulsory drug treatment programmes which are likewise to be introduced under the Act. Moreover, it is likely that the probation service will be asked to become increasingly involved in the supervision of offenders who are subject to electronic monitoring, a measure whose application the government seems keen to expand. Curfew orders with electronic monitoring are to be made available for three new groups of offenders under the Crime (Sentences) Act 1997: fine defaulters, petty persistent offenders and juveniles aged 10 to 15. The Crime and Disorder Act 1998 goes further, permitting the release of short-term prisoners (those serving less than four years) up to two months before their normal release date, subject to an electronically monitored 'home curfew detention' which will be combined with supervision by the probation service. It also includes the power to specify those who will be responsible for monitoring the released offender's whereabouts, which could include probation officers despite their traditional opposition to the principle of electronic tagging[51]—opposition which may however be currently declining, as we shall discuss shortly. Finally, probation officers will also have a key role in implementing the government's 'Welfare to Work' programme following a commitment to extend its training and access to work provisions to offenders on their release from prison. All of these developments represent an expansion of the traditional supervisory and welfare functions of the probation service.

However, other proposals are more consistent with the first tentative steps towards a gradual transformation of the probation service into something resembling Mike Nellis's portrait of a community-based organization that is actively engaged in the pursuit of restorative justice. A number of the youth justice reforms contained in the Crime and Disorder Act[52] can be interpreted in this light. They include the provisions for reparation orders and action plan orders as new community penalties that will be available to the youth court and, possibly, the new final warning procedure which seems intended to extend the use of 'caution plus' procedures of the kind that have been pioneered in Northamptonshire and elsewhere. All of these measures have the potential to encourage the use of mediation and reparation schemes on a far wider scale, and this in turn could help to stimulate a more active involvement on the part of probation services, especially if similar measures are extended from the youth to the adult criminal justice system.

While there are some grounds for cautious optimism in relation to some of these developments, other signs have been much less hopeful. Firstly, and most ominously, there has been no serious attempt as yet to halt the Conservative government's vicious 'incarceration spiral', in spite of inheriting a rapidly deteriorating prison numbers crisis. Indeed, the Home Secretary has gone on record as accepting that prisons are 'essentially a demand-led service'[53] (unlike virtually all other publicly funded institutions), and that his priority (like that of his predecessor) is not to reduce the prison population but to 'secure the protection of the public'—implying that these two goals are mutually exclusive. At other times he has spoken of the problems caused by the growth of the prison population over the past few years, and the need to reverse this trend.[54] However, in reiterating the need for community punishments to be 'credible' enough to command the confidence of the courts and the public,[55] and in emphasising that the probation service's primary duty is to protect the public by implementing and enforcing the orders of the court, his language is still coloured by much of the punitive rhetoric associated with his predecessors. And while there are some provisions in the Crime and Disorder Act which are consistent with a restorative justice approach, many other measures are much more redolent of a traditional, punitive, Strategy A approach.

In view of these mixed messages—and the tensions which they suggest go right to the heart of the government's criminal justice policy-making—the future of community punishment in general, and the probation service in particular, remains shrouded in uncertainty, at least until we know what will be the final responses of the Labour government to a series of crucial reviews that were established shortly after it took office. The first of these was a major cross-Departmental review of the entire criminal justice system, announced shortly after Labour took office, which in July 1998 resulted in the publication of the formidable Home Office research publication *Reducing Offending*.[56] We discuss this report and its significance in *Chapter 8*.

The second was the 'Prisons-Probation Review', commenced in July 1997. The purpose of this review was to examine the structure and organization of both the probation service and the Prison Service, including options for closer and more integrated work between the two services. The fact that the review was asked to examine 'international models of good practice' (notably Sweden and Canada) prompted fears[57] of a possible merger between the two services, and the creation of a North American-style 'Department of Corrections'.

Such fears might have been misplaced, particularly if lessons really had been learned from the Swedish experience.[58] Although nominally located within a central government department dealing with prison and probation, the administration of the two services in Sweden is devolved on a regional basis, and probation is made accountable to a local supervision board (consisting of judges and co-opted members) rather than the prison service. Far from swallowing up the local identity of probation by combining it with an over-centralised prison service, the Swedish experience appears to offer a method of combining the benefits of local accountability (and increased confidence in the implementation of non-custodial penalties) with a greater degree of integration and planning at regional and national levels. Indeed, the implications of adopting a 'Swedish' model could be even greater for the Prison Service than for the probation service.

In the event, however, no such merger seems likely. A consultation paper issued in August 1998 on the publication of the Review's final report[59] rejected a merger and favoured the option of keeping the prison and probation services separate, but integrating the two more closely and harmonising their structures, particularly in terms of coterminous boundaries and similar lines of accountability (including a clear line of accountability up to the Home Secretary). The government's preference was to amalgamate the existing 54 separate probation services into one national service (albeit one organized in 42 local area units coterminous with police and Crown Prosecution Service areas), which would probably strike against any notion of local communities having any serious input into 'community sentences'. The government also favours 'rebranding' both the service itself and community sentences such as probation and community service orders, with the service acquiring a new name such as 'Public Protection Service' or 'Community Justice Enforcement Agency' and probation officers losing their historic statutory duty to 'advise, assist and befriend' the offenders they supervise. The document concentrated on the perceived need to give probation and community sentences a less 'soft' image, continuing the Conservatives' attempt to detach probation from the values and ethos of social work. It seemed to envisage that any reorientation of community punishment should be in the general direction of even greater (real or perceived) 'toughness' rather than towards restorative justice. Thus, the strongest themes in the government's response to the review were, firstly, a concern for Strategy B managerialism, and secondly a wish for community penalties to have a tough image.

Finally, a third review which could also affect the future of the probation service and community punishment in general was an inquiry by the (all-party) House of Commons Home Affairs Committee into Alternatives to Prison Sentences, which reported on 10 September 1998. The committee's unanimously agreed report warned that 'the huge rise in the prison population during the last five years is unsustainable. Unless halted—and in due course reversed—it will end badly.' It 'noted' estimates by the Chief Inspector of Prisons that 30 per cent of prisoners (and 70 per cent of female prisoners) need not be in prison. Its prescription was for more offenders to receive community sentences, in particular expressing a desire to see electronic tagging extended nationally. To achieve this shift in sentencing patterns, it adopted the familiar approaches of the 'strategy of encouragement' and 'punishment in the community': community penalties should be rigorous and more strictly enforced to make them credible with sentencers as alternatives to custody.

While it is too soon to be sure of the future trends in this important area of government policy, we will conclude this chapter by taking bearings on some possible future directions for community penalties.

What future for punishment and the community?

If we are to take a broad strategic view of community penalties, the first question is the basic one: what are community penalties for?

One could say—truthfully, but begging the question somewhat—that community punishment can serve almost all the purposes that are served by other forms of punishment such as imprisonment. Community penalties can operate as retribution, as deterrents, as denunciation of wrongdoing, as attempts to reform offenders, as reparation, and as a vehicle for 'reintegrative shaming' (see *Chapter 2*). For some of these purposes—reparation, reform and reintegrative shaming—it seems fairly safe to say that in most cases we are much more likely to be able to pursue these ends effectively by keeping the offenders in the community than by locking them up. As regards reform, research evidence to date seems to show that, although reformative programmes of certain kinds can show some success in custodial settings, similar methods are more effective without incarceration[60]—as common sense might suggest, since the 'prison as university of crime' effect will be absent, and the training takes place while the offenders are already living in the community in which they have to try to go straight. Again, it will for obvious reasons usually be far more difficult for offenders to make either financial or non-financial reparation to victims or to the community as a whole if they are locked up, and in a manner which severely reduces their future job prospects. And, while prison certainly shames, it does so in an excluding and stigmatising manner which removes the offender from the community (in every sense of the word), making effective reintegration that much more difficult.

As for retribution and denunciation—if these are legitimate penal purposes at all[61]—there is no reason in principle why these could not be satisfied by community penalties as well as by imprisonment, *if only* we could get over the obsession that prison is the only real 'proper punishment'—more on which shortly. What of deterrence? Intuitively it might seem unlikely that potential offenders might desist from crime out of dread of receiving a probation or community service order—or even the major interference with liberty and stigma of a curfew enforced by tagging—rather than because there is a chance of going to prison. But the empirical evidence we surveyed in *Chapter 2* shows that, to put it no higher, there is very little if any greater deterrent effect to be gained from a very high rather than a very low use of imprisonment. Effective and economical deterrence requires the latter.

At the end of the day, there are only two purposes which custody can achieve but community penalties (currently at least) cannot. One of these is the last-resort imposition of a sanction on an intransigently uncooperative offender. Most community penalties, and most methods of enforcing them, depend to some extent on the co-operation of the offender[62] (even if, since section 38 of the Crime (Sentences) Act 1997 came into effect, they do not legally require the offender's prior consent in order to be imposed by the sentencing court). With deprivation of liberty, the offender can ultimately be seized and detained forcibly. Perhaps advancing technology will eventually produce a viable sanction for non-cooperators to supplant the relatively crude business of imprisonment, but for the moment it is probably needed as a back-up sanction of last resort. It should not, however, have to be one which is often used (the lonely hour of the last resort may never arrive)—and when it is used for this purpose, there may be no need for the period of confinement to be a long one. A very short period of 'time out'—for example for the persistent and out-of-control 'Duck Boy' discussed in *Chapter 7*—may be all that is needed.

The other effect which only custody can have is *a certain kind of incapacitation*. While imprisoned, a person is physically prevented from committing some crimes for the time being. We should not ignore the fact that a great many crimes are committed in prison, notably drug offences and assaults, but also many property offences. But it is true to say that, for example, joyriding and house burglary are usually hard to do from prison. It can be doubted whether we can really justify the extreme sanction of imprisonment for offences of this kind, especially given the evidence summarised in *Chapter 2* about the utter inefficiency of incapacitation. Nevertheless, we accept that there are some violent and sexual offenders who pose such a vivid threat to others that incarcerating them in conditions of high but humane security is both justifiable and right for reasons of incapacitation. If these were the only people imprisoned, however, the prison population would be minuscule. A brief excursus is in order here about the possibility, in this high-tech age, of incapacitation in the community by electronic means. Some community penalties already incapacitate to some extent. Attendance centre orders[63] can keep hooligans away from football matches and disqualification can stop traffic offenders from driving, but only if they obey the order. Once they disobey, there is nothing to stop them offending. It is probably an important part of the appeal of electronic tagging that it gives the *impression* of creating effective incapacitation in the community in a way that these other penalties do not. It is, however, a false impression.

Interestingly, tagging of offenders was first introduced at the urging of a New Mexico judge who had read a comic in which Spiderman was tagged by one of his villainous enemies. Presumably what happened to Spiderman was not a curfew in his home but electronic *tracing* or *tracking*, whereby the person's every movement is electronically monitored. This may be the image which tagging presents, but is not the reality. Although (expensive) electronic tracing devices do exist, tagging is quite a different matter. The tag does not set off an alarm leading the police to pounce as soon as, for example, the paedophile approaches the school playground or the shoplifter enters Marks and Spencer. All the tag can do is to *enforce a home curfew*, currently for a maximum of 12 hours in the day.[64] If the offender leaves home during the curfew period, the breach should be logged and sanctions can be administered retrospectively. But once the offender has left home in breach of the curfew—and during the other 12-plus hours in the day—the tag and its bearer could be almost anywhere, getting up to anything.[65] Jack Straw has talked of tagging as 'the future of community punishment' and has suggested that it 'may in future be used to monitor offenders wherever they are in the community; it could be used to track their movements and make sure, for example, they stay away from certain areas'.[66] If so, then it could indeed rival imprisonment as a method of non-custodial incapacitation; but the day still seems far off.

Consequently, the purposes which can rationally be propounded for tagging at present can only be retribution, denunciation and deterrence. Tagging on its own seems unlikely to reform anyone. However, some senior probation officers[67] are at present moving towards limited acceptance of the electronic tag, while insisting that it should be used as an alternative to prison for 'high tariff' offenders and that it is unlikely to succeed in reformative terms unless it is *combined* with help and supervision from a human being such as a probation officer. The use envisaged for the tag in the Crime and Disorder Act 1998—for prisoners released early, in combination with parole supervision—marks an interesting development in this respect.

So—apart from incapacitation and last-resort enforcement sanctioning—community penalties can do almost anything that imprisonment can do, and usually much cheaper. But one thing it cannot do as well as prison is *make offenders suffer*, so advocates of Strategy A who are motivated (whether overtly or covertly, consciously or unconsciously) by this kind of punitive desire will still wish to use prison as much as possible—doubtless while insisting, however disingenuously, that this is only because 'prison works'. For Strategy A supporters, community penalties may still be appropriate for some lesser offences, but they should be made as punitive, restrictive and unpleasant as possible. This could certainly be done—the Conservative government made giant strides in this direction—and represents one possible future for community punishment.

Strategy B reformers, on the other hand, would care little one way or the other about how much offenders suffer. But they should be impressed by the relative cheapness and effectiveness of most community penalties compared with custody, and seek to maximise their use accordingly.

However, for the Strategy C reformer—particularly if an advocate of restorative justice—it may not simply be a question of 'anything custody can do, community penalties can do just as well and cheaper'. A long term restorative justice strategist would seek to change the whole thrust of punishment away from its current orientation. This of course brings us back to the way in which 'punishment' is conventionally conceptualised, and particularly the tendency to equate it with the use of custody which we discussed at the beginning of this chapter. One of the biggest mistakes associated with the Strategy A approach is its repeated assertion that this curiously impoverished concept of 'punishment' must be the primary, if not the only, aim of the criminal justice system. Thus, for example, Strategy A sees the community service order as only of value to the extent that it restricts liberty and is unpleasant for the offender, with its restorative element at best being merely subordinate.

This problem was perhaps compounded by the managerialist and desert-based sentencing reforms contained in the 1991 Criminal Justice Act which, as we have seen, sought to equate community punishment with the loss of liberty which it entails and to measure its intensity in terms of its negative effect on the offender's liberty. Whatever its intentions might have been, one tendency of such a restrictive approach is to confirm the status of imprisonment as setting the gold standard with regard to punishment, compared with which all other penalties are likely to be dismissed by sentencers and public alike as base metal counterfeits: not simply soft options, but not really punishments at all. Once this mind-set is established, no amount of tough talking or even tough action is going to compensate for the fact that, when it comes to restricting a person's liberty, custody is in a league of its own. Consequently, attempting to enhance the 'credibility' of non custodial sentences by making them ever more restrictive seems doomed to failure. Instead of seeking to repackage the various community-based penalties in terms of the restrictive punitive discourse that has come to prevail in recent years—as the Labour government still seems intent on doing, to judge from its response to the Prisons-Probation Review—there is an urgent need to confront and challenge these conventional understandings of what punishment means and what it can (and cannot) achieve. In particular, it would help if people could be encouraged to think of community criminal justice as something which can be constructive and positive, not merely punitive in a negative sense. This is the kind of 'replacement discourse' we spoke of in *Chapter 1* as necessary if any real progress is to be made in transforming the penal scene.

It could almost be said that the desert-based framework which underpinned the 1991 sentencing reforms failed to acknowledge even the possibility (let alone the desirability) of other more constructive responses to the problem of offending. Thus, the 1991 Act's almost complete silence on the issue of compensation for victims (not to mention other forms of reparation) affords mute testimony to the inadequacy of the overall conceptual framework which the Act sought to establish. While—as we acknowledged earlier—it may be necessary in the case of certain serious offences to restrict the liberty of the offender in order to protect the public, we need to recognise that in the great majority of less serious cases for which punishment in the community is more appropriate, we should look beyond the restriction of liberty for its own sake.

We believe that there are principled and pragmatic arguments supporting the introduction and development of non-custodial measures that are demanding in the sense that they seek to make offenders accountable for what they have done, and also constructive in the sense that they seek wherever possible to meet and respect the legitimate needs of victims. We therefore favour the development and application of restorative measures where appropriate, such as victim/offender mediation and community or family group conferencing in which meetings are arranged which may include not just victim and offender but also members of their families and other interested members of the community.

It would be a mistake, however, simply to graft these measures onto the existing stock of punitive disposals since there is a danger that they would be seen and used as instruments of punishment and exclusion, in which case much of their potential value would be lost. There is an urgent need to reopen the question of penal aims specifically in relation to non-custodial penalties and to abandon the strict desert-based model which sees them purely as negative constraints on the offender's liberty. This is not to say that we should lose sight of the fact that community penalties *do* infringe the liberty of the individual in very real ways, and that this is not a matter to be taken lightly merely because it takes place outside the prison walls. Consequently, we would wish to retain a place for the 'just deserts' principle that sanctions should be in proportion to the offender's wrongdoing, at least to the extent that the principle of proportionality should act as an upper constraint on the severity of the sanction, even if this takes a 'restorative' form.[68] We would favour the prioritisation of restorative measures wherever possible, but believe there is also a place for other forms of intervention including reformative or educational measures in appropriate cases. There is thus a need for 'targeting' to ensure that the different measures are applied to the most appropriate groups of offenders.

There is also a need to ensure that restorative measures are developed in a coherent and principled way rather than leaving it up to the individual initiatives of interested individuals or agencies. In our view there is a strong case for assigning a lead role in the development of such measures to one key agency—the probation service (or whatever it ends up being called) being the most obvious and appropriate choice— and to ensure that it is adequately resourced in order to fulfil its responsibilities.

Another danger is that, as with any new 'crime control' measure, unrealistic expectations may be raised about the effectiveness of restorative justice measures and their impact on overall crime rates. We are in favour of restorative justice (provided it is implemented sensitively and sensibly) because it respects the rights of both victims and offenders and appears to avoid some of the harmful consequences that are associated with more punitive methods, not because we expect it to drastically reduce the likelihood of reconviction. Indeed, we reiterate the need for penological realism which warns against looking to the penal system as a solution to the problem of crime.

In the long term, there is much to be said for applying restorative justice principles beyond the criminal justice system, to the development of broader social policies—for example in the fields of education, housing, employment and welfare—that seek to promote the goal of social inclusion, and to avoid the negative consequences (including increased levels of crime) that are associated with the all-too pervasive phenomenon of social exclusion.[69] Indeed, if the government is serious about its famous commitment to being 'tough on the causes of crime' as well as crime itself, then the two go hand in hand. This again raises questions about the philosophy of communitarianism which underpins much of the discussion about restorative justice and its potential. For, as we pointed out in *Chapter 2*, communitarianism comes in a number of guises. And, while the more liberal and progressive version is based on a socially inclusionary vision, backed by appropriate policies such as the introduction of a decent minimum wage, enhanced educational and employment opportunities and appropriate levels of financial and other forms of support for those in need, there is also a more authoritarian version which is uninterested in pursuing inclusionary social policies and seeks to include in the community only those who adhere to a rigid set of 'strong moral values', excluding those who fall outside a fairly narrowly defined consensus.[70] We hope and believe that New Labour is more closely aligned to the liberal 'inclusive' version of communitarianism than the more authoritarian 'exclusive' version. Nevertheless it would be surprising if there was no element of tension in relation to the precise form it espouses or the way its policies will develop in the future. It is no exaggeration to say that the future not only of punishment in the community but the entire New Labour project may depend on how this tension is resolved over the coming months and years.

ENDNOTES: *Chapter 4*

1 See Michael Cavadino and James Dignan, *The Penal System: An Introduction* (2nd ed., London, Sage Publications, 1997), 207-8.
2 Speech to the Police Foundation on 10 July 1997 (*NACRO Digest* No. 93, July 1997).
3 In 1996 only 64,900 of the 301,400 people sentenced for indictable offences were sent to prison (21.5 per cent) compared with 86,000 who received community sentences (28.5 per cent), 55,100 who were discharged (18 per cent) and 84,900 who were fined (28 per cent) (Ricky Taylor and colleagues, *Cautions, Court Proceedings and Sentencing England and Wales 1996*, Home Office Statistical Bulletin 16/97 (London, Home Office, 1997).
4 Anne Worrall, *Punishment in the Community* (Harlow, Addison, Wesley Longman, 1997): 46. See also Anthony Bottoms, 'The Philosophy and Politics of Punishment and Sentencing' in Chris Clarkson and Rod Morgan (eds.),

The Politics of Sentencing Reform (Oxford, Clarendon Press, 1995); Nicola Lacey and Lucia Zedner, 'Discourses of Community in Criminal Justice', *Journal of Law and Society*, 23 (1995): 301-25; Adam Crawford, *The Local Governance of Crime: Appeals to Community and Partnerships* (Oxford, Clarendon Press, 1997): ch. 5; and Ian Brownlee, *Community Punishment: A Critical Introduction* (Harlow, Addison, Wesley Longman, 1998), 56-9.

[5] Bottoms, op. cit., pp. 34-6.

[6] Which was sometimes though not always backed by the payment of a sum of money or 'surety'.

[7] Bill McWilliams, 'The Mission to the English Police Courts 1876-1936', *Howard Journal*, 12, (1983): 129-47 at p. 134.

[8] Robert Harris, 'Probation Round the World: Origins and Development' in Koichi Hamai, Renaud Villé, Robert Harris, Mike Hough and Ugljesa Zvekic (eds.), *Probation Round the World: A Comparative Study*, (London, Routledge, 1995).

[9] Bill McWilliams, op. cit., p. 130, and Ian Brownlee, op. cit., p. 65.

[10] In the Summary Jurisdiction Act 1879.

[11] Now known as pre-sentence reports since the Criminal Justice Act 1991.

[12] David Haxby, *Probation: A Changing Service*, (London, Constable, 1978): 51.

[13] Peter Sheriff, *Summary Probation Statistics England and Wales 1997*, Home Office Statistical Bulletin 12/98 (London, Home Office, 1998). To the 1997 figure must be added a further 1,919 probation services' officers (formerly known as ancillary workers), 4,131 clerical, secretarial and administrative staff, 842 non-probation staff working in approved probation and bail hostels and 768 other probation employees.

[14] At present there are 54 probation areas in England and Wales, most of which are county-based; but see below for recent government proposals to create a national probation service.

[15] We noted in *Chapter 3* that another important influence on the content of the 1991 sentencing reforms was the 'just deserts' model, and have already discussed its impact on the *use* of community penalties. However, its effect on the reform of the probation service as such has been much less profound and far less pervasive.

[16] The terms 'consumerist' and 'systemic' are derived from Bottoms (op. cit., p.24).

[17] See Tim Newburn, *Crime and Criminal Justice Policy* (London, Longman, 1995): 86.

[18] Bill McWilliams, 'The Probation Officer at Court: From Friend to Acquaintance', *Howard Journal of Criminal Justice*, 20 (1981): 97-106.

[19] For example, the ratio of supervisory to maingrade officers increased from 1:6 in the early 1950s to 1:3 by 1975 (Haxby, op. cit.).

[20] See Christopher Humphrey, 'Calling in the Experts: The Financial Management Initiative, Private Sector Management Consultants and the Probation Service', *Howard Journal of Criminal Justice*, 30 (1991), 1-18.

[21] op. cit., p. 30ff.

[22] op. cit., p. 72.

[23] Home Office, *National Standards for the Supervision of Offenders in the Community* (London, Home Office, 1992), para. 1.3.6.

[24] Home Office, *National Standards for the Supervision of Offenders in the Community* (London, Home Office, 1995), para. 1.4.

[25] Tim Newburn, op. cit., p. 96.

[26] Cm 424 (London, Home Office, 1988).

[27] *Tackling Offending: An Action Plan* (London, Home Office, 1988).

[28] Audit Commission, *The Probation Service: Promoting Value for Money* (London, HMSO, 1989).

[29] Home Office, *Supervision and Punishment in the Community*, Cmnd 966 (London, HMSO, 1990).

[30] op. cit., para. 3.2.

[31] Powers of Criminal Courts Act 1973, section 2(1), prior to amendment by the Criminal Justice Act 1991.

[32] *Thinking About Crime* (New York, Basic Books, 1975). See *Chapter 8*, esp. pp.180ff.

[33] Ian Brownlee, op. cit., p. 17.

[34] *National Standards for Community Service Orders* (London, Home Office, 1988).

[35] Sections 12 and 13, Criminal Justice Act 1991.

[36] Section 11, Criminal Justice Act 1991.

[37] According to the government White Paper, *Crime, Justice and Protecting the Public: the Government's Proposals*, Cm 965 (London, HMSO, 1990).

[38] *Strengthening Punishment in the Community: A Consultation Document*, Cm 2780 (London, HMSO, 1995).

[39] Home Office, *Protecting the Public: The Government's Strategy on Crime in England and Wales* (Cm 3190, London, HMSO, 1996): para. 7.1.

[40] See e.g. the Association of Chief Probation Officers, *More Demanding than Prison* (Wakefield, ACOP, 1988), published in response to the Green Paper *Punishment, Custody and the Community* (op. cit.); also ACOP, *Probation Works Better than Prison: A Briefing Paper* (London, ACOP, 1996).

[41] 'A Non-treatment Paradigm for Probation Practice', *British Journal of Social Work*, 9 (1979), 159-202.

[42] Other contributions to the debate about the future role of the probation service have been even more vulnerable on this score. They include Hilary Walker and Bill Beaumont's *Probation Work: Critical Theory and Socialist Practice* (Oxford, Blackwell, 1981) which called for a radical socialist approach to probation work, founded on an analysis of the role of capitalism, poverty and oppression in the genesis and perpetuation of crime. Although popular with sections of the Probation Service, including the National Association of Probation Officers, such views were unlikely to influence the terms of the debate.

[43] Mike Nellis, 'Probation Values for the 1990s', *Howard Journal of Criminal Justice*, 34 (1990), 19-41; John Pendleton, 'More Justice, Less Law' in David Ward and Malcolm Lacey (eds.) *Probation: Working for Justice* (London, Whiting and Birch, 1995); and Guy Masters, 'Values for Probation, Society and Beyond', *Howard Journal of Criminal Justice*, 36 (1997), 237-47.

[44] The latter are principally involved in the resolution of neighbour and community disputes, but many of these incidentally involve responding to criminal actions which give rise to (or are committed during) disputes.

[45] Tony Marshall, 'The Evolution of Restorative Justice in Britain', *European Journal on Criminal Policy and Research* 4, 4 (1997), 21-43.

[46] One pre-court diversion project and three court-based projects. See Tony Marshall and Susan Merry, *Crime and Accountability: Victim Offender Mediation in Practice* (London, Home Office, 1990).

[47] See Marshall and Merry, op. cit.; and James Dignan 'Repairing the Damage: Can Reparation be Made to Work in the Service of Diversion?', *British Journal of Criminology*, 32 (1992), 453-72.

[48] See Dignan, op. cit.

[49] op. cit., note 45 above, p. 31.

[50] *New Millennium – New Training for Probation Officer Recruits* (Home Office Press Release 185/97, 29 July 1997).

[51] See George Mair and Ed Mortimer, *Curfew Orders with Electronic Monitoring*, Home Office Research Study No. 163 (London, Home Office, 1996): 29. One of the conclusions of the study was a need to clarify the role of the probation service in view of the fact that 'many of those tagged need support to cope with the demands of the sentence and it is not the task of the [service providers] to supply this' (p. 40).

[52] See *Chapter 7*; see also James Dignan 'The Crime and Disorder Act and the Prospects for Restorative Justice', [1999] *Criminal Law Review*, 48-60.

[53] Interview with Home Secretary Jack Straw on BBC Radio 4's *Today*, 30 July 1997; quoted in Ian Brownlee, op. cit., p. 190. See also HC Deb. 2 March 1998, col. 690, where Mr Straw said: 'Within the sentencing framework set by Parliament, who is sent to prison and for how long is a matter for the courts.'

[54] For example in his first formal speech as Home Secretary to probation staff: Jack Straw, *Role of Probation Service Essential in Improving Criminal Justice System* (Home Office Press Release 233/97, 18 September 1997).

[55] E.g. 'The Government is also committed to providing more effective and tougher community punishments' (HC Deb. 2 March 1998, col. 690), and 'I am seeking to strengthen the credibility of probation supervision and ensure that community punishments are administered correctly.' (Letter from Jack Straw to Paul Cavadino, Chair of the Penal Affairs Consortium, 5 September 1997).

[56] Peter Goldblatt and Chris Lewis (eds.), *Reducing Offending: An Assessment of Research Evidence on Ways of Dealing with Offending Behaviour*, Home Office Research Study No. 187 (London, Home Office, 1998).

[57] See e.g. Mike Nellis 'Time for Reflection', *Guardian Society*, 1 October 1997.

[58] See John Harding 'The Walls of Ignorance', *Guardian Society*, 1 October 1997.

[59] *Joining Forces to Protect the Public*; *Prisons-Probation Review Final Report* (both London, Home Office, 1998).

[60] Goldblatt and Lewis, op. cit., p. 104; Julie Vennard, Carol Hedderman and Darren Sugg, *Changing Offenders' Attitudes and Behaviour: What Works?* Home Office Research Study No. 171 (London, Home Office, 1997), p. 3; D. A.

Andrews, Ivan Zinger, Robert D. Hodge, James Bonta, Paul Gendreau and Francis T. Cullen, 'Does Correctional Treatment Work? A Clinically Relevant and Psychologically Informed Meta-Analysis', *Criminology*, 28 (1990), 369-429 at p.382; Mark W. Lipsey, 'The Effect of Treatment on Juvenile Delinquents: Results from Meta-Analysis', in Friedrich Lösel, Doris Bender and Thomas Bliesener (eds.), *Psychology and Law: International Perspectives* (Berlin, Walter de Gruyter, 1992), 131-43 at p. 138.

[61] See Cavadino and Dignan, op. cit.., ch. 2.

[62] Some do not: e.g. seizure and sequestration of property and assets; but these are of course of limited application to most offenders who typically do not have much property.

[63] These require the offender to attend a centre run by the police or some other agency, typically for a few hours on a Saturday afternoon.

[64] Criminal Justice Act 1991, section 12. For an overview, see Dick Whitfield, *Tackling the Tag: The Electronic Monitoring of Offenders* (Winchester, Waterside Press, 1997).

[65] Nor is tagging a cheap disposal compared with other community penalties, although it is cheap compared with prison. The latest evaluation research on the pilot schemes currently under way estimated that if tagging were to be extended throughout the whole of England and Wales, and *if* it were used by the courts to a much greater extent than it has been in the pilot areas, then a *three-month* curfew would cost £1,900. This compares with an *annual* cost of £2,200 for a probation order and £1,700 for a community service order (Ed Mortimer and Chris May, *Electronic Monitoring in Practice: The Second Year of the Trials of Curfew Orders*, Home Office Research Study No. 177, London, Home Office, 1997), 42. (Prison currently costs on average £24,000 per year.)

[66] Home Office Press Release, *Electronic Monitoring – the Future of Community Punishment*, 12 November 1997.

[67] This is currently the position of the Association of Chief Officers of Probation: see Paul Cavadino, 'Electronic Tagging – The Evidence So Far', *Criminal Justice*, vol. 15, 2 (May 1997), 4-5.

[68] 'Just deserts' may also be of abiding use as a 'default setting', fixing an appropriate amount for a fine or community service sentence in cases where the negotiation of a more individualised measure of reparation to the victim is either impossible or inappropriate. Cf Michael Cavadino and James Dignan, 'Reparation, Retribution and Rights', *International Review of Victimology*, 4 (1997), 233-53.

[69] See David Faulkner, *Darkness and Light: Justice, Crime and Management for Today* (London, Howard League for Penal Reform, 1996); and James Dignan, "'Restorative Crime Prevention' in Theory and Practice", *Prison Service Journal*, 123 (1999), 2-5.

[70] See also James Dignan (1999), *Restorative Justice in Northern Ireland Review Report*, Northern Ireland Criminal Justice Review Commission (forthcoming).

CHAPTER 5

Imprisonment: The Hard Cell

In the absence of capital punishment, imprisonment represents the ultimate form of social exclusion, whatever punitive or other effects it might have. Yet for the great majority of imprisoned offenders, their exclusion will only be temporary, and at some point they will return to the community from which they have been exiled. So what happens to them while they are in prison, and whether they are likely to have changed for the better or for the worse by their experience of imprisonment following their release are questions that one might expect to loom large in debates over prison policy. But have they? In this chapter we examine some of the most important developments in prison policy during the post-war period in the light of the different strategies that have been deployed in this and other areas of criminal justice policy making, and assess the prospects for a reform of prison policy which addresses its impact on the broader problem of social exclusion.

PRISON POLICY IN THE PRE-MANAGERIAL ERA

During the early post-war period, the Prison Service shared with the probation service a 'sense of mission' (at least at a rhetorical level) that was also founded on the rehabilitative ideal. For many years this was symbolically encapsulated in Prison Rule Number One, which adopted as the primary aim of imprisonment the attempt to ensure that prisoners would lead 'a good and useful life' on release.[1] During the period of rehabilitative optimism it was widely believed that this might be achieved by equipping offenders with skills such as literacy and numeracy which would enable them to desist from crime, and by setting them a positive example.

However, the early post-war period was also characterised by a sharp and sustained increase in the rate of recorded crime,[2] and this soon began to have an impact on prison numbers. One immediate problem was that of overcrowding, particularly since the capacity of the prison estate had contracted during the inter-war period, following a halving of the average daily prison population between 1908 and 1938.[3] The problem was made worse by the ageing and deteriorating state of the prison estate which, with only two exceptions,[4] was made up of prisons that were over 100 years old. Moreover, it was compounded by a reluctance on the part of central government to spend money, whether on expanding or improving the prison estate or on significantly increasing staffing or other resources. Instead, the authorities responded pragmatically by 'doubling-up' (or in some cases 'trebling-up') the occupancy of each cell, while presiding over a steady deterioration of prison conditions.

The only major departures from the predominantly *laissez faire* approach which characterised prison policy (as it did probation policy: see *Chapter 4*) during the first three decades following the second world war were those forced upon policy makers by external events such as the 'crisis of containment',[5] which unfolded as a result of a succession of well-publicised prison escapes involving several high profile prisoners. However, the response to the problem involved a tightening of prison security throughout the system following the decision to keep 'Category A' prisoners who were deemed to present a high security risk[6] in a number of 'dispersal' prisons along with 'Category B' inmates, with the result that security in these prisons' had therefore to be substantially (and expensively) upgraded. The effect of this dispersal policy compounded the many problems from which the system was already suffering since it drastically skewed the deployment of resources and subordinated all other objectives (such as training, education, work, recreation and the quest for better rights and conditions) to the single overriding goal of security.

Another unintended consequence of this dispersal policy was to heighten problems *within* the increasingly fortified prison perimeters, as the maintenance of control became increasingly problematic; and the repressive measures which were adopted in response[7] proved to be ineffective at best, and in some cases counter-productive since they frequently provoked further disturbances.

The difficulties facing the prison system during this *laissez faire* era were further compounded by a long-running and steadily deteriorating industrial relations problem. In part this revolved around the 'traditional' concerns of pay and conditions, but it also reflected a much more profound 'crisis of authority',[8] which stemmed from resentment on the part of prison officers over a wide range of issues. These included changes in the role of prison officers; their relations with inmates and other grades of staff; and changes in the philosophy, style and structure of prison management; plus a growing sense of disquiet over the direction of government policy towards prisons.

Finally, another long-term consequence of the growing post-war crime rate to which we referred earlier was to cast increasing doubt on the basic premise that offenders were susceptible to reform, which underpinned the era of rehabilitative optimism. These seemingly insurmountable problems exposed the inadequacy of the conventional *laissez faire* approach to prison policy, and set the scene for the emergence of a very different approach, often referred to as managerialism, which is associated with Strategy B.

STRATEGY B: MANAGING—& MARKETING— CONFINEMENT

The adoption of a managerialist approach within the prison service is reflected in a number of key changes: changes in the structure of management; changes in the style of management; and a number of management-inspired changes in the aims and objectives of the Prison Service that over the years have become associated with a radically different policy agenda for the prison system. We will examine each of these changes in turn.

Rearranging deck chairs on *The Titanic* . . . changes in the structure and style of Prison Service management
Between 1877[9] and 1963 the administration of the prison system in England and Wales was the responsibility of the Prison Commission and was heavily influenced by the personality and predilections of the Chairman of the Prison Commissioners—with all the strengths and weaknesses of this form of autocratic domination. The first Chairman, Sir Edmund du Cane, was notorious for the ruthless way in which he imposed his own uncompromisingly deterrent and punitive philosophy on the entire prison system (making him an early exponent of Strategy A) while many of his successors on the Prison Commission promoted a humanitarian and reformist approach that had more in common with Strategy C. Notable among these successors was the charismatic Sir Alexander Paterson, whose abiding influence was as immense as his reforming zeal, despite the fact that he was never actually Chairman of the Commission.

For the next 30 years following the abolition of the Prison Commission in 1963, responsibility for administering the system lay directly with the Home Office. This 'made it easier for government ministers to impress their will on the prison system',[10] though for most of this time, as we have seen, little was done to tackle the increasingly serious problems besetting it. However, the style of prison management was undoubtedly transformed during this period, from a highly personalised exercise of power by a charismatic leader to a more hierarchical, bureaucratic model, in which authority is increasingly derived from a system of general rules and regulations rather than personal edicts.[11]

As with other criminal justice agencies such as the police and the probation service, one of the characteristic features of this managerialist approach to prison policy-making is its 'systemic' nature.[12] The term 'systemic' refers in part to its preoccupation with the abstract relationships between the various agencies making up the criminal justice system, as opposed to the personal relationships that subsist between, for example, prison officers and inmates, between prison officers and prison management, and between prison management and policy makers. However, the weakness of this impersonal, 'top-down' and highly bureaucratic managerial style was cruelly exposed by the Strangeways riot of 1990, during which the Strangeways governor was obliged to consult his superiors within the prison service, many of whom had no direct operational experience.[13] The Woolf Inquiry[14] which was set up to investigate the 1990 prison disturbances was highly critical of the gulf it identified between Home Office ministers and policy makers, Prison Service management at Prison Headquarters, and those working at all levels within the service itself. Lord Woolf's proposed cure for this malaise was to call for 'clear and visible leadership' of the service by someone recruited internally, which contained distinct echoes of a much earlier style of personalised prison service management. He also called for a less directive approach on the part of ministers and civil servants and increased delegation of responsibility for implementing prison policy, to the Director General of the Prison Service in the first instance and, beyond that, to the governors of each individual prison establishment.

Changes in the managerial and the organizational structure of the prison system had been proposed even before the Strangeways riot, following a recommendation by the Conservative government's 'Efficiency Unit' as part of its 'Next Steps' initiative.[15] This was in keeping with the government's 'new public management' approach which, as we saw in *Chapter 4*, adapted private sector techniques of '*technocratic managerialism*' to a variety of public sector agencies including both the probation service and the prison service. The proposals were not adopted immediately, however, and it was only following yet another review of Prison Service management[16] in the wake of an embarrassing escape by two IRA suspects from Brixton prison in 1991 that they were finally accepted.

Under the changes, which were introduced in April 1993, the Prison Service became an executive agency which, in theory at least, was intended to operate at arm's length from central government, under the leadership of its Director General. Whereas Lord Woolf had looked for 'clear and visible leadership' from within the Prison Service, the Government followed its ideological instincts in selecting Derek Lewis as the agency's first Director General. A business executive with no previous experience of prisons, his prime qualification for the post was his perceived ability to apply 'modern managerial methods' to the running of the prison system.[17] The ostensible aim of the reforms was to achieve a clearer demarcation between policy-making and resource allocation, responsibility for which was retained by the Home Secretary, and the conduct of 'operational' matters, responsibility for which was devolved to the Director-General of the Prison Service. Beyond that, much of the responsibility for implementing specific policies and the meeting of agreed 'targets' was supposed to be further devolved to individual prison governors. However rational they may have appeared on paper, these changes in the managerial structure of the prison service failed to achieve any of their declared objectives, though few could have foreseen how soon, how brutally and how decisively their shortcomings were to be exposed when put to the test.

Shortly after the new managerial structure had been introduced, two spectacular prison breakouts occurred, the first involving a number of armed prisoners who managed to effect a brief escape from the Special Security Unit at the new 'dispersal' prison at Whitemoor in September 1994. Government embarrassment at the security lapse was compounded by the discovery of Semtex explosives and detonators at the prison, and the inquiry[18] set up to investigate the incident was brutally frank, concluding that so many things were wrong with procedures and policies that it was 'a disaster waiting to happen'. But worse still was to come. In January 1995, three life sentence prisoners escaped from Parkhurst dispersal prison on the Isle of Wight; again, their recapture did nothing to contain the political fall-out resulting from the episode.

The initial response to the latter escape was the reluctant removal of the Parkhurst prison governor by the Director General, amid claims of political interference on the part of Home Secretary Michael Howard, claims which were subsequently and devastatingly confirmed by his own junior Minister at the time, Ann Widdecombe. The Director General of the Prison Service, Derek Lewis, was himself summarily sacked by the Home Secretary in October 1995 on the publication of Sir John Learmont's report[19] on the Parkhurst breakout, which documented 'a chapter of errors at every level' and was implicitly critical of ministerial interference in the running of prisons. (One reading of these events is that a Strategy A Home Secretary felt impelled to exercise such personal hands-on influence on the prisons that what had been a Strategy B reorganization came under intolerable strain.) The Home Secretary meanwhile refused to accept responsibility for what he insisted were purely 'operational' matters even though he was later shown to have been actively involved in the decision to remove the prison governor. Derek Lewis subsequently received £220,000 compensation for wrongful dismissal. An independent study of the performance of the Next Steps agencies, including the Prison Service, found the model to be deeply flawed, and was particularly critical of the attempt to separate policy and operational issues, concluding that the extent to which it is either feasible or desirable is questionable.[20]

FROM MORAL MISSION TO MISSION STATEMENT: MANAGEMENT-INSPIRED CHANGES IN FOCUS AND POLICY

Changes in the style and structure of Prison Service management have been accompanied by equally profound changes in the service's professed aims and objectives, policies and priorities. The service's sense of moral mission which was once symbolically prioritised in Prison Rule Number One has gradually given way to the more prosaic terminology that is used to articulate managerially inspired goals and institutional mission statements. An early indication of the more limited aspirations that would come to characterise the managerialist agenda for the Prison Service was set out in a statement of aims published by the Prisons Board[21] in 1984. It defined the task of the Prison Service as being 'to use with maximum efficiency the resources of staff, money buildings and plant made available to it by Parliament in order to fulfil four basic functions'. These included the tasks of bringing unsentenced prisoners to the right court on time,[22] and holding them in custody in the meantime; keeping sentenced prisoners in custody until the end of their sentence; providing inmates with 'as full a life as is consistent with the facts of custody' and 'helping prisoners to keep in touch with the community and prepare them for their return to it (if possible)'.

This set the scene for a dramatic change of focus, in which the terms of discussions about prisons shifted from the aims of and justification for imprisonment to a growing preoccupation with the goals of financial and managerial probity; and in which the agenda for the Prison Service has come to be shaped by the three familiar managerialist 'virtues' of economy, efficiency and effectiveness to the virtual exclusion of more fundamental values and purposes. Indeed, the much vaunted 'new public management' approach appears to have much in common with the notion of 'penological pragmatism' which Tony Bottoms[23] has used to describe the response of successive post-war British governments to the problems facing the penal system. Both approaches are reactive rather than proactive, and merely seek to manage the continuing resource crisis 'with no clear or coherent philosophical or other theoretical basis'. This picture was not radically changed by the publication of a 'Statement of Purpose, Vision, Goals and Values' by the Prison Service in 1993 when it became an executive agency. Despite its routine deployment of humanistic sentiments such as 'Our duty is to look after them [prisoners] with humanity and help them lead law-abiding and useful lives in custody and after release', it also tellingly contained the goal to 'deliver prison services using the resources provided by Parliament with maximum efficiency.'

One of the earliest products of the new managerialist approach took the form of a new set of working practices for prison officers which was optimistically called 'Fresh Start'. In the wake of a report produced jointly by the Prison Department and a team of management consultants,[24] which castigated existing shift and overtime practices, the new package required prison officers to work without overtime, but with an improved basic salary. At the same time, new management structures were introduced which made prison governors answerable to area managers. Although it was hoped that the introduction of 'more efficient' working practices would result in enhanced prison regimes, the improvements which were anticipated failed to materialise; indeed the quality of prison regimes was found to have deteriorated significantly following the changes.[25] Prison officers claimed that this was because insufficient staff were recruited to make the new system work. If this was true, the responsibility probably lay in another set of managerialist reforms which were introduced by the government just before Fresh Start itself. These led to the imposition of individual budgets for each prison (analogous to the system of cash limits applied to health and social services) the effect of which was to restrict the amount that could be spent on staff in each prison. Whatever its merits or shortcomings, Strategy B was exerting a growing influence on the running of the prison system by the end of the 1980s.

Even the Woolf report had a predominantly managerialist orientation, despite the almost universal acclaim with which it was greeted on the part of politicians, commentators and penal reform organizations alike.[26] (As with the Criminal Justice Act of 1991 which we examined in *Chapter 3*, however, it would be wrong to portray it as the embodiment of Strategy B, for it did also contain significant Strategy C elements, as we shall see). This is reflected in the report's relatively restricted terms of reference, which precluded any fundamental questions about the aims or legitimacy of imprisonment, and even forestalled any attempt to examine the broader context in which the Prison Service operates, including the sentencing policies of the courts.

Instead, the authors confined themselves largely to the broadly administrative questions which they were asked to address, notably those relating to the maintenance of order and control in prisons and the prevention of future disturbances.

Many of Woolf's recommendations are consistent with the objectives of 'systemic managerialism' which we have encountered already, notably the call for a national inter-agency Criminal Justice Consultative Council (augmented by similar local bodies) 'to promote better understanding, co-operation and co-ordination in the administration of the criminal justice system'. We have already commented on Woolf's proposals for reforming the management and organizational structure of the prison service which were also strongly redolent of Strategy B. Likewise, Woolf's response to the steady decline in prison conditions in the period leading up to the Strangeways riots also chimed in well with the target-setting approach favoured by Strategy B—although it could be said that Woolf was attempting to employ Strategy B techniques in the pursuit of an ultimately Strategy C goal (justice for inmates).[27] Woolf's approach involved the introduction of a national system of minimum standards for prisons. When first introduced, these standards would only be 'aspirational' and therefore unenforceable; and indeed when the Prison Service did publish its first set of Operating Standards in April 1994[28] it was made clear that they were not intended to give prisoners any legal entitlements.

A strongly managerialist agenda was also clearly discernible in respect of two additional sets of proposals relating specifically to prison inmates and prison staff respectively. For prisoners, Woolf advocated the introduction of 'contracts' or 'compacts', specifying the facilities and provisions they might expect to be provided, and also their responsibilities. The proposal can be seen as a managerial response to the control problem faced by the authorities since, by making their entitlements progressive, and dependent on their degree of compliance with the regime, an important aim could be to 'depoliticise' inmate resentment by recharacterising their status as 'consumers', rather than simply convicts.[29] With regard to prison staff, Woolf suggested that the main priority was to improve their morale and self esteem. In order to achieve this, and in recognition of the additional responsibilities placed on them in delivering the higher standards which inmates might expect to experience, he advocated improvements in staff training and an enhanced role in their dealings with inmates. This also represents an administrative response to the 'crisis of authority'[30] that has beset the prison system for many years. But by characterising it as essentially an industrial relations issue (to do with status and recognition), the Woolf report failed to address the contribution which staff attitudes and behaviour made to the other key problems afflicting the system: notably the 'control' problems and 'legitimacy' problems it has experienced. Significantly, the Woolf report had very little to say about the state of relations between prison staff and inmates and how these might be improved. But as we noted in *Chapter 2*, many of the techniques that have come to be associated with modern managerialism are not noted for either their sensitivity or their success in nurturing the relationships on which all effective social organizations depend, regardless of the sector of the economy in which they operate.

MARKETING CONFINEMENT: THE 'HARD SELL'

One consequence of the 'managerial revolution' that was unleashed by the Conservative governments led by Margaret Thatcher was to expose public sector institutions to the 'disciplines' of the market place. Initially, the most visible manifestation of this cultural transformation in relation to the Prison Service was a growing proliferation of strategic planning documents, including Business Plans and Corporate Plans, setting out targets and also 'key performance indicators'[31] by which progress in meeting those goals could be measured. However, the 'Financial Management Initiative' (FMI) which was introduced in 1982 also helped to prepare the ground for an even more radical transformation in the management of the prison system, with the private sector operating not just as role model but as direct competitor in a burgeoning market for prison services.

Although this was the logical outcome of the Financial Management Initiative, there appeared to be little enthusiasm for extending the concept of privatisation to the Prison Service during the first decade of Conservative rule, despite some active lobbying and a favourable report by the Parliamentary Home Affairs Committee in 1986.[32] However, the pace began to quicken during the debates on the Criminal Justice Act 1991, which authorised the management of any prison to be 'contracted out' to the private sector.[33] After its somewhat hesitant start the Conservative government under John Major threw caution to the wind and committed itself to an ambitious prison privatisation programme despite the momentous changes which it entailed, and without waiting for the evaluation of the first prison to be privatised (Wolds).[34] By the time of the 1997 General Election, there were four privately operated prisons in England and Wales, all of them new, with another three in the pipeline, though this still fell some way short of the target figure which the outgoing Conservative government had set itself of ten per cent of the prison estate in England and Wales under private management. Court escort services had also been privatised, as had a range of ancillary services including catering and medical facilities, and also prison educational services. Moreover, in 1992 the government launched the Private Finance Initiative, a process whereby the private sector finances, designs and builds public assets, and continues to run the relevant services in return for payments from the procuring authorities, usually on the basis of a 20 or 25 year contract. Under the rules of the initiative, no new public expenditure can be agreed by the Treasury unless the use of private finance has first been considered. The Conservative government announced that all new prisons were to be commissioned on this basis, and a wide range of other Prison Service functions was also under consideration for privatisation in the same way.

There have now been some reasonably authoritative assessments of the relative performance of public and private prisons, including their relative costs. One review was carried out by the Parliamentary Home Affairs Committee, and was published in March 1997 shortly before the General Election.[35] This concluded that, at least in their early years (and while acknowledging the difficulties of ensuring that comparisons are made on a 'like with like' basis) privately managed prisons appear to have delivered to the prison service cost savings of a little over ten per cent per prisoner.[36] Another review, by Jo Woodbridge of the Home Office, concluded that private prisons are eight to 15 per cent cheaper than their publicly-operated equivalents, but the state has started to close the gap.[37] These differences are rather less than the 15-25 per cent cost advantage which the Conservative government had repeatedly claimed.

It would be surprising if there were no cost savings to be made by having prisons run privately, since private prisons employ fewer staff on lower pay and with worse conditions than their public sector counterparts. However, the argument over costs is not conclusive, since (for example) privately managed prisons have experienced higher levels of assaults on staff and inmates and a range of other shortcomings,[38] which are sufficiently serious and persistent to cast doubt on claims that privatisation affords an easy remedy for the multitude of problems besetting the prison system. Indeed, the independent evaluation of Wolds prison[39] concluded that, with regard to the quality of provision for inmates some of the new public sector prisons are able to deliver 'similar, and some might argue better achievements' than are to be found in the private sector.

A more fundamental objection to the policy of prison privatisation (which is also applicable to any strategy of unalloyed managerialism in general) is its tendency to skew the debate over prison policy by concentrating on technical issues of competence and efficiency while relegating or excluding altogether the much more important policy questions relating to the aims and purposes of imprisonment. These include the justification for pursuing an expansionary prison policy at the expense of other, arguably more constructive, policies for preventing crime and the need to find better ways of dealing with the vast majority of less serious offenders who are currently sent to prison. By concentrating exclusively on the comparative costs of public and private sector custody, attention is deflected away from the much more important issue of the 'opportunity costs' that are incurred by squandering such huge sums of money on imprisoning offenders while restricting other forms of social spending. For this reason, critics of prison privatisation are apt to see it at best as a damaging diversion from the need to fundamentally reform the entire prison system. And at worst it is seen as a possible obstacle to reform, both because of its destructive short term impact on the prison numbers problem, and on account of its even more damaging long-term implications for the shaping of criminal justice policies—to the extent that these are likely to be influenced by powerful private corporations acting out of corporate self interest as opposed to the broader public interest.

When viewed in this light, the most significant aspect of the prison privatisation saga may be that in the early 1990s it helped to pave the way for a much more virulent version of Strategy A by appearing to remove some of the practical economic and political constraints that had previously inhibited governments from making excessively profligate use of custody, whatever their ideological preferences might have dictated.

Strategy A: The 'prison works' mantra

Strategy A was not of course invented by Michael Howard, even though he has been its most notorious exponent in this country in recent times. Indeed, we saw previously that the first Chairman of the Prison Commission, Sir Edmund du Cane, was himself an early exemplar of this approach, although the size of the prison population actually contracted by over 40 per cent[40] during his regime (which lasted from 1877 to 1895). This was something over which he had no direct control. Indeed, it is even possible that the very severity of custodial punishment during this era may have encouraged the development of alternatives such as probation. Even during the 'era of rehabilitative optimism', vestiges of Strategy A lingered on: notably in the use of physical force on those who resisted 'good order and discipline' while in custody. And although corporal punishment within prisons was abolished in 1967, the use of physical force persisted, particularly in response to the growing incidence of disorder following the security clamp-down of the 1960s.

The latest resurgence of Strategy A was already under way prior to February 1993. It was, however, something of a defining moment when

Prime Minister John Major urged society to 'condemn a little more and understand a little less', while announcing a 'crusade against crime' in the wake of widespread public revulsion following the murder of two year old James Bulger by two ten-year-old boys. With fellow crusader Michael Howard installed as Home Secretary in May 1993, the rebirth of Strategy A formed an integral part of the Conservatives' 'Back to Basics' campaign which was launched at the party's annual conference in October 1993. This conference also marked the first proclamation of Mr Howard's 'prison works' mantra and the unveiling of a 27-point plan for 'getting tough on criminals'. In relation to prison, the package contained plans for the construction of six new private prisons, compulsory drug testing for prisoners and a much tougher prison regime, described by Mr Howard as being 'decent but austere' (with the emphasis on 'austere').

In keeping with the 'hands-on' approach for which he was to become notorious, Mr Howard let it be known that he was vehemently opposed to the introduction of in-cell television (even though this was first introduced by the Conservative government in 1991, and had been associated with a reduction of prison violence in France). Prison governors were given substantially increased powers to award disciplinary punishments,[41] and prisoners' entitlement to home leave was cut back by a massive 40 per cent. Restrictions were also imposed on the practice of temporary release prior to the ending of a sentence, and a new offence of absconding while on temporary leave was introduced. In addition to the deliberate toughening of prison regimes, the amount of time spent out of cell or in educational or other facilities was further curtailed, partly as a result of renewed security concerns following the Whitemoor and Parkhurst breakouts and partly as a result of Treasury-inspired budget cuts. Although Strategy A involved the curtailment of many existing rights for prisoners, a new 'national incentives scheme' was introduced in July 1995, which introduced a limited number of *conditional* privileges. These were extended only to prisoners who earned them, by behaving responsibly and taking part in constructive activities. They included access to private cash over and above the normal limits, additional or improved visits, eligibility to participate in enhanced earnings schemes and (for certain groups of prisoners only) earned community visits.

The particularly abrasive nature of Michael Howard's promotion of Strategy A was well illustrated by his dealings with both the Chief Inspector of Prisons and the Prisons Ombudsman.[42] As Chief Inspector, Judge Stephen Tumim had been a long-standing critic of prison conditions, and the Home Secretary's refusal to renew his contract in October 1995 confirmed beliefs that Mr Howard could not tolerate his outspoken and critical views. Judge Tumim himself commented on the day of his retirement that the Home Secretary no longer seemed to want independent advice. Michael Howard also played an active part in the selection of the first Prisons Ombudsman, vetoing on political grounds all three of the candidates who were originally short-listed for the post. He subsequently criticised[43] the performance of the Ombudsman he did appoint, Sir Peter Woodhead, for upholding too many prisoners' complaints (51 per cent in the first six months) and went on to curtail his terms of reference by excluding the investigation of complaints involving the effect of ministerial decisions on prisoners.[44]

By far the most damaging effect of Strategy A has been its impact on the prison population and the associated crisis of resources. Following his chilling warning in October 1993 that the government would no longer judge the success of the criminal justice system by a fall in the prison population, both the Home Secretary and the Prime Minister appeared to go out of their way to encourage sentencers to adopt a more punitive approach in their dealings with offenders and suspects. Little exhortation was needed, since sentencing was already becoming harsher, and the prison population rising, even before the government signalled its change of rhetoric. In December 1992 the prison population stood at 40,600. By the time of the General Election in May 1997, this had increased by almost exactly 50 per cent to just over 60,000.

Quite apart from the human misery which the resurgence of Strategy A has inevitably inflicted on prison inmates and their families, there has also been a considerable financial cost. Although it is difficult to be precise, some idea of the price tag that needs to be attached to the 'prison works' rhetoric can be gleaned from the fact that in late 1993 an additional sum of £620.3 million was assigned to new prison building for 1994-7, to which a further sum of £117 million should be added for the provision of 2,000 extra prison places at existing prisons by the building of additional houseblocks (announced in January 1994). This does not include the cost of additional quotas which the government agreed should be paid to private prison contractors in order to accommodate the additional prisoners they could be expected to take beyond their Certified Normal Accommodation. More sobering still is the increase in the proportion of public spending that was devoted to law and order and public safety during the Conservative period in office. This more than doubled from 2.6 per cent in 1979 to 5.5 per cent in 1994 (though it fell back to 4.9 per cent in 1996).[45] Other forms of social spending, particularly on housing and other welfare benefits were all slashed during the same period, though the 'savings' which accrued were more than cancelled out by the increased spending on enforcement and punitive strategies. In short, the bitter legacy of Strategy A represents not just a wasted opportunity and a waste of resources, but a triumph of perversity over hope.

Strategy C: Hope springs eternal?

Strategy C is the direct antithesis of Strategy A, which appears to be based on the belief that offenders can be intimidated or cowed into obedience and, where this proves impossible, that they should be contained and incapacitated with little regard for their status as citizens or even their humanity. In marked contrast, Strategy C is founded on a 'strong empathy with the delinquent as a fellow human being . . . a person, on the one hand, needing help and, on the other, entitled to certain basic rights. In other words compassion, co-responsibility and a deep sense of humanity . . . '[46] Above all, a commitment to Strategy C would require a determination to avoid the use of imprisonment in favour of more constructive approaches wherever possible, and to minimise the pain and suffering caused by imprisonment in those cases where it cannot be avoided.

A key concept in Strategy C is the notion of legitimacy, which sociologists define as *power which is perceived to be morally justified.*[47] The meaning of the concept has been further elaborated by David Beetham,[48] a political philosopher, who has proposed three prerequisites which need to be satisfied for power to be legitimately exercised: (1) *conformity with established rules,* which are (2) *justified on the basis of shared beliefs;* and to which (3) *express consent, authenticated by actions, is given by the subordinate party.* Where, and to the extent that, these conditions are satisfied, the subordinate party in a relationship is afforded moral grounds for compliance; and conversely, where they are not, the subordinate party is afforded moral grounds for withholding that compliance. The concept's particular relevance to the debate about the morality of imprisonment has been highlighted by criminologists such as Richard Sparks and Tony Bottoms.[49] They point out that 'a defensible and legitimated prison regime demands a dialogue in which prisoners' voices . . . are registered and have a chance of being responded to'. They go on to argue that legitimacy 'demands reference to standards that can be defended externally in moral and political argument' and in addition requires 'the recognition of prisoners in terms both of their citizenship and their ordinary humanity'.

This analysis has profound implications for the three criminal justice strategies we have been considering in this book. It suggests that Strategy A is likely to incur a serious and unavoidable 'legitimacy deficit' by virtue of its reliance on coercive measures that deny prisoners both the respect to which their humanity entitles them and also their residual civil status as members of the moral community of citizens. To the extent that Strategy B is used in pursuit of the coercive ends identified by Strategy A (what we have called 'punitive managerialism'), it is likely to incur a similar legitimacy deficit. Such a deficit can only hope to be avoided by respecting the humanity of all prisoners, and by regarding them as members of the moral community of citizens whose civil status, albeit diminished, affords them certain basic constitutional and civic rights. This approach has only been convincingly advocated by some of those who adhere to Strategy C, though as we argue in this book it is perfectly possible to imagine some of the managerialist techniques associated with Strategy B being deployed in pursuit of Strategy C goals.

We can discern elements of a Strategy C approach in certain of the policies and practices relating to imprisonment over the years, though it is fair to say that this has never formed a coherent and paramount objective. Early examples include the humanitarian and reformist aspirations of a number of Prison Commissioners, notably Sir Alexander Paterson, during the inter-war period. Indeed Paterson's insistence on 'the primacy of rehabilitation as an ideal and an objective'[50] represents one distinctive strand of Strategy C. A more recent example is the report of the government-appointed Control Review Committee,[51] which criticised the controversial use of 'control units' in which disruptive prisoners were segregated and confined in exceptionally Spartan conditions during the 1970s. The committee favoured instead the adoption of a liberal and humane but highly secure regime in which the emphasis was on resocialisation rather than repression. These recommendations formed the basis for the establishment of a small number of 'Special Units'. The best known example of this kind of unit was the one which was set up in Barlinnie prison in Scotland in 1973. But in spite of some remarkable (and all too unusual) success stories, two of these units (including the one at Barlinnie) were closed down in 1995: victims of the blinkered obsession with punishment and security that is associated with Strategy A.

Many of the recommendations contained in the Woolf report[52] were also consistent with Strategy C, though it could be said that its overall preoccupation with the managerial and operational problems confronting the prison system (in which due regard was paid to the need to retain control over prisoners and maintain high levels of security) were even more strongly redolent of Strategy B. The report came much closer to adopting a Strategy C agenda in its emphasis on the need for justice to be given a much higher priority within the prison system, and for urgent action to be taken to address the widespread feelings of injustice on the part of inmates, which Woolf accepted were genuine. The duty to provide reasons for any decision which adversely affects a prisoner, and for an adequate grievance procedure to be made available—which would allow complaints to be investigated and appropriate forms of redress to be provided—are essential prerequisites for any relationships that claim to acknowledge the principle of respect for others. Even here, however, it can be argued that Woolf erred in restricting access to an external complaints adjudicator (or ombudsman) to the apex of the complaints system, instead of introducing an independent element at an earlier stage, much closer to the point of dispute.[53]

Another set of recommendations which also contains a significant element of Strategy C was Woolf's proposal that prisoners should be given better opportunities to maintain their links with their families and communities, through more visits and home leaves, and also by ensuring that they are located as close to their homes as possible (which would also remove another major source of grievance). Woolf took the idea further by recommending a major reorganization of the prison estate into a network of 'community prisons' which would be situated, where possible, near to major centres of population. Woolf believed that such a system would be conducive both to the rehabilitation of offenders and their reintegration on release, and also to the smooth running of the prison system. The proposal failed to materialise though there were limited moves to develop the idea. However, the wider issue of the relationships that ought to exist between prisons, inmates and their local communities was not addressed, as it would need to be, in any thorough-going version of Strategy C.

Another key issue for Strategy C which was also neglected by Lord Woolf concerns the nature of the relationships between prison staff and inmates and the basis on which these are founded. The importance of the issue was recognised by Joe Pilling who was Director General of the Prison Service from 1991 to 1993, but who was passed over as head of the new 'executive agency' Prison Service by Kenneth Clarke in favour of Derek Lewis. In a lecture in 1992,[54] Joe Pilling highlighted the Prison Service's essential purpose of looking after prisoners with 'humanity', and argued for prisoners to be treated with 'respect, fairness, individuality, care and openness'. In sharp contrast to some of his colleagues and successors, he spoke of the need for leaders within organizations such as the prison service to articulate clearly the values to be applied at all levels within it, from policy makers to those who implement it, particularly those who have contact with prisoners.

But although there have been beacons of Strategy C enlightenment over the years, the quest for moral legitimacy and respect for human rights has never consistently illuminated the direction of government policy towards prisons or the manner of its implementation. At best it has provided a rhetorical halo which has all too often masked a mainly pragmatic or even deliberately harsh approach to prison policy. This is the somewhat depressing context in which we come to examine the promise and the performance of the new Labour administration during its first year in office.

NEW LABOUR: NEW PRISONS POLICY?

The purpose of the criminal justice system . . . is first of all to try and prevent crime arising altogether. Secondly, to divert as many people as possible from the necessity of custody. Thirdly to imprison those whom it is necessary to imprison, only. Fourthly to understand that the purpose of imprisonment is to ensure that the best chance of rehabilitation is given to those that are in prison. What we require is not a series of policy initiatives that are reflex responses to particular events occurring in our [s]ociety, but a thought out policy, a strategy . . . that deals with all the various aspects of the problems that we face and doesn't attempt to isolate the Prison Service from the rest of the Criminal Justice System.

These are not our words, but those of the present Labour Prime Minister, Tony Blair, when he was Shadow Home Secretary.[55] The Labour Party's 1997 election manifesto sounded less visionary on the subject of prisons, stating only that 'the Prison Service now faces serious financial problems. We will audit the resources available, take proper ministerial responsibility for the service, and seek to ensure that prison regimes are constructive and require inmates to face up to their offending behaviour', and promising to 'attack the drug problem in prisons'.[56]

Since the General Election of May 1997, perhaps the most notable change in the governmental approach to prisons has been New Labour's marked and welcome change of rhetoric, symbolised in the ditching of the 'prison works' slogan. But when it comes to the crucial issues of how many people we keep in prison and how they are treated, there are few signs so far that the policy agenda is about to be released from the iron grip of Strategy A. There have been a few minor concessions, for example a return to the policy of introducing televisions in prisoners' cells (a privilege for which prisoners have to pay out of their meagre prison earnings).[57] When £660 million extra money was allocated to the Prison Service in July 1998 it was stated that some of this would go towards developing more constructive prison regimes, but it seemed likely that most of it would be swallowed up in accommodating the increased numbers of prisoners. And Mr Straw has offered prison officers a limited restoration of their legal right to undertake industrial action—albeit only in return for a no-strike agreement, with the Home Secretary retaining reserve powers to forbid industrial actions—along with an independent pay review body and a new disputes procedure which will seek to remove some of the most contentious issues from the traditional arena of collective bargaining.

Beyond that, however, there has so far been little movement— particularly with regard to the key question of the sheer massive size of the prison population, which has continued to rise inexorably since the General Election. We noted earlier that by 1 May 1997 it had already reached 60,000. By the end of April 1998 it had increased still further to 65,507, which represents a staggering rise of 61 per cent since December 1992. Remarkably, Jack Straw's reaction has been to assure doubters that 'there is no danger of the prison population getting out of control.'[58] Far from ensuring that as many people as possible are diverted from the necessity of custody, and that custodial sentences are reserved only for those whom it is necessary to imprison, Jack Straw has suggested that prisons are 'essentially a demand-led service' asserting, in words that his predecessor might have used, that his priority was not to reduce the prison population but 'to secure the safety of the public'.[59] Accordingly, as we have noted, still more money was found in order to meet this 'demand' from sentencers,[60] even though other forms of public expenditure were being held within the tight spending limits inherited from the government's Conservative predecessors. The only attempt to ease some of the growing pressure on the prison population has been the relatively modest plan in the Crime and Disorder Act 1998 to release up to three thousand prisoners slightly earlier than normal, subject to electronic monitoring; but the current rate of increase in the prison population is likely to cancel out any advantage well before the measure is brought into effect.

While still in opposition, Jack Straw asked the pertinent question what had happened to the Woolf Report, commenting that

> it is extraordinary that such an authoritative report, hailed as a masterly piece of work by everyone involved in the prison system . . . has been so quickly neglected. The Woolf Report offered us a unique opportunity to reform the prison system. We should return to its guiding principles of security, control and justice.[61]

As we write in the second year of the new Labour government, the question he posed is just as relevant, yet the agenda proposed by Woolf remains just as becalmed as it was then. Although the fetters imposed on the jurisdiction of the Prisons Ombudsman by Michael Howard were subsequently removed,[62] reports by the government's Chief Inspector of Prisons, Sir David Ramsbotham, show that conditions and regimes continue to deteriorate throughout the prison system. Moreover, an even more transparent U-turn has taken place with regard to the issue of prison privatisation.

Before the General Election Mr Straw had said,

> Let me reiterate that I regard privatisation of the prison service as morally repugnant. It is not appropriate for people to profit from incarceration, and we intend to take privatised prisons back into the public sector as soon as contractually possible.[63]

However, the newly elected government started backtracking almost immediately after the election. On 8 May 1997, Mr. Straw announced ' . . . if there are contracts in the pipeline and the only way of getting the [new prison] accommodation in place very quickly is by signing those contracts, then I will sign those contracts.'[64] Just over a month later, he reported that he had renewed the management contract for Blakenhurst, one of the first privately run prisons, and had agreed to two new privately financed, designed, built and run prisons. One year later, on 19 May 1998, Mr Straw told the Prison Officers' Association that all new prisons in England and Wales were to be privately built and run. He indicated that his decision was based in part on the findings of the Labour members of the House of Commons Home Affairs Select Committee in 1997 (see above), and in part on two Prison Service Reviews which he had commissioned the previous year, but whose findings have never been made public. The first of these had reportedly found that the option of using private finance to build new prisons while retaining the management function was not affordable and did not offer value for money. The second one reportedly concluded that 'the immediate transfer of existing private prisons is not affordable and cannot be justified on value for money grounds'. The only concession he made was to allow the Prison Service to bid for the chance to take over the management of existing privately managed prisons when the contracts next expire.

This turn-around indicates that Mr Straw has adopted without demur the managerialist arguments of his predecessors on the subject of privatisation. On the subject of imprisonment generally, his government so far seems unwilling to publicly repudiate Strategy A (presumably for fear of being outflanked by the Conservative Party) let alone commit themselves wholeheartedly to Strategy C. Yet unless this is done, it is difficult to see how the government will be able to tackle the problems of the penal system effectively, certainly while retaining the previous government's tight public expenditure totals.

Perhaps the best that might have been hoped for, at least in the short to medium term, was that the review of prison and probation services which we mentioned in *Chapter 4* might result in more radical reforms for the prison service as well as probation. Perhaps, for example, lessons really could have been drawn from the Swedish model of prison organization.[65] There, all but the larger secure prisons are organized on the basis of correctional care regions, which attempt to maximise the influence of surrounding communities on small local prisons by providing for extended leave arrangements, conjugal visits, day release for vocational training and employment, and pre-release hostels. Such an arrangement sounds not too dissimilar to Lord Woolf's concept of community prisons. But there was little sign of anything like this in the government's consultation paper on the prison and probation services published in August 1998. The closest it came to this agenda was perhaps its expression of a pious desire to see more prisoners accommodated close to their homes, which was almost inevitably combined with regrets that limited resources gravely limited what could be achieved in this respect.[66] And indeed, the resources which would be needed to turn Woolf's vision into reality do seem to represent an insuperable stumbling block; unless (and this is a really big 'unless') the government could summon up the courage and confidence both to jettison Strategy A completely and to commit itself to a new beginning for criminal justice founded on Strategy C.

One key element in such a strategy would be to rethink the purpose of custody, and work towards creating a system where (as we suggested in *Chapter 4*) confinement is used only for genuinely dangerous offenders who need to be prevented from committing really serious offences, and very occasionally as a 'last resort' sanction for failing to comply with court orders when all other sanctions fail. Another would be to drastically reform the prison regime by gearing it towards respect for prisoners' rights, encouraging the practice of reparation, facilitating the (voluntary) rehabilitation of offenders and working for the reintegration of all offenders subject to the need to safeguard public safety.[67] It is tempting to say that, on the evidence we have seen to date, the prospect of these sorts of major shift in penal orientation occurring is exceedingly remote. But we shall return to this issue in our concluding chapter, when we may find greater cause for optimism.

ENDNOTES: *Chapter 5*

1 The rule was adopted for the first time in 1949, but reflected a process of 'humanisation' and reform that had gathered momentum throughout the inter-war years, particularly when Sir Alexander Paterson was a prominent member of the Prison Commission.

2 The level of recorded crime doubled between 1955 and 1964, having risen steadily during the late 1940s before levelling off slightly in the early 1950s: Mike Maguire, 'Crime Statistics, Patterns and Trends' in Mike Maguire, Rod Morgan and Robert Reiner (eds.), *The Oxford Handbook of Criminology* (2nd edn., Oxford, Oxford University Press, 1997), 135-88 at p.159.

3 As a result, 25 local prisons were closed between 1914 and 1929, and no new

capacity was added to the system apart from Borstal institutions for young offenders until after the war: Andrew Rutherford, *Prisons and the Process of Justice* (Oxford, Oxford University Press, 1986), 131.

4 Camp Hill prison on the Isle of Wight which was built in 1912 and Everthorpe which was opened in 1957: Terence Morris, *Crime and Criminal Justice Since 1945* (Oxford, Blackwell, 1989), p. 125.

5 See Michael Cavadino and James Dignan, *The Penal System: An Introduction* (2nd edn., London, Sage, 1997), 116-9.

6 Under the classification system proposed by Lord Mountbatten's *Report of the Inquiry into Prison Escapes and Security*, Cmnd 3175 (London, HMSO, 1966).

7 These included the use of physical force, segregation and reallocation or transfer to another establishment.

8 See Cavadino and Dignan op. cit., pp.133-7.

9 When the prison system was first centralised. Before then, long-term convict prisons had been administered by the Home Office, while local gaols had come under the jurisdiction of local magistrates.

10 Morris, op. cit., p.129.

11 This has been described as a 'bureaucratic-lawful model' by I. Barak-Glanz 'Towards a Conceptual Schema of Prison Management Styles', *The Prison Journal*, 61(2) (1981). See also John Ditchfield, *Control in Prisons: A Review of the Literature*, Home Office Research Study No. 37 (London, HMSO, 1990). Max Weber proposed a three-fold typology of authority comprising 'traditional', 'charismatic' and 'legal' authority *(Economy and Society,* New York, Bedminster Press, 1968), and the shift we are discussing here can be seen as a move from the second to the third of these forms of authority.

12 See Anthony Bottoms, 'The Philosophy and Politics of Punishment and Sentencing' in Chris Clarkson and Rod Morgan (eds.), *The Politics of Sentencing Reform* (Oxford, Clarendon Press, 1995): 17-49.

13 See Cavadino and Dignan, op. cit., pp. 135-6.

14 Lord Woolf and Judge Stephen Tumim, *Prison Disturbances April 1990*, Cm 1456 (London, HMSO, 1991).

15 See the Home Office, *Improving Management in Government: The Next Steps* (Government Efficiency Unit, London, HMSO, 1988): para. 19; and Home Office, *HM Prison Service – Review of Organization and Location above Management Level* (London, HMSO, 1989).

16 See Sir Raymond Lygo, *Management of the Prison Service: A Report* (London, Home Office, 1991).

17 The former Granada Television executive was also appointed as chief policy adviser to the Home Secretary on all prison issues including the introduction of greater private sector involvement in the prison service, both as a competitor and as a stimulus for innovation (see section on privatisation, below).

18 Sir John Woodcock, *The Escape from Whitemoor Prison on Friday 9th September 1994* ('The Woodcock Enquiry'), Cm 2741 (London, HMSO, 1994).

19 Sir John Learmont, *Review of Prison Service Security in England and Wales and*

the Escape from Parkhurst Prison on Tuesday 3rd January 1995, Cm 3020 (London, HMSO, 1995).

[20] Centre for Public Services, *Reinventing Government in Britain – The Performance of the Next Steps Agencies: Implications for the USA* (Centre for Public Services, Sheffield, 1997).

[21] *Report on the Work of the Prison Department 1983* (London, HMSO, 1984): para. 7.

[22] This was before the privatisation of court escort services.

[23] Anthony Bottoms and Ronald Preston (eds.), *The Coming Penal Crisis: A Criminological and Theological Exploration* (Edinburgh, Scottish Academic Press, 1980), 4.

[24] Home Office, *HM Prison Service* (London, Home Office, 1986).

[25] Kathleen McDermott and Roy King, 'A Fresh Start: The Enhancement of Prison Regimes', *Howard Journal of Criminal Justice*, 28 (1989), 161-76.

[26] See for a rare exception Joe Sim, 'Reforming the Penal Wasteland? A Critical Review of the Woolf Report' in Elaine Player and Michael Jenkins (eds.) *Prisons After Woolf: Reform Through Riot* (London and New York, Routledge, 1994), 31-45.

[27] The same could be said, e.g. of Woolf's call for a timetable for the provision of integral sanitation in all prison cells which would finally eliminate the humiliating and degrading practice of slopping-out. But although the government claimed to have eradicated the practice by April 1996 this proved to be premature. Reports published by the chief inspector of prisons more than three years later disclosed that inmates in at least two prisons were still having to 'slop out' (*Guardian*, 20 July 1999; 12 August 1999).

[28] HM Prison Service, *Operating Standards* (London, HM Prison Service, 1994).

[29] See Sim, op. cit., pp. 38-41.

[30] See Cavadino and Dignan, op. cit., pp. 133-7.

[31] These included, for example, numbers of escapes, capacity, levels of overcrowding, time out of cell, visiting entitlements and cost per prison place.

[32] House of Commons Home Affairs Committee, *Contract Provision of Prisons* (Fourth Report, Session 1986/7, HC 291, London, HMSO, 1987).

[33] See Cavadino and Dignan, op. cit., ch. 6 for a more detailed history of prison privatisation.

[34] See Keith Bottomley, Adrian James, Emma Clare and Alison Liebling, *Monitoring and Evaluation of Wolds Remand Prison and Comparisons with Public-Sector Prisons, in particular HMP Woodhill* (London, Home Office Publications Unit, 1997).

[35] House of Commons Home Affairs Committee, *The Management of the Prison Service (Public and Private)*, Second Report, Session 1996/7 (London, The Stationery Office, 1997).

[36] Para. 179.

[37] Jo Woodbridge, *Prison Service Research Report No. 3*, December 1997.

[38] See Cavadino and Dignan, op. cit., ch. 6 for details.

[39] See Bottomley et al., op. cit., p. 52.

40 Figure extrapolated from information cited by Rutherford, op. cit., p. 123.
41 These included an across-the-board increase of 50 per cent in the level of virtually all penalties available to governors, in April 1995.
42 And with prison trade unions: legislation was introduced in the Criminal Justice and Public Order Act 1994 to suppress dissent on the part of prison officers by severely curtailing their ability to take part in industrial action.
43 *The Independent*, 20 October 1995.
44 *The Guardian,* 9 May 1996.
45 *Social Trends,* 28 (London, The Stationery Office, 1984): *Table* 6.21 and 1998: *Table* 6.20, p. 120.
46 Willem de Haan, *The Politics of Redress* (London, Unwin Hyman, 1990: p. 69), as quoted in Andrew Rutherford's 'Penal Policy and Prison Management', *Prison Service Journal*, 90 (1993): 26-9.
47 See Cavadino and Dignan, op. cit., p. 21.
48 David Beetham, *The Legitimation of Power* (London, Macmillan, 1991).
49 Richard Sparks and Tony Bottoms, 'Legitimacy and Order in Prisons', *British Journal of Sociology*, 34 (special issue, 1995: 45-62 at p. 59). See also Richard Sparks, Tony Bottoms and Will Hay, *Prisons and the Problem of Order* (Oxford, Clarendon Press, 1996); Adrian James, Keith Bottomley, Alison Liebling and Emma Clare, *Privatising Prisons: Rhetoric and Reality* (London, Sage, 1997); and Cavadino and Dignan, op. cit.
50 Terence Morris, op. cit., p. 73.
51 Home Office, *Managing the Long Term Prison System: the Report of the Control Review Committee* (London, HMSO, 1984).
52 op. cit.
53 Andrew Coyle, 'Prisons for Whose Profit?', *Prison Service Journal*, 90 (1993), 30-4 at p. 32.
54 The Eve Savill Memorial Lecture to the Institute for the Study and Treatment of Delinquency, 11 June 1992.
55 Tony Blair, 'The Future of the Prison Service', *Prison Service Journal*, 90 (1993), 20-5 at p.20.
56 Labour Party, *New Labour: Because Britain Deserves Better*, General Election manifesto 1997.
57 A limited extension of in-cell television was announced on 1 June 1998. The weekly charge is likely to be about £1 against average weekly prisoner earnings of £7.50.
58 H C Deb. 2 March 1998, col. 691.
59 Interview with Jack Straw, on BBC Radio 4's *Today,* 30 July 1997.
60 £43 million extra was allocated to the Prison Service in July 1997, a further £70 million in February 1998, and a massive £660 million in July 1998 following the completion of the government's Comprehensive Spending Review.
61 Jack Straw, 'The Penal System in Crisis', in David Bean (ed.), *Law Reform for All* (London, Blackstone Press, 1996): 30-42 at p. 41.
62 Prisons Ombudsman Annual Report 1998/9, Cm 4369 (London, Prisons Ombudsman, 1999).

63 op. cit. at pp. 41-2.

64 Prison Reform Trust, 'UK: Labour's Prison U-turn Complete', *Prison Privatisation Report International*, 21 (1998): p.1.

65 John Harding, 'The Walls of Ignorance', *Guardian*, 1 October 1997.

66 *Joining Forces to Protect the Public* (London, Home Office, 1998), paras. 3.12-3.13.

67 See Cavadino and Dignan, op. cit., p. 307.

CHAPTER 6

Just Fine? (Or, Never Underestimate the Power of a Crisp Packet)

Once upon a time the fine was a quiet, unassuming part of the British criminal justice process. It was used as the penalty for the great majority of summary offences dealt with by the courts and about half the indictable offences, and most people paid their fines, one way or another. The people who didn't were regarded as the feckless or society's small time losers, and something of a nuisance, and some of them went to prison for a while. Because it went quietly about its business most of the time, the fine attracted less attention than its more glamorous brothers and sisters in the penal armoury, such as imprisonment or community service. Less research was conducted on fines than these other measures, and it seldom made the news. But its moment came in the spring of 1993 when suddenly the nation stood aghast to learn that someone had been fined £1,200 for dropping a crisp packet. The government of the day immediately leapt into determined and resolute action: something must be done when an upstart like the lowly fine starts throwing its weight about. Legislation was enacted, and the fine meekly subsided back into the obscurity whence it came.

The story of how this came about, and its relationship to the development of broader criminal justice policy, is the subject of this chapter. It finds its place in this book precisely because we believe that the fine (and the related topic of compensation) have not received sufficient consideration in the context of penal strategy. The fine is most naturally of interest for a Strategy B approach since, aside from default and imprisonment for default, it offers a very cost-effective way of dealing with offenders. So, not surprisingly, it was at the time in the late 1980s when managerialism was in the ascendancy that there was most interest in the problems of, and prospects for the fine. Although primarily punitive in nature, the fine is a 'low-tariff' (relatively lenient) penalty, and therefore has little appeal for a Strategy A approach. As a consequence, apart from the question of how to enforce financial penalties, use of the fine received less attention from 1993 onwards. Fines have also held little appeal for proponents of Strategy C thus far— although this is something that we feel could be given more attention. But more of that later. Let us first look at how a mainstay of the criminal justice system came to be in a fine old mess.

MEANS-RELATED FUSS

What caused all the fuss in 1993 was something called a unit fine, which was introduced into English magistrates' courts in October 1992 as part of the reform package that was the Criminal Justice Act 1991. It did not last long, for in May 1993 Home Secretary Kenneth Clarke announced that it was to be completely abolished, a demise swiftly administered by the Criminal Justice Act 1993.[1] 'Unit fine' was the term given in England and Wales to a method of imposing financial penalties on offenders that takes account of their means in a systematic way. Similar methods have been used for many years in other countries, where they are often known as 'day fines'. This term has the potential to cause confusion, since it may be taken to imply that so much is paid every day, whereas in fact it refers to the way the fine is calculated in terms of days' pay. In this chapter we will use the general term 'means-related fines' to describe such systems of fining.

So what are means-related fines? Essentially they are a way of imposing a financial penalty in such a manner as to distinguish between the gravity of the offence and the means of the offender. The intended consequence is that penalties are equally onerous on those who commit comparable offences even though their financial circumstances may be very different. For example, a moderately well off offender could be sentenced to pay 25 units to reflect the gravity of the offence at £10 per unit, totalling £250. Someone who has less disposable income than the first person but who commits a similar offence might also be fined 25 units, but could be assessed at, for example, £5 for each unit and would pay £125 in total.

Such a system has a number of advantages. In the first place it seems much more equitable if fines have 'equality of impact'[2] upon comparable offenders, and if parity and proportionality of sentencing are a concern then it appears to be more fair and just. This is an argument in favour of means-related fines as a matter of principle—one which should appeal particularly to advocates of the 'just deserts' line of thinking. There is also a pragmatic argument which should appeal to those of a Strategy B disposition. If fines are fixed at a level which is adjusted to match peoples' means, then they are more likely to pay them, and this reduces the burden of enforcement, and ultimately the cost of imprisoning them for non-payment. A third consideration, which came increasingly to the fore in England and Wales during the 1980s, is that such a system should result in a reduction in variations between the amounts of fines imposed by different courts. (For differing reasons, both Strategy B and 'just deserts' adherents disapprove of such disparities: fines should be equally fair everywhere for the former, and efficiently standardised for the latter.)

On the basis of these arguments (and the example given), it might be concluded that the means-related system appears both simple and persuasive. But there are problems. One of the main ones is how to assess people's means. This can be problematic if you have to rely on the person concerned telling you what their means are. Again, in order for means-related fines to work, all offences have to be within a framework which enables various gravity levels to be reflected in the calculation of the fine. On top of this, the range of units and the monetary amounts per unit have to be set carefully so that the product of the two makes it possible to implement a flexible sliding scale that can be used to take account of a wide range of circumstances, without there being excessive variation in the totals imposed—if, that is, you want to avoid the worst off in society paying what might be viewed as derisory amounts for relatively serious offences and the better off paying very large sums for (say) dropping a crisp packet. In this regard particular attention needs to be paid to those at the very bottom of the scale who are on state benefit, and who are regarded as having little or no excess income to be deprived of.

Another problem for means-related fining systems concerns the attitudes and traditions of sentencers. In Britain—as we saw in *Chapter 3*—sentencers have been very jealous of their powers to determine what sentence is imposed on an individual basis. And well before unit fines were introduced it was apparent that many magistrates and justices' clerks viewed with suspicion a development that they thought would reduce their ability to set a penalty as they saw fit. We will discuss this aspect of the story further in due course. First, however, to understand developments in recent years we need to look at fines over a longer period.

Fines in England and Wales prior to 1991

Along with physical punishment, depriving someone of money is one of the oldest means of penalising people, and there has probably always been some recognition, albeit crude and subjective, that this needs to take account of what an offender can pay. Before the advent of unit fines this recognition was enshrined in the provision in the Magistrates' Courts Act 1952, section 31 (and later in the Magistrates' Courts Act 1980, section 35) whereby magistrates were required 'to take into consideration among other things the means of the person on whom the fine is imposed so far as they appear or are known to the court'.[3] This requirement was, however, vague and in practice rather hit and miss. John Wheeler, an MP with experience of the penal system and once a

Chairman of the All Party Penal Affairs Group, said of the Magistrates' Courts Act provision that 'the whole process is a mixture of bluff and chance'.[4] A study for the US Vera Institute of Justice found that 'in setting fine amounts, magistrates emphasise the severity of the offence and do not always review thoroughly the information available to them on offenders' means. Thus the total fine amounts set are often high and inconsistent with offenders' means'.[5] The requirement was further limited by the fact that, in practice, it was interpreted as meaning that adjustments for means could only operate in one direction: the amount of a fine could be reduced for the less well off, but could not be increased for the better off.

The possibility of introducing a 'day fine' type of system was considered in 1970 by the Advisory Council on the Penal System in its report *Non-Custodial and Semi-Custodial Penalties*.[6] While the Council was attracted to the idea, it felt that such a system could not be introduced at that time, for two main reasons. The first was that the Council took as its model the day fine system in Sweden, where it was much easier for courts to obtain details about offenders' means than in England and Wales because information about individuals' incomes and tax codings was more readily available. The second reason was that introducing such a system at that time would have entailed a revision of the system of maximum penalties, including a considerable number of summary offences each with their own statutory and often quite small maxima. The consequence of the Advisory Council's conclusions was that the whole issue of fines and their reform faded into the background for several years, and the use and enforcement of fines was over-shadowed by other developments during the 1970s, including the introduction of community service orders (recommended by the Council in the same report) and other 'alternatives to custody'.

Nonetheless, there was increasing concern during the 1970s over a rise in the number of offenders imprisoned for fine default from just over 10,000 in 1973 to 17,000 in 1979. This was not because more people were being fined, but because of an increase in the proportion who were imprisoned as a result of default: this increased from six per 1,000 persons fined in 1973, to ten per 1,000 in 1979.

In 1979 the National Association for the Care and Resettlement of Offenders (NACRO) convened a prestigious Working Party, chaired by Lady Howe, to inquire into the problem of fine enforcement and default. The Working Party made a series of recommendations and concluded, 'the first step in securing the payment of fines and other sums is to ensure they are within an offender's means to pay. We suggest ways of achieving this and look at the important related issue of obtaining information about means'.[7] (NACRO, 1981, para. 6.7). The Working Party went on to recommend,

> that courts adopt the principle, already used in some courts, of estimating the weekly amount an offender can pay and reflect the gravity of the offence in the number of weeks pay to be affected. These two elements of the fine should be stated in court.

> that the obstacles to introducing something similar to a day fine system are not insuperable and such a system should be considered, . . . and we welcome the government's undertaking to pursue the possibility further.

The Working Party also recommended the piloting of a means assessment form.[8]

Support for looking again at the possibility of introducing a day fine system had also come from the House of Commons Expenditure Committee. In its reply to the Committee the government of the day pointed out once more that to overcome inconsistencies in the relationship of financial penalties to each other a comprehensive review of such penalties would be necessary, but made a commitment that, 'as soon as it is possible to undertake such a review, the Government will ensure that the possibility of changing to a day fine system is fully explored'.[9] A number of the NACRO Working Party's recommendations were subsequently implemented in the Criminal Justice Act 1982. These included a review of maximum penalties, which involved setting levels which could incorporate summary offences and be more readily altered to reflect the changing value of money. Clearly the wholesale introduction of a day fine style system required more consideration over a longer period of time, but the reports of both the House of Commons Expenditure Committee and the NACRO Working Party put such a system back on the agenda and set in train deliberations which were to lead to pilot experiments towards the end of the decade.

THE SOCIAL AND ECONOMIC CONTEXT

At this point it is important to look at the broader social and economic aspects of fines and their enforcement. As indicated earlier, the fine is generally regarded by those involved with criminal justice matters as being a successful measure, and is used more than any other sanction. For many years the main focus of concern in relation to the fine was the minority who failed to pay their fines and the even smaller minority who ended up in prison as a consequence. Studies highlighted the fact that prominent amongst such defaulters were the socially inadequate and persistent petty offenders, habitual drunken offenders, those who regarded fines as an occupational hazard, such as illegal street traders, and prostitutes, those on the lowest incomes, and those who simply 'played the system' for as long as possible. In other words, socially marginal groups of people.

A 1978 Home Office research study, *Fines in Magistrates' Courts*[10] reported that most of the defaulters studied had very restricted means and this contributed to their failure to pay. A study of men discharged from three prisons in Yorkshire[11] found that it was the most socially isolated men in the sample who were most likely to be in prison for fine default, and a small study of fine defaulters received at Winson Green prison at around the same time found a similar group of what were termed 'social inadequates' amongst the fine defaulters there.[12]

While the main basis of concern about the fine during the 1970s was the rise in the numbers imprisoned for fine default, another phenomenon was developing that was to cause further consternation. This was the rising level of unemployment. Fines work quite well in a relatively affluent society with near full employment, where almost everyone has a level of disposable income in excess of their basic needs. It is being deprived of this excess that acts as a penalty and restricts peoples' liberty to spend their money as they wish. In such circumstances non-payment and sanctions for default will tend to be limited to the socio-economically marginal groups mentioned above, or can be attributed to those who display a wanton disregard of the law and therefore deserve to be punished by deprivation of other forms of liberty. However, if unemployment becomes widespread then the fine becomes a less viable option This is precisely what happened during the 1980s.

Fines in Magistrates' Courts had found that although unemployed offenders were less likely to be fined than others, they were more likely to be imprisoned for default. Further Home Office research in 1983 found that the likelihood of being committed to prison for not paying a fine was significantly greater in areas of high unemployment.[13] A Scottish Office study of the experimental introduction of fines enforcement officers in certain courts in Scotland found that default was greater among the unemployed than those in employment, and that a large proportion of defaulters were living on low incomes, many at subsistence level, and were having difficulty making ends meet, even for essentials such as housing, fuel and food.[14] A study for the Vera Institute of Justice found that 'if they do not pay their fines, the unemployed men tend to end up in prison for non-payment regardless of their prior record' and that 'the combination of large fine amounts and declared low income contribute to prison time being served for non-payment'.[15]

It is not too difficult to envisage what happens in court. The sentencer concludes on the basis of the information presented that a fine is the right sentence, but that in order to reflect the gravity of the offence the fine needs to be quite a heavy one. However, confronted with unemployed offenders in an area where there are few realistic opportunities for lawful employment, sentencers are faced with the dilemma of either imposing a sum which they feel does not reflect the gravity of the offence, or one which offenders are very unlikely to be able to pay, with the result that they may well end up as part of the prison population. Not surprisingly courts will in many cases start to think less in terms of a fine and more often turn to other penalties.

A study in the mid-1980s looked at the sentencing of property offenders at six magistrates' courts in areas of the country with contrasting levels of unemployment and found, as the earlier Home Office study had, that unemployed offenders were less likely to be fined. While some received conditional discharges instead, others received 'higher tariff' non-custodial disposals, such as probation orders and community service orders, which were particularly popular with the courts as an alternative to a fine for the unemployed. There was also a small but significant tendency for imprisonment to be used more often in such cases.[16] The study also found that when fines were imposed, although unemployed people were generally required to pay less than those in work, the differences were not great and there were cases of unemployed people receiving fines of more than £400 (which would be greater now allowing for inflation in the intervening years). Bearing in mind that fines usually had to be paid within twelve months of imposition, it was not surprising that unemployed people were more likely to default and more likely to be imprisoned for default. One of the points that comes across from several of the studies referred to above is that, for most people on low income, fines are often one of a number of debts. Hence, as unemployment grew and more people were forced into debt, fine default became another aspect of the growing problem of debt at this time, and it has sometimes been argued that imprisonment for fine default is reminiscent of the imprisonment of debtors.[17]

The inevitable consequence of the above was that use of the fine declined over a period of years. Up until 1979 the fine had been used to deal with 50 per cent of all indictable offences (give or take a per cent). But during the 1980s its use declined steadily to 38 per cent in 1987. Indeed, as the following chart shows, use of the fine was inversely related to the level of unemployment:

Figure 6.1: Unemployment Rate (adjusted to OECD concepts) and Use of the Fine
(for Indictable Offences)

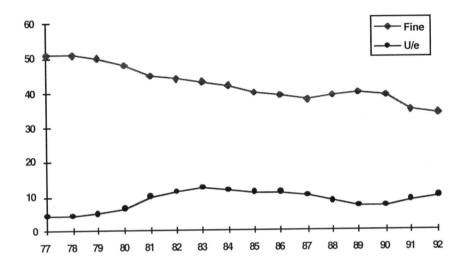

This link was officially recognised in the *Criminal Statistics* in 1984, which
stated: 'The reduction since 1977 in the proportionate use of the fine. . .
may be associated with the higher levels of unemployment in recent
years affecting the ability of some offenders to pay.'[18]

Despite concern about the minority of offenders imprisoned for
default, most of those with an interest in criminal justice agreed that the
fine was by and large satisfactory. It was a useful 'low tariff disposal',
reconviction rates were as good as any other sentence, and it cost very
little; indeed, fines generated income. It was therefore important to
safeguard the position of the fine as the basis for dealing with most
cases. This wish not to do anything to undermine the fine was often
given as one of the main reasons for not abolishing imprisonment for
default, the fear being that if the sanction of imprisonment was removed
sentencers would use it much less. However, by the later part of the
1980s the fine was in decline in any event. Attention had shifted from the
small group of social inadequates who had previously gone to prison for
default to the more substantial threat posed by large scale
unemployment, affecting a much wider group of the population. In this
context the government's commitment in response to the House of
Commons Expenditure Committee's report to look again at the
possibility of a day fine system became more significant. Anything that
held out the prospect of containing the mounting costs of imprisonment,

whether directly by bolstering a non-custodial sanction, or indirectly by reducing the possibility of imprisonment for non-payment, was likely to be considered more favourably than in the past. In addition the main obstacles that the Advisory Council had said stood in the way of day fines had either been removed (a review of maximum fines had been included in the Criminal Justice Act 1982), or were no longer so significant (systems other than that in Sweden, such as the German *Tagesbussensystem*, had shown that day fines could work well without the kind of access to personal financial information that operated in Sweden). The opportunity to do something came with the Criminal Justice Bill of 1990-91.

UNIT FINES AND THE CRIMINAL JUSTICE ACT 1991

Criminal Justice Acts prior to 1991 had usually consisted of an assortment of measures, and while they may have reflected a trend in overall criminal justice policy, they tended not to have a unified, coherent framework. Thus, it would have been possible, given a similar Act in 1991, to introduce unit fines as a measure that could be justified in their own right. However, the Criminal Justice Act of 1991 was different to previous Acts in that it sought to introduce a coherent framework. How did fines, and unit fines in particular fit into this? As far as fines in general are concerned there was no great problem. They are intended to be punitive and unlike some other measures, such as probation or community service, have never claimed to have a rehabilitative component or address other objectives. The basis of the 1991 Act was the deprivation of liberty on a 'just deserts' model. The way in which the various types of sentence related to this central objective are set out in the Home Office guidelines for the subsequent Criminal Justice Act 1991, where it is stated that:

> Most penalties restrict the offender's liberty in some way. It is that restriction of liberty which is the punishment for the offence.

> Although fines and other financial penalties do not restrict the offender's liberty in quite the same way as a community or custodial sentence, they deprive the offender of money and therefore of the ability to spend that money in other ways. . . .

> Community sentences . . . restrict the offender's liberty, though to a lesser degree than custody. . . .

The severest restriction of liberty is imprisonment. It is right that this penalty should be reserved for the most serious offences. [19]

Thus, together with compensation and absolute and conditional discharges, fines formed the lowest tier in the three tier sentencing framework introduced by the Act, below custody and 'community sentences'.

As far as *unit* fines are concerned the key notion is that of proportionality in sentencing. This is fulfilled by having units that reflect the gravity of the offence, and in many ways the unit fine seemed to be ideally suited to the principles of the 1991 Act. However, unit fines also take account of means. If the criterion is deprivation of the liberty to spend one's disposable income in the way one wishes, then the well off person will need to be deprived of a greater monetary amount in order to be deprived of this freedom to the same extent as the less well off. In a 'just deserts' approach the sentence should normally reflect the gravity of the offence rather than the circumstances of the offender. Hence less weight is accorded to the offender's social background and personal circumstances. Where unit fines differed from other aspects of the Criminal Justice Act 1991 was that they *did* take account of individual circumstances—albeit in a way which could be regarded as contributing to 'equality of impact' and hence of genuinely proportional punishment. Nevertheless, it could be said that in a sense unit fines were working in the opposite direction to the tenor of the Act as a whole. For a number of years the trend had been towards focusing more on the offence and to be less inclined to accept the offender's circumstances as a mitigating factor. Although to our knowledge it has never been said explicitly, it may be that this aspect of unit fines also contributed to their less than enthusiastic reception by some of those involved in dispensing criminal justice.

However this may be, the prospects for the practical implementation of a system of means-related fines had been under consideration by the Home Office for some time. As previous research[20] had indicated, there were already some courts where a rudimentary implementation of the principle was developing. As a result of the high proportion of unemployed defendants (around 60 to 70 per cent) appearing before many courts during the 1980s, some had adopted the practice of calculating that an unemployed offender could reasonably be required to pay £3 per week out of their benefit (this was the DHSS's pay back rate at the time for any excess benefit owed by the beneficiary). Since it had been ruled that fines should be paid within 12 months some courts had already determined that the maximum realistic fine that could be levied on unemployed offenders was in the region of £150 (£3 x 50 weeks). Some courts saw merit in developing such a principle further, and in the latter part of the 1980s, about the same time that the Green Paper that preceded the Criminal Justice Act 1991 came out, a pilot experiment in the use of unit fines was carried out at four courts.

The pilot study

Information on the imposition and enforcement of fines was recorded for fines set for seventeen types of offence for six months before and six months after the introduction of unit fines.[21] The results showed that courts were able to obtain sufficient means information from defendants, using a simple form and without undue difficulty. Although there was no overall change in the proportionate use of the fine at the four courts, there was a significant drop in the proportion of those fined who were imprisoned for default. Fines were paid more quickly, disparities between courts in fines imposed on poorer offenders were significantly reduced, and a small supplementary study at one of the courts showed that many people could afford to pay more than the local norm. In addition the magistrates and court staff at the four courts were agreed that unit fines were an improvement on the previous system and continued to use them after the experiment ended. The researchers noted that if such a system were to be adopted nationally then it would be important for courts to adopt a common basic approach to assessing disposable income and guidance would be needed where fines were being imposed together with costs and compensation orders. Thus, by and large the pilot experiment was a success and demonstrated the viability of the unit fine system.

However, it is important to note certain things about the experiment. As Bryan Gibson (a justices' clerk) pointed out, even before the Criminal Justice Act 1991 some press and media were lining themselves up to oppose the system, suggesting that it was a method of punishing wealth.[22] The pilot courts were therefore careful to set parameters in order to avoid 'derisory' fines at one end and excessive fines at the other. The latter was particularly important since at the time it was not clear that fines could be increased for the better off. The Criminal Justice Act 1982 established five levels of fine, according to the seriousness of the offence, with a maximum for each level. At the time the maximum amount that could be imposed by a magistrates' court for a level 5 offence was £2,000. Thus with a maximum of 50 units being used to mark the gravity of the offence, in theory the maximum multiplier for each unit during the pilot study was £40; in practice three courts set a local norm of £20 and the fourth one of £10. However, it was known that the government was likely to increase the maximum levels at which fines could be set. Gibson illustrated the possible effect of this by referring to a case in which the Duke of Westminster (then reputedly Britain's wealthiest man) had been fined for speeding at 106 miles per hour, a level 4 offence for which the maximum was then £1,000. If the Duke had come up at three of the four pilot courts during the experimental period the offence would have been likely to attract a fine of perhaps 15 units, but with a maximum multiplier of £20, resulting in a fine of £300. However if the maxima were to be revised to an upper limit of £5,000 (as in fact happened) then the corresponding fine for Britain's wealthiest person would be £1,500. Hence it was clearly known prior to the introduction of unit fines nationally what the effects of a substantial increase in the maxima at the same time would be.

IMPLEMENTING UNIT FINES: REACTIONS

Unit fines were introduced into magistrates' courts (but not Crown Courts) on a national basis along with most of the provisions of the rest of the Criminal Justice Act 1991 in October 1992. From this point there are two main stories to be told. One concerns the reaction and rhetoric that surrounded the new system and the other is what actually happened in terms of the use of unit fines in sentencing.

We shall first look at how unit fines were received by those involved in using them, and for this purpose will refer to the study of the Act which we carried out in four areas of the North of England.[23] The first point to note is that many magistrates knew relatively little about the provisions of the Criminal Justice Act 1991 until the summer of 1992. When we approached courts in the North of England during the spring and early summer of 1992 asking if we could do some interviews prior to implementation of the Act in order to establish a baseline of expectations, we were told by court clerks that there was not much point in interviewing magistrates because as yet they would not know much about the Act. Many magistrates were still preoccupied with absorbing the implications of the Children Act 1989, which had been implemented the previous autumn. Although magistrates were aware of the impending introduction of the Criminal Justice Act 1991, they did not know much about the detail, and training sessions were scheduled for during the summer to acquaint them with it.

However, even at this stage there was apprehension amongst court clerks, not so much about the principle of unit fines as about the levels at which the fines were to be fixed, the likely public reaction to larger fines for better off motorists, and other worries about how the unit fines would be received, particularly by the press. Those interviewed at one of the larger courts echoed the others when they said that it was a mistake to accompany the introduction of unit fines with a big increase in the overall level of fines. This court went to the trouble of preparing a press release prior to implementation to try to explain the provisions to the press and try to forestall misunderstanding. At only one of the four magistrates' courts were reservations expressed at this time about the *principle* of unit fines.

Six months after implementation of the Act a survey of magistrates was carried out in the four areas covered by the study,[24] which yielded two main findings regarding unit fines. The first was that at all four courts in the study a small majority of the magistrates who responded (54 per cent) thought that unit fines were good in principle but had been badly implemented in practice. Second, asked about the kind of problems encountered as a consequence of the introduction of unit fines, the most commonly cited problems were not to do with unit fines as such, but were concerned with the possibility of adverse press comment (95 per cent of magistrates mentioned this) and public disapproval (88 per cent). This suggests that it was the way in which unit fines were introduced and the publicity that accompanied them that was the main source of concern, but that most magistrates could have accepted the reform if it had been better implemented.

It was clear from observations carried out in the four magistrates' courts involved in the research study shortly after implementation of the Act that there was some initial confusion over the use of unit fines.[25] Lay magistrates in particular seemed to lack confidence when fining, and there was a tendency to give a monetary sum and then work out how it converted into units. At one court magistrates tended only to specify the number of units being imposed without placing a value on the unit. Some defendants thought they were only being fined £15, when in fact they were being fined 15 units at £4 per unit. At another court several defendants were dealt with for personal possession of drugs, in similar circumstances, following a raid on a 'rave' club in the town. The first three defendants were unemployed and were fined £50 with £35 costs, with no mention of units or unit values. When a fourth defendant said he was employed the magistrate reverted to the unit system and awarded 10 units at a rate of £32. At a third court total fines were read out and the clerk had the job of breaking the total down into a number of units and the value of each unit. Only one of the four courts adopted a clear and consistent approach from the outset, with magistrates announcing a number of units and the rate per unit on each disposal.

However, the indications are that after a while such initial uncertainties were resolved and when interviews were carried out nine months to a year after implementation of the Act the consensus was that, in terms of administration, unit fines had worked well. Some clerks said that in many respects they were preferable to the previous system. The main problems had arisen as a result of the failure of some defendants to provide means information, as a result of which two different approaches had emerged. At two of the courts, when there was no means information, a guideline rate of a certain amount of weekly disposable income per unit was set. It was feared that one consequence of this was that the guideline rate might be too low for some people, and in one of the courts magistrates were given discretion to vary the rate on the basis of where defendants lived, whether they had a car or job, etc. To avoid this problem the other two courts adopted the response of always imposing a maximum fine where no means information was available. This was done on the basis that it was up to the defendant to provide such information and if they had not done so they must be prepared for the consequences. The assumption was that defendants who could not afford the maximum rate would then come back to the court and request a reduction. As a result many reviews were expected and took place at these two courts, the size of the fine being adjusted accordingly once the defendant provided the necessary information.

This is how the infamous crisp packet incident arose. An unemployed 20 year-old, Vaughan Watkins, was fined £1,200 at Cwmbran in April 1993 for dropping a crisp packet. He had been asked by an off-duty police officer to pick the packet up, but refused and swore at the officer, even though there was a litter bin a short distance away. Mr Watkins failed to attend court or supply details of his circumstances to the court, and therefore, in line with the procedure adopted by many other courts at this time, the maximum penalty was imposed, a penalty that was reduced on appeal to £48. The public in general at the time were not aware of this procedure and some sections of the press either did not realise it, or did not want to spoil a good story by explaining it.

Apart from this, the main reaction of magistrates interviewed in the summer after implementation was that while many of them accepted the principle of unit fines they found the method for imposing them to be too rigid and inflexible and would have liked more opportunity to vary the rates. Of the nine circuit judges interviewed about the Act, all but one approved of the principle of unit fines, but said that the way they had been implemented was disastrous. Several of the judges made the point that they could not understand why, since the pilot schemes worked, the system had been completely altered when unit fines were introduced nationally. Unit fines were never introduced in the Crown Court, so judges only had to deal with them when cases were brought on appeal. In only one instance was something similar to a unit fine approach used for such cases. Most judges simply used a monetary amount as previously, although a couple of judges mentioned that they were quite likely to substitute a conditional discharge instead of a fine.

The point made by the judges about the difference between the pilot study and the Act was one made again by a visiting member of the New Zealand Ministry of Justice, who came to this country to investigate the implementation of unit fines, and urged that 'Any scheme subsequently adopted should take heed of the experiences from the pilots.'[26]

Implementing unit fines: The impact on sentencing

The impact of unit fines on sentencing was significant and effective. Use of the fine for indictable offences in magistrates' courts stood at 42 per cent during the first three quarters of 1992, but increased to 45 per cent in the fourth quarter of 1992, following implementation of the Criminal Justice Act 1991. However, it subsequently fell again to 38 per cent by the last quarter of 1993 following the abolition of unit fines (which took effect on 20 September 1993). In the Crown Court, where unit fines were not introduced the use of the fine continued to be around 6 per cent throughout 1992, where it had also been in 1991. It declined to 4.6 per cent by the end of 1993.[27] Since then, the fine has resumed its long-term decline. In 1996 it was used for 36 per cent of offenders in the magistrates' court (compared with 63 per cent in 1975); in the Crown Court for only 5 per cent (17 per cent in 1975).[28] The overall figure for all indictable offenders in all courts was an all-time low of 28 per cent, compared with 51 per cent in 1975.

Figure 6.2: Use of the Fine, Magistrates' Courts

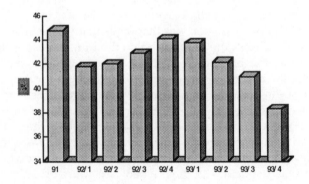

Figure 6.3: Use of the Fine, Crown Courts

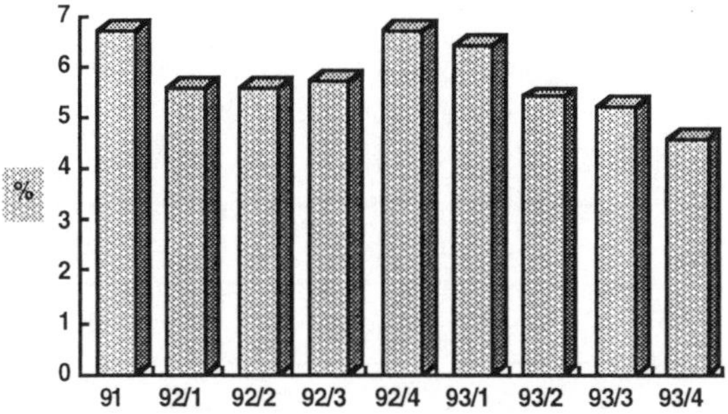

The rise in the proportionate use of the fine during late 1992 and early 1993 was most apparent among the unemployed, rising from 30 per cent in summer 1992 to 43 per cent in early 1993 (for theft and handling from 31 per cent to 48 per cent). The decline in the use of the fine in later 1993 affected all employment status groups, but was most marked amongst the unemployed. In this group the use of the fine fell back from the high of 43 per cent to 32 per cent by late 1993.

Between summer 1992 and early 1993, for males aged 21 and over sentenced at magistrates' courts, there was an increase in the average amount of fines from £144 to £233 for those in employment, and a decrease from £88 to £66 for the unemployed. Subsequently the average fine imposed on the employed decreased to £158 and increased for the unemployed to £78.

Table 1:   Average fines in Magistrates' Courts 1992-1993

Status	Jul-Aug 1992	Jan-Feb 1993	Nov-Dec 1993
Employed	£144	£233	£158
Unemployed	£88	£66	£78

Thus in the context outlined earlier, unit fines could be said to have very largely fulfilled intentions and expectations in the short term. Their impact is further emphasised by the subsequent decline in use of the fine following the abolition of unit fines, and the fact that this decline was most marked amongst the unemployed.

Further evidence that the rise in the use of the fine following implementation of the 1991 Act can be linked to increased use for those on low incomes is seen when one looks at the number and amount of units imposed. *Table 1* compares employed and unemployed offenders who were fined at the four magistrates' courts in the study we conducted in the North of England during the first quarters of 1991 and 1993.

Table 2: Use of the Fine for Employed and Unemployed Offenders, Males aged 18, in four courts in the north of England, first quarters of 1991 and 1993.

	Employed		Unemployed	
	'91	'93	'91	'93
% fined	52	55	31	46
Mean Fine	£121	£180	£93	£78
Mean No. Units	—	15.7	—	16.2
Mean Amount p. Unit	—	£14.6	—	£4.2
Total n	196	134	606	671

Table 2 shows not only that use of the fine increased more for the unemployed during the January to March 1993 period, but that the average amount of fine went down for the unemployed and up for the employed because, while both groups received a comparable number of units, the unemployed were fined a much smaller amount per unit.

Despite this demonstrable practical success of unit fines, it was the reactions of certain members of the magistracy and the media that gained the upper hand at a time when the government of the day was experiencing political setbacks from several quarters. We have argued elsewhere that the repeal of sections of the Criminal Justice Act 1991, including unit fines was largely a political act rather than one dictated by the needs of criminal justice.[29] Kenneth Clarke's announcement on 13 May 1993 that unit fines were to be abolished is a good illustration of the principle that,

the essential attractiveness of the punitive response is that it can be represented as an authoritative intervention to deal with a serious, anxiety ridden problem. Such action gives the appearance that "something is being done" here, now, swiftly and decisively.[30]

DEVELOPMENTS SINCE THE CRIMINAL JUSTICE ACT 1993

Unit fines were abolished by section 65 of the Criminal Justice Act 1993. They were replaced by a relatively vague statutory provision requiring courts which impose fines to inquire into the offender's means and to fix the amount according to those means and the seriousness of the offence.[31] As we have seen, the use of fines fell following the demise of unit fines. When they were abolished the Magistrates' Association issued a new set of guidelines for courts, although as with previous guidelines the Association emphasised that these were only a basis for magistrates to use when determining what they felt was appropriate. Out of four courts we studied in the North of England, one proposed continuing its own modified 'unit fine' approach, but the others adopted the Magistrates' Association's guidelines.[32] Research undertaken since the 1993 Act found that 55 per cent of courts followed the Magistrates' Association guidelines, with a further 28 per cent using local variations of the guidelines and only 17 per cent adopting an informal 'unit fine' approach.[33]

This study also found that the courts still using the 'unit fine' approach were more consistent in their sentencing decisions, graduating fines more in accordance with defendants' incomes, whereas non-'unit fine' courts made little distinction between low-income and medium-income defendants. Although 'non-unit fine' courts were less likely to take account of means when deciding the size of fines, they did do so when fixing the *rate* at which fines were to be paid. This meant that the period over which payment was spread could be very different between the different courts. In interviews undertaken for this research it was once again found that in courts which used the 'unit fine' approach, 'they did not see the failure of the statutory unit fines as being due to the principle but rather to the method in which it was implemented'.[34] However, it was also noted that whereas statutory unit fines were associated with a proportionate increase in use of the fine, those petty sessional divisions (PSDs) using a unit fine approach after their statutory abolition did not make proportionately greater use of fines than did courts adopting a different approach. Such PSDs did, however, tend to experience lower arrears than non-'unit fine' PSDs.

However, the main feature of developments following repeal of unit fines was a reversion to the kind of concerns that preceded their introduction: once again default, enforcement and imprisonment became the focus of discussion. In 1994 the National Association of Probation Officers published details of 35 case studies of defaulters convicted of low level offences, suggesting that the main problems in most cases were related to poverty and debt. Fines were 'so high that custody was inevitable', and prison was sometimes avoided only by incurring debts elsewhere by leaving bills unpaid.[35] A paper from the Penal Affairs Consortium (a grouping of organizations with an interest in penal matters) in 1995 brought together many of the concerns current at the time, and put forward eleven proposals for reform, including the reintroduction of a means-related fines system, 'based on the best aspects of the 'unit fine' scheme'. This paper again highlighted the problems of poverty and debt as significant features of the non-payment of fines[36] and the theme was taken up by a *Guardian* feature article, 'The Poor Laws' in February 1996. Such concerns were supported by a Home Office survey of imprisoned fine defaulters which found that three quarters of imprisoned defaulters were unemployed and in receipt of benefit.[37]

Concern has focused especially on default and imprisonment for television licence evasion, and the fact that a high proportion of those convicted for this offence are women in difficult circumstances.[38] In 1993, 63 per cent of those prosecuted for using a television set without a licence were women. This was 38 per cent of the women prosecuted for all offences during that year. In 1994, 77 per cent of all the women fined had been charged for failure to buy a television licence. In 1996 of 330 receptions into prison for non-payment of fines imposed for using a television without a licence, 90 (just over a quarter) were females.[39] Another common link between fine default and women offenders is the fact that a high proportion of those convicted of prostitution offences are fined and fail to pay their fines. The Home Office survey of imprisoned defaulters found that almost a third of the women defaulters were in prison for fines imposed for prostitution offences.[40] Other research studies have found that sentencers show a reluctance to fine women for certain offences.[41] This can result in a more lenient sentence, a discharge, but for some it results in a more severe community penalty.

Before imprisoning fine defaulters, magistrates' courts are under a legal obligation to hold an inquiry into the means of the defaulter and only to commit to prison if they find that the default is due to 'wilful refusal or culpable neglect' on the part of the defaulter. The court also has a clear statutory duty not to use imprisonment without having considered all other methods of enforcement (of which quite a bewildering variety exists).[42] A particularly common complaint has been that courts have not in practice given adequate consideration to all the options before imprisoning defaulters. One reason for this is the pressure on courts to clear unpaid fines as a measure of their efficiency, and one of the easiest ways to do this is by committal to prison. It has also been suggested that fine defaulters are particularly unlikely to attract the sympathy of the courts. In a study of a magistrates' court undertaken by someone with 15 years experience of being a magistrate, Gordon Read concluded that on the whole magistrates' courts are a fair and considerate service. But he singled out as an exception the treatment accorded to fine defaulters:

> But the Fines Enforcement court was singled out as the one area where humiliation and embarrassment do intentionally form part of the courtroom procedure . . . In these courts humiliation is used in order to communicate to the defendants that not only are they 'working the system' but the court knows they are . . . The defendants who appear to be at the forefront of the displeasure which is demonstrated in the magistrates' courts are the fines defaulters . . . The questioning in these courts is quite often aggressive.[43]

Read explained that the reason for this was that the defaulter was seen to be someone who had flouted the court's decisions.

It might be thought that there should hardly ever be any need to imprison fine defaulters since the introduction (by the Criminal Justice Act 1991, section 24) of the power to order that unpaid fines be deducted from income support, adding to existing powers to recover fines by ordering attachment of earnings and seizure of goods. In fact, court-ordered deductions from benefit are rare. Home Office research found that just over half of a sample of imprisoned defaulters were on income support, but the option was explored in only 13 per cent of cases and used in only three per cent.[44] Perhaps, however, we should not overexaggerate the blameworthiness of the courts in this regard. The same research found that the average amount of outstanding fines at the point of imprisonment was £1,305 (and 46 per cent of defaulters had other outstanding debts as well); given the strict statutory limits restricting the amount that can be deducted from benefits per week magistrates presumably feel that this is a far from satisfactory solution in such cases. Recent research in Scotland has found that one common reason given by sentencers for not deducting unpaid fines from benefit is the fear that this would cause hardship to defaulters and their families.[45] Some courts may even feel they are doing defaulters a favour when they wipe out their outstanding fines by sending them to prison for a short time as a preferable alternative to dragging more and more money out of someone in poverty and deep debt.

In the wake of continuing concern about the imprisonment of fine defaulters there was speculation at the beginning of 1996 that the then Home Secretary Michael Howard was considering options to end imprisonment for fine default. Indeed, for someone so strongly committed to the use of imprisonment Mr Howard uncharacteristically expressed the (Strategy B) view that fine defaulters 'impose an additional and unwelcome burden on hard-pressed local prisons' (*The Guardian* and *Daily Telegraph*, 14 February 1996). It subsequently became apparent that less radical measures were envisaged. The White Paper, 'Protecting the Public' said that,

> improvements can be made in two ways. First existing powers and procedures must be made as effective as possible, and used to the full. Second, new ideas should be considered, to widen the range of options open to courts so that even in difficult cases, they are able to enforce payment without resorting to imprisonment unless absolutely necessary.[46]

It was announced that the Lord Chancellor's Department would set up a Working Group on the Enforcement of Financial Penalties to examine what improvements could be made, and that if legislative change was necessary it would be brought forward as a priority. The Lord Chancellor's Working Group published guidance to magistrates' courts on 10 July 1996. This included timetables for reviews of payments, monitoring of enforcement methods, greater use of money payment supervision orders, and fines clinics. Later the same month a consultative paper[47] put forward proposals that fine defaulters and low level offenders could be sentenced to community service and curfew orders monitored by electronic tagging. The Crime (Sentences) Act 1997 implemented these proposals and also brought in other provisions to avoid or deal with fine default along these lines. Thus, the Act allowed courts to impose a community service order as a penalty for fine default (section 35), allowed courts to impose an attendance centre order as penalty for fine default on offenders up to the age of 25 instead of 21 as previously (section 36), enabled magistrates to impose a period of disqualification from driving instead of imprisonment for fine default and other financial penalties imposed by the courts (s. 40), and provided for the imposition of a community service order in cases where the offender has outstanding fines that result in the offender having insufficient means to pay a further fine (section 37).[48] These provisions were brought into force between October 1997 and January 1998. The Act also provided for an extension in the use of electronic monitoring to deal with fine defaulters and petty persistent offenders and juveniles.[49]

Perhaps the most significant development since the abolition of unit fines has come, not as a result of legislation or government policy, but as a result of a Court of Appeal judgment in November 1995. For many years the number of receptions for fine default was around the 20,000 mark, with the number in prison at any one time being several hundred—usually two per cent or so of the prison population.[50]

However, the number of receptions dropped from 20,200 in 1995 to 8,555 in 1996 and the number held in default of payment of a fine dropped from 520 on 30 June 1995 to 140 at the same time in 1996, just 0.3 per cent of the total sentenced prison population.[51] The main reason for this fall is most likely to have been the judgment in *R v Oldham Justices ex parte Cawley*[52] in November 1995, which re-emphasised the legal requirement which many in the courts seemed to have forgotten or overlooked: that magistrates must consider all other methods of enforcement before committing a fine defaulter to prison. This also had the effect of increasing the number of people starting a money payment supervision order (supervised by a probation officer) from 3,318 in 1995 to 6,400 in 1996, an increase of 94 per cent—although the figure was to drop again to 4,800 in 1997.[53] Thus, there has been progress in reducing the imprisonment of fine defaulters, but use of the fine has not recovered, and its use for just 28 per cent of indictable offences in 1996 was the lowest ever. In addition, the amount of total fines in arrears has risen from £112 million in 1993 to £138 million in 1996 (*Sunday Telegraph*, 24 August 1997:7).

Following a change of government in May 1997 the new Home Secretary was reported as intending to halt the jailing of fine defaulters (*The Guardian*, 16 May 1997) and expressed a wish to see a greater use of fines:

> I am very concerned indeed that in a period when living standards have risen in the last ten years and unemployment has fallen, the use of the fine has dramatically fallen. There are half as many fines issued today as there were ten years ago for no very good reason.[54]

It might be pointed out that those most likely to incur a fine are those least likely to have experienced rising living standards over the period in question and most likely to have experienced unemployment. As we have seen, the problem is precisely that of how to deal with a relationship between default and enforcement on the one hand and poverty, debt and unemployment on the other. Unit fines held out the prospect of making a start on resolving this dilemma, but never had the chance.

WHERE NOW?

There has undoubtedly been some progress in the management of financial penalties in recent years. However, much of the discussion since the repeal of unit fines in 1993 has been a re-run of that which preceded their introduction: concern about minor and less well off offenders clogging up the courts and the local prisons, followed by proposals and measures to improve enforcement and use other options. The decline in the use of the fine is an unsolved problem, and with the measures introduced in the Crime (Sentences) Act 1997 it appeared to be accepted as inevitable. There is, however, some governmental interest in reviving the fine, which should increase if notice is taken of cost-conscious Home Office recommendations that 'the resources of the Probation Service should not be dissipated on those for whom a fine would serve as well'.[55] Part of the solution might be sentencing guidelines (see *Chapter 3*) which encourage greater use of fines rather than more intensive community penalties in a greater range of cases; but the difficulties of relating fines to offenders' means and the associated issue of default would still remain.

Unit fines may not have been a magic recipe for the problems of the fining system, but they worked in the sense that they achieved what they were intended to achieve while they existed. They did not exist for long because their implementation was botched and they did not have enough support to overcome the inevitable teething problems.[56] Any attempt to revive unit fines as a national system is unlikely in the foreseeable future. Of course it may be hoped that courts will make use of the looser formulation of the principle of relating means to the amounts of fines resulting from the 1993 Act and revised Magistrates' Association guidelines. The national government could even try to foster the gradual reintroduction of the unit fine by the back door, by positively encouraging courts who wish to do so to use a unit system on a non-statutory basis (as some already do). But past experience is not too encouraging, and disparities in local fining and enforcement practices are likely to mean considerable variations in the experience of justice.

There could, however, be some further scope for strengthening national guidelines to courts with the aim of bringing about better tuning of the size of fines to offenders' means, which could in turn encourage greater use of fines rather than higher-tariff (and more expensive) community penalties for less well-off offenders. This might be especially effective if courts could be given financial incentives to follow such guidelines rather than simply to dispose of cases (which is quite easily done by committing to custody for default). One particular device which has existed for many years is the power of enforcement courts to remit fines in whole or part if the offender's financial circumstances change for the worse following the fine's imposition.[57] Studies show that this power is only used very rarely even though adverse changes of circumstance are a common factor in default;[58] there must surely be scope for encouraging courts to use this provision in the way Parliament presumably intended.

Despite the problems of default and enforcement the fine has generally been regarded as one of the more successful ways of dealing with offenders. This is in large measure because it appeals to different penal viewpoints. It has practical advantages in being relatively simple to administer, most offenders do pay their fines eventually, and it is better than cheap—it brings in revenue. Thus, for those with a Strategy B approach to criminal justice it is almost the ideal sentence. It is also clearly punitive. As the guidelines for the Criminal Justice Act 1991 put it, fines deprive the offender of the freedom to enjoy certain financial benefits. It therefore finds favour with the Strategy A school of thinking, even if it is not their main concern. Those of a more liberal, Strategy C persuasion see the fine as an accpetable 'low tariff' sentence, preferable to more directly intrusive custodial and non-custodial methods.

However, there is a relatively neglected aspect of the fine, and that is its restorative potential. We saw in *Chapter 4* that other non-custodial penalties such as community service can be conceptualised in significantly different ways, either as punishments intended to impose suffering on offenders and deprive them of freedom, or as reparation to the community. The same is true of the fine. As well as being a punishment in the negative sense, financial penalties are quite literally a way of paying for what one has done. At the moment financial penalties take three forms: fines, compensation and costs. Compensation constitutes the most direct form of reparation—to the victim—while the fine might be thought of as paying one's debt to society, which is also done by making a contribution to the costs of a case. At present, the way in which compensation works is far from ideal. Compensation orders are not always considered (despite a statutory duty on courts to do so), and when imposed may not represent the full amount that the victim has lost as a result of the crime, especially where the offender has committed a number of offences with multiple victims. Furthermore, the victim often has to wait for compensation to be paid in small sums according to the means of the offender, not infrequently having to go back to the court when instalments are not paid. Organizations acting on behalf of victims have in the past argued for a central fund out of which victims can be paid at the time, leaving the courts to recoup the amount from the offender.

There is a lot to be said for emphasising the reparative element of the fine as well as compensation and perhaps working towards closer links between the two. In recent years legislation has been passed to deprive those convicted of serious drug offences of the gains they have made as a result of their activities, and it had been expected that the monies received would be distributed to programmes working to combat drug misuse. There have been complaints that in practice the money simply goes to the Treasury,[59] but more recently the government has moved to rectify this.[60] The principle is a good one, and might usefully be extended to other financial penalties. The income from fines and confiscations could be used to create a 'Reparation Fund' from which victims are compensated immediately, thus making a much more explicit link between crime which infringes the rights and well-being of others and reparation for such wrongs. Such a fund could be used to ensure that victims immediately received the full amount of compensation they have been awarded by the court. The fund could then be reimbursed by the offender at whatever rate the court feels is appropriate after taking account of the offender's financial circumstances.

Throughout this book we have emphasised a rights-based (Strategy C) approach to criminal justice, taking account of both victim and offender. Although unit fines should not be seen as the only answer to the problems of fines and fine default, they offered the prospect of being one of the most just and equitable ways of imposing penalties. In an ideal world, justice should not depend on changing economic conditions and circumstances. If unit fines are no longer a viable option for the time being, then at least relating the offender's means and abilities to the losses and needs of victims offers a more soundly based moral justification for the penalty that is imposed.

ENDNOTES: *Chapter 6*

[1] Section 65, which came into force on 20 September 1993.

[2] See Andrew Ashworth, *Sentencing and Criminal Justice* (2nd ed., London, Butterworths, 1995), 262.

[3] A similar, non-statutory rule applied in the Crown Court.

[4] John Wheeler, *Who Prevents Crime?* (London, Conservative Political Centre, 1980), 10.

[5] Silvia Casale and Sally Hillman, *The Enforcement of Fines as Criminal Sanctions* (Vera Institute of Justice, 1986) .

[6] Advisory Council on the Penal System, *Non-Custodial and Semi-Custodial Penalties* (London, HMSO, 1970).

[7] NACRO, *Fine Default: Report of a NACRO Working Party* (London, NACRO, 1981), para. 6.7.

[8] ibid., paras. 3.10 - 3.18 and recommendations 8-11.

[9] House of Commons, *Fifteenth Report from the Expenditure Committee: The Reduction of Pressure on the Prison System* (London, HMSO, 1978).

[10] Paul Softley, *Fines in Magistrates' Courts*, Home Office Research Study No. 46 (London, HMSO, 1978).

[11] John Corden, Jo Kuipers, and K Wilson, *After Prison: a Study of the Post-release Experience of Discharged Prisoners*, Papers in Community Studies No. 21 (York, University of York, 1978).

12 Geoff Wilkins, *Making Them Pay: a Study of Some Fine Defaulters, Civil Prisoners and Other Petty Offenders in a Local Prison* (London, NACRO, 1979).

13 David Moxon, 'Fine Default: Unemployment and the Use of Imprisonment', *Research Bulletin*, No. 16: 38-41 (Home Office Research and Planning Unit, 1983).

14 Anne Millar, *The Experimental Introduction of Fines Enforcement Officers into Two Sheriff Courts* (Central Research Unit, Scottish Office, 1984).

15 Casale and Hillman, op. cit.

16 Iain Crow and Frances Simon, *Unemployment and Magistrates' Courts* (London, NACRO, 1987).

17 Nick Davies, 'The Poor Laws', *Guardian 2*, 8 February 1996, 2-3.

18 *Criminal Statistics, England and Wales, 1984*, Cmnd 9621 (London, HMSO, 1985), para. 7.17.

19 *A General Guide to the Criminal Justice Act 1991*, (London, Home Office, 1991), paras. 2.2 to 2.5.

20 Crow and Simon, op. cit.

21 David Moxon, Mike Sutton and Carol Hedderman, *Unit Fines: Experiments in Four Courts*, Research and Planning Unit Paper 59 (London, Home Office, 1990).

22 Bryan Gibson, *Unit Fines* (Winchester, Waterside Press, 1990), 22.

23 Iain Crow, Michael Cavadino, James Dignan, Valerie Johnston and Monica Walker, *Changing Criminal Justice: The Impact of the Criminal Justice Act 1991 in Four Areas of the North of England* (University of Sheffield, Centre for Criminological and Legal Research, 1996).

24 Iain Crow, Valerie Johnston, James Dignan, Michael Cavadino and Monica Walker, 'Magistrates' Views of the Criminal Justice Act 1991', *Justice of the Peace*, 158 (1994), 37-40.

25 Crow et. al., op. cit. note 23, p. 19.

26 Angela Cook, *Unit Fines: A Study of Their Operation* (New Zealand, Department of Justice, 1993).

27 *Monitoring of the Criminal Justice Act 1991 – Data from a Special Data Collection Exercise*, Home Office Statistical Bulletin 25/93 (London, Government Statistical Service, 1993). Statistics in this section are taken from this bulletin and also from: *Cautions, Court Proceedings and Sentencing, England and Wales, 1993* and *Monitoring of the Criminal Justice Acts 1991 and 1993 – Results from a Special Data Collection Exercise*, Home Office Statistical Bulletins 19/94 and 20/94 (both London, Government Statistical Service, 1994).

28 Claire Flood-Page and Alan Mackie, *Sentencing Practice: An Examination of Decisions in Magistrates' Courts and the Crown Court in the Mid-1990s*, Home Office Research Study No. 180 (London, Home Office, 1998), 16.

29 Iain Crow, 'Le Choix des Peines et les Recent Changements Legislatifs en Grande-Bretagne', *Déviance et Société*, 20 (1996): 3-16; Michael Cavadino and James Dignan, *The Penal System: An Introduction* (2nd ed), (London, Sage Publications, 1997), 296.

30 David Garland, 'The Limits of the Sovereign State', *British Journal of Criminology*, 36 (1996): 445-71 at pp. 460-1.

[31] Section 18, Criminal Justice Act 1991, as substituted by section 65 of the Criminal Justice Act 1993.

[32] Crow *et al*, op. cit. note 23, pp. 28-9.

[33] Elizabeth Charman, Bryan Gibson, Terry Honess and Rod Morgan, *Fine Impositions and Enforcement Following the Criminal Justice Act 1993*, Research Findings No. 36 (London, Home Office Research and Statistics Directorate, 1996).

[34] ibid., p. 2.

[35] *Fines, Defaulters and Debtors' Gaol* (National Association of Probation Officers, 1994).

[36] *The Imprisonment of Fine Defaulters* (London, Penal Affairs Consortium, 1995), 5.

[37] David Moxon and Claire Whittaker, *Imprisonment for Fine Default*, Research Findings No. 35 (London, Home Office Research and Statistics Directorate, 1996).

[38] Clive Walker and David Wall, 'Imprisoning the Poor: Television Licence Evaders and the Criminal Justice System' [1997], *Criminal Law Review*, 173-186; Christina Pantazis and David Gordon, 'Television Licence Evasion and the Criminalisation of Female Poverty', *Howard Journal*, 36 (1997), 170-186.

[39] Philip White and Jo Woodbridge, *The Prison Population in 1996*, Home Office Statistical Bulletin 18/97 (London, Home Office Research and Statistics Directorate, 1997), para. 16.

[40] Moxon and Whittaker, op. cit.

[41] Carol Hedderman and Lizanne Dowds, *The Sentencing of Women: A Section 95 Publication*, Research Findings No. 58 (London, Home Office Research and Statistics Directorate, 1997); Flood-Page and Mackie, op. cit., p. 121.

[42] Magistrates' Courts Act 1980, section 82(3) and (4).

[43] Gordon Read, *A Qualitative Study of Social Interaction in a Magistrates' Court* (Unpublished M Phil thesis, Sheffield Hallam University, 1997), 55, 90.

[44] Moxon and Whittaker, op. cit.

[45] Ian Clark, 'The Use of Direct Deductions from Benefits in Scottish Courts', *Howard Journal of Criminal Justice*, 37 (1998), 291-305.

[46] Home Office, *Protecting the Public: The Government's Strategy on Crime in England and Wales*, Cm 3190 (London, HMSO, 1996), para. 5.33.

[47] *Alternative Penalties for Fine Defaulters and Low Level Offenders* (London, Home Office, 1996).

[48] But for these new provisions a community service order (or curfew order) would have been ruled out by the provisions in the Criminal Justice Act 1991 (section 6) categorising community service as a 'community sentence' which cannot be passed unless the offence is 'serious enough to warrant' a sentence in this middle tier of that Act's sentencing framework (see *Chapter 1*). The provisions also address the problem noted by Moxon and Whittaker (op. cit., p.2) that: 'although the court is required to take means into account when sentencing and may link individual fines to the offenders' ability to pay, they often do not know whether the offender has other outstanding fines at the time of sentence. In this way offenders can accumulate large amounts of fines which become difficult both to pay and to enforce.'

[49] See Ed Mortimer and Chris May, *Electronic Monitoring in Practice: the Second Year of the Trials of Curfew Orders*, Home Office Research Study No. 177 (London, Home Office, 1997). These provisions are to be piloted experimentally during 1998, and the results are unknown at the time of writing.

[50] There is a significant difference between the number of receptions for fine default and the number of defaulters in prison at any one time because fine defaulters spend a relatively short period of time in prison (one week on average).

[51] White and Woodbridge, op. cit., paras. 11 and 16.

[52] [1997] QB 1.

[53] Peter Sheriff, *Summary Probation Statistics England and Wales 1997*, Home Office Statistical Bulletin 12/98 (London, Home Office, 1998), para. 10 and Table 2.

[54] H.C. Deb, 25 November 1997.

[55] David Moxon, 'The Role of Sentencing Policy', in Peter Goldblatt and Chris Lewis (eds.), *Reducing Offending: An Assessment of Research Evidence on Ways of Dealing with Offending Behaviour*, Home Office Research Study No. 187 (London, Home Office, 1998), 85-100, at p. 98; Flood-Page and Mackie, op. cit., p. xii.

[56] Crow, op. cit; also Iain Crow, *Sentencers' Decisions and Recent Legislative Change in the UK*. Presented to 'Judging and Decision Making', 2nd Annual Conference of the Institute for the Study of the Legal Profession, University of Sheffield, September 1994.

[57] Magistrates' Courts Act 1980, section 85.

[58] For example, Moxon and Whittaker (op. cit.) found this power had only been used for six per cent of imprisoned defaulters.

[59] Her Majesty's Inspector of Constabulary, *An Examination of Police Force Drugs Strategies* (London, Home Office, 1996).

[60] *Tackling Drugs to Build a Better Britain: The Government's Ten-Year Strategy for Tackling Drug Misuse*, Cm 3945 (London, HMSO, 1998).

CHAPTER 7

Young Offenders: Tough on Youth?

Along with all their other irritating habits, young people have a tendency to take centre stage in both public and private discussions about criminal justice policy. The Conservatives took power in 1979 with 'short, sharp shock' detention centres as their highest-profile policy on law and order. Their 18 years in power ended as Labour highlighted its election promise to set up a 'fast track' for persistent young offenders and halve the time it took them to reach court, confident that this pledge could compete electorally with the Conservatives' record in introducing 'boot camps' and planning to bring in secure training orders.

In this chapter we look at the problem of youthful offending, the different strategies which have been and could be tried to deal with it, and assess the prospects for a rational and humane youth justice policy.

THE PROBLEM OF YOUNG OFFENDERS

Young people rarely commit the very worst violent crimes, although it goes without saying that it is a matter of serious concern when they do. But the main contribution of young people to the crime problem is one of quantity. Forty-two per cent of those convicted of or cautioned for indictable offences in England and Wales in 1996 were under 21,[1] and the peak age for committing a detected offence is currently 18 for males and 15 for females. Although most of their crimes may be relatively petty, the sheer number of thefts, burglaries and car crimes which they commit has a harassing and depressing effect on the everyday lives of ordinary people.

Allied with the fact that grownups are constantly prepared to bemoan the state of the younger generation as a potent symbol of the way the country is clearly going to the dogs, this may well explain why the crimes and treatment of young offenders tend to have such a high profile among law and order issues. But there is an arguable case that the best thing we could do would be to take a more relaxed (or less alarmist) attitude towards youthful offending and generally respond to it as little as possible, since our responses and interventions are unlikely to help matters much and may make them worse.

'Leave those kids alone'?

This anti-interventionist argument proceeds from the facts that (as already noted) young people rarely commit the serious crimes, and that official figures suggest, if anything, a declining amount of youthful offending in recent years. The number of offenders under 21 found guilty or cautioned for indictable offences in 1996 was 34 per cent fewer than in 1985 and 14.5 per cent down on 1992, only part of this decline being attributable to a reduced number of young people in the population generally. Such official figures are regarded with scepticism by some. Academics such as David Farrington[2] and politicians such as the Labour ministers Jack Straw and Alun Michael[3] have claimed that these trends in the official statistics, which contradict 'common sense' impressions that crime by young people *must* be on the increase, are illusory. They argue that the apparent decrease in youthful offending has been brought about by developments such as mounting use of 'informal warnings' given to young offenders by the police, with the result that increasing numbers of young criminals fail to appear in the official statistics. Since informal warnings are usually not recorded at all,[4] it is difficult to decide this point empirically one way or the other; nevertheless, a careful but somewhat overlooked piece of recent Home Office research tentatively concluded that the fall in the number of recorded male offenders under 18 between 1985 and 1995 was *not* fully accounted for by increased police use of informal warnings. This research calculated that the number of young male offenders known to the police in 1995 *including* those informally cautioned was significantly less than the number found guilty or cautioned in 1985; and that at least for the 10 to 13 age range this represented a genuinely declining *rate* of offending per 100,000 young people in the population.[5]

The anti-interventionist argument continues by drawing on criminological 'labelling theory' to contend that heavier intervention against young offenders is likely to make matters worse. Offending is a phase which very many young people go through, and if we resist the urge to intervene and leave them alone they will '*grow out of crime*'.[6] On the other hand, the argument goes, if a young offender is officially 'labelled' as a criminal by being formally punished, he or she is likely to be excluded from the company of law-abiding peers, to be impelled to associate more and more with other offenders in a 'deviant subculture', and ultimately to adopt a progressively more ingrained 'deviant self-image'. The result is a 'deviancy amplification spiral' which leads to an increased level of offending and perhaps even a long criminal career.

There are different versions of this 'minimum intervention' approach, all of them belonging under the general heading of our Strategy C. Perhaps the most extreme is 'radical non-intervention' which simply (some would say simplistically) advocates that we 'leave kids alone wherever possible'.[7] A more sophisticated and politically streetwise position is the 'systems management' approach which gained great popularity among youth justice workers in the 1980s and succeeded in influencing policy makers and juvenile justice practices in many local areas and at the national level.[8] This approach seeks to minimise rather than abolish official responses to youth crime (although its proponents would like to see the end of penal custody for juveniles). This minimisation is to be brought about by essentially managerial (Strategy B) techniques, notably systems analysis and monitoring; inter-agency cooperation; diversion of offenders from prosecution by means of cautioning and from custody by the provision of alternative court disposals; 'targeting' of more intrusive community-based interventions on young offenders who are genuinely at risk of custodial sentences; and generally seeking to keep young offenders as far 'down the tariff' of official punishments as possible.

Different again—to the extent that it may be stretching a point slightly to lump it in with the others as 'anti-interventionist'—is the attractive 'developmental approach' put forward by Andrew Rutherford.[9] While still wishing to minimise formal interventions against young offenders (and especially incarceration or other drastic interventions involving removal from home or the community), 'the developmental approach does not mean ignoring or taking no action on youth crime'. Rather, Rutherford advocates interventions which *help* young people to grow out of crime by strengthening the ability of the family and the school to 'hold on' to them effectively rather than removing them as a punishment.

All of these 'minimum intervention' positions, of course, run completely counter to the 'common sense' view of crime and punishment, which assumes that punishment is an effective 'individual deterrent' to those who receive it. According to this way of thinking, it is important precisely *not* to leave young offenders alone, for if they offend with impunity there will be no deterrent to prevent them offending again. Rather, once a young person offends they should be punished with swiftness and certainty in an attempt to 'nip things in the bud'. This is the policy of '*zero tolerance*' which has been so fashionable recently and in which Tony Blair and Jack Straw have repeatedly declared their faith. 'Go around our adult jails, as I do', Mr Straw told the 1997 Labour Conference in characteristic manner, 'and you will see them full of people who first started getting into trouble like this when they were young. We do those children no favour by excusing their behaviour or by indulging in the fantasy that they "will all grow out of it".' Clearly for Mr Straw the policy of minimum intervention is reminiscent of *Porridge*'s Mr Barrowclough.

What do we know about the general merits of the arguments over non-intervention and minimum intervention? Jack Straw's interpretation of the evidence is simple and straightforward: 'For too long we have assumed that young offenders will grow out of their offending if left to themselves. The research evidence shows that this does not happen.'[10] We beg to differ. On the contrary, it seems clear from research that most young offenders *do* 'grow out of crime'—although Mr Straw is quite right to point out that not all do, and that most adult offenders started their criminal careers young. But with the peak age of known male offending at 18 it is clear that many criminal careers must be relatively shortlived. According to Home Office estimates, 26 per cent of all males born in England and Wales in 1968 had received a criminal conviction before the age of 25, but 60 per cent of known male offenders have an official 'criminal career' lasting less than one year. (One fifth have a series of convictions extending over more than ten years—which does not necessarily mean that they are offending constantly over that period— but only one in 20 acquire a reconviction 20 years or more after their first offence.)[11] So if you go around the prisons you will certainly find that many of the prisoners started offending young; but the much larger number of people who offended when young but have since grown out of it will not of course be there for you to meet.

Some have drawn contrary conclusions from a recent 'self report' study of offending, which found different 'peak ages' for different types of crime, and a slightly higher proportion of 22 to 25 year old males *currently participating* in acquisitive property crime (but not in violence, vandalism and drug offences) than younger people, although offending *less frequently*.[12] This study categorically does *not* disprove the notion that young offenders grow out of crime, or show that they no longer do so. It does indicate that some have not grown out of crime by the age of 25— although the nature of their offending may change—while others (about 30 per cent of offenders in this age group, according to the study) take up crime in their twenties.

There *may* have been a tendency in recent years for fewer young offenders to grow out of crime than did so in the past, although it would be wise to hesitate before basing too much policy on assuming that this is the case. If it is so, the explanation presumably lies in those 'causes of crime' on which New Labour promises to be tough. Youthful offending and its cessation are largely brought about by the process of adolescence; but this does not mean that they are simply and directly caused by biological factors such as hormones. If they were, then one would expect an explosion of offending at puberty and a gradual tailing off thereafter, and the earlier puberty of today's young people would have led to a reduction in the peak age of offending rather than the opposite, which is what has occurred.[13] Rather, juvenile crime is a response to *the social situation of adolescence*, the period between dependent and powerless childhood and adulthood, which changes its character as society and the economy alter. Not least in importance, in our opinion, is the employment situation;[14] rates of youthful offending are likely to be significantly affected by the current and future job prospects for young people, which alter their perceptions of whether legitimate options for material rewards and fun are worth pursuing. (This suggests that if the recent improvements in the unemployment figures continue and the government's 'Welfare to Work' and 'New Deal' youth employment policies are successful, young offenders could be *more* likely to grow out of crime in the coming years.) The accumulated criminological evidence certainly indicates that such factors are of considerably more importance than the workings or failings of the criminal justice system for young offenders.

Is it true that 'leaving the kids alone' is more likely to produce the desired result of their growth out of crime? There is some evidence to support this 'labelling theory' hypothesis. The classic longitudinal self-report study by Donald West and other Cambridge University researchers did suggest that the best way to prevent a repeat offence by a boy growing up in London might be *not to catch* the culprit in the first place.[15] If we do catch them, there is also some evidence that gentler treatment may often have better results. For example, between 75 and 87 per cent of young people who received police cautions in 1985 and 1988 were not convicted of an offence in the next two years, and Home Office research has calculated that young adults (aged 17 to 20) are less likely to reoffend if they are cautioned rather than taken to court.[16] This suggests that official action to 'nip in the bud' offending by young people which is not yet serious or persistent may more often have the opposite effect, of 'amplifying deviance'.

Nevertheless, although the gentle touch usually seems to work, it does not always do so. Perhaps a 'one size fits all' policy is not appropriate for all those who commit crimes in adolescence. Some young offenders persist in their criminal activities and for a long time show no sign of 'growing out of crime'. Who are these *persistent* young offenders, and what can be done about them?

DUCK BOY: PERSISTENT AND SPREE OFFENDING

With grim regularity, the media (usually in alliance with their contacts in the police) bring to our attention persistent young offenders glorying in nicknames like 'Rat Boy' or 'Spider Boy'. Presumably before the rest of the bestiary is exhausted we shall hear about Duck Boy—so called, of course, because he is always being picked up by the Bill. The Duck Boys of this world are described as mini-crime waves whose offending sprees grossly inflate the local crime statistics (one was christened 'Blip Boy' for this reason) and who are supposedly able to offend repeatedly with impunity. Even when charged with an offence, Duck Boy is given bail, allowing him to reoffend yet again, or if remanded in local authority accommodation he absconds and commits more crimes, pausing only briefly to pose for the media cameras wearing a fetching balaclava. He never actually seems to be sentenced for anything, because the delays in the criminal justice system mean he has always committed more offences before he is tried for the last lot. Well-meaning lawyers, magistrates and court administrators keep ensuring that his case is adjourned so that all his offences can be tried together; but of course during the adjournment he always offends again . . .

It is Duck Boy (and successive Home Secretaries) whom we have to thank for bringing us the secure training order, a new custodial sentence for persistent offenders aged between 12 and 14. Provision for this sentence and the new secure training centres in which they are to be served was contained in the Conservative government's Criminal Justice and Public Order Act 1994. Although the then Labour Opposition criticised this creation at the time, preferring a policy of providing more places in secure care accommodation for young offenders who needed to be detained, the new Labour government has begun to introduce it, although it may prove to be only a temporary measure. The first of five planned secure training centres opened at Medway in Kent in April 1998, but the government hopes ultimately to abolish the secure training order as a specific sentence when it introduces the new 'detention and training order' contained in the Crime and Disorder Act 1998 (see later in this chapter).

Various attempts have been made to measure the size and scale of the 'persistent young offender' problem. Often it is the least satisfactory surveys which receive the largest amount of publicity. For example, a study conducted and published by Northumbria Police in 1996[17] calculated that 58 local young offenders were responsible for 1,079 detected offences in 1995. This averages out at 19 offences per offender, itself rather less than the claims often made of some young offenders committing in excess of fifty or a hundred crimes in a short space of time. But additionally, the study was flawed by its use of 'offences taken into consideration' as a basis for calculation. The practice of asking or persuading detected offenders to admit to previously unsolved crimes to be 'taken into consideration', thus enabling the police to improve their official 'clear-up rate', is notoriously unsound as a procedure for determining who has actually committed which crimes, allowing as it obviously does for a combination of police pressure and youthful bravado to generate false admissions.

A somewhat sounder Home Office study attempted to get police forces to identify all people under 17 who were known or alleged to have committed ten or more offences within a three-month period in 1992.[18] The total number of such offenders, provided by 33 forces, unfortunately not including the Metropolitan Police, was (only) 106, two thirds of them aged 15 or 16. One of the most satisfactory surveys to date,[19] carried out by Ann Hagell and Tim Newburn of the Policy Studies Institute in London and the Midlands in 1992, found that young repeat offenders were not responsible for anything like the high proportion of local crime that myth suggests. The known and alleged offences of the most persistent six per cent of the repeat offenders accounted for no more than 15 per cent of recorded juvenile crime in the locality.[20] Moreover, very few young repeat offenders were 'persistent' according to more than one definition of the term; and even among those who could be defined as 'persistent', few continued to offend for more than six months. Only a tiny number were still persisting in their offending after a year. The picture painted by this research was one of sad, mixed-up and immature but rarely malicious young people with very disrupted family lives and chaotic lifestyles, some of whom indulged in 'sprees'—intensive but short-lived and self-terminating phases of (usually relatively petty) offending. It seems from this that there are not very many Duck Boys, that they represent a smaller problem than we have been led to believe, and that even Duck Boy is likely to grow out of crime. It also suggests that punishment is likely to have little deterrent effect on Duck Boy. For his profile as it emerges from this research is uncannily reminiscent of the following passage about the limitations of deterrence from a 1990 White Paper:[21]

> There are doubtless some criminals who carefully calculate the possible gains and risks. But much crime is committed on impulse, given the opportunity presented by an open window or unlocked door, and it is committed by offenders who live from moment to moment; their crimes are as impulsive as the rest of their feckless, sad or pathetic lives. It is unrealistic to construct sentencing arrangements on the assumption that most offenders will weigh up the possibilities in advance and base their conduct on rational calculation. Often they do not.

Nevertheless, Duck Boy still represents a serious challenge to the anti-interventionist approach. He may grow out of it at some stage, but in the meantime can we really sit back and allow him to carry on with impunity, disrupting his own life as well as other people's while waiting for this to happen? Moreover, how much evidence is there that *at this level of persistence* intervention is likely to be counter-productive? For example, there is some empirical evidence suggesting that, while cautioning a young offender up to three times may be more effective or at least as effective as prosecution in discouraging reoffending, a fourth caution is less effective than taking the young offender to court.[22] It also seems a little implausible to suggest that Duck Boy has not yet got a 'deviant self image'[23] and is going around innocently unaware that he is doing anything wrong. Despite everything we have seen about the inefficiency of deterrence, there sometimes comes a point with a Duck Boy (or even a mini, duckling boy) when his perception of impunity becomes a problem and some intervention is called for. In our opinion, *this does not invalidate a general minimum-interventionist approach*, for generally speaking less harsh interventions do work well with young offenders. But there is no *a priori* inevitability about either labelling theory or deterrence theory. It is a contingent or empirical question in any instance whether intervening is likely to be effective or counter-productive. Sometimes (perhaps usually, especially with less persistent offenders) it is counter-productive. But sometimes, especially with persistent offenders, there is no escaping the need to intervene.

But when we do need to intervene, what form should our intervention take? What is likely to work?

WHAT WORKS WITH YOUNG OFFENDERS?

From the early 1970s until very recently, the criminological orthodoxy was that 'nothing works' either to reform or deter offenders, including young offenders: whatever you do with them will make no difference to their chances of offending again in future. Increasingly, there seems to be good evidence that *some things do work*: some kinds of programmes can have measurable (albeit not necessarily dramatic) effects in reducing the likelihood that a young offender will commit further crimes. Other things don't work well: we have already seen that for first and second-time offenders, prosecution (whatever court disposal may ensue from it) looks as if it may be counter-productive when its results are compared with a simple caution. It also seems as if both programmes based exclusively on traditional punishment and those based on traditional psychotherapeutic thinking (such as general counselling and family casework) are equally ineffective,[24] perhaps helping to explain why data from the 1960s and 1970s tended to show no difference between the results of these two approaches. On the other hand, there are definite signs that well-designed and implemented programmes which use a more focused and 'cognitive' approach can make a real positive difference to the subsequent behaviour of at least some young offenders.

Such programmes aim at improving the reasoning and social skills of the offenders, getting them to think about their offending and its consequences and teaching them skills which will assist them to act in less anti-social ways.[25] Importantly, it seems that for these schemes to be most effective they need to be *community-based*[26]—taking place as the young person is living a normal life to which the lessons can be related— rather than within the peculiar closed world of an institution full to the brim with other young people who have a disposition to commit crimes.

There are various ways of trying to deliver such programmes. They can be ordered by a court following conviction by making participation in the programme a condition of a supervision or probation order (known as 'intermediate treatment', 'intensive supervision' or 'intensive probation'). Alternatively, with the offender's agreement, they can be attached to an enhanced type of police caution, until now usually called 'caution plus', so that no prosecution and court proceedings take place. Or they can be offered on a voluntary basis to young people who may not even have officially offended yet but have been somehow identified as being 'at risk' of doing so. We could also legally require a young person to participate in such a programme without any finding of guilt; hitherto this has not been possible under English law, but the government's Crime and Disorder Act 1998 contains provisions for such compulsory programmes for 'pre-delinquents' under the aegis of 'child safety orders' (see below).

It may also be the case—although here the evidence is so far less compelling—that similar beneficial effects can be achieved by programmes aimed at the *parents* of young offenders and potential ('at risk') offenders. It certainly seems well established that harsh, erratic and uninvolved ways of bringing up children make them more likely to offend.[27] (Incidentally, taking the children away from inadequate parents is certainly no cure-all: more than a quarter of prison inmates and almost two-fifths of young prisoners were taken into care before their sixteenth birthdays.)[28] The idea that parents can be trained and helped to improve their parenting skills, with beneficial effects on their children's propensity to keep or break the law is a notion which has obvious appeal and is currently much in favour with government, but as yet such parental training programmes have not been adequately evaluated.[29] As with interventions aimed directly at young offenders themselves, there is a danger in going too readily overboard in espousing such programmes, which is the danger that labelling theory might be right. It might well be that any positive effects of the parenting programme could be outweighed by negative 'labelling effects' caused by the young person being stigmatised as a criminal in the making, which could become a self-fulfilling prophecy. These adverse labelling effects could even occur in respect of young people who have been *falsely* identified as likely to offend in the future, turning potential non-offenders into real criminals.[30] We do not yet know how well or badly such programmes are likely to work; an 'evidence-based' strategy would be concerned to pilot, monitor and evaluate schemes of this kind before adopting them as a magic panacea.

As advocates of the concept of *restorative justice*, we would like to be able to claim that restorative measures are effective in making young offenders less likely to reoffend—but we can't, or at least not yet. So far, hard evidence is lacking about the rehabilitative effectiveness of restorative schemes, despite occasional (and occasionally extravagant) claims to the contrary. One such claim received wide publicity in October 1997, when the media reported that a restorative 'caution plus' project run by Thames Valley Police in Aylesbury, Buckinghamshire had 'cut reoffending' from 30 per cent (for a young offender undergoing a usual police caution) to four per cent for participants in the scheme.[31] We would be surprised if crime reduction of this magnitude is verified when the scheme is definitively evaluated, and there is a danger that inflated claims of this kind could raise unrealistic expectations of the restorative approach.

We do not see restorative justice as a magic fix for juvenile crime. Nothing is. As we saw in *Chapter 2*, it is unrealistic to expect the workings of the criminal justice system to have a dramatic impact on crime levels, however it operates. But we would certainly expect restorative measures to be at least as effective in crime prevention as more punitive and less positive approaches.[32] Indeed—as we said in *Chapter 2*—we think that restorative justice has great potential to develop into a system of responding to crime which does reduce reoffending by promoting the 'reintegrative shaming' of offenders, especially if it is implemented in such a way as to promote offenders to reflect upon and acknowledge the harm and upset caused by their actions and to take action to make amends and achieve reconciliation with victims and the wider community. But our advocacy of restorative justice does not depend upon its being more effective in reducing reoffending than other methods (although we would be embarrassed in the unlikely event of it proving *less* effective). Restorative justice seems to us worth pursuing in the interests of victims and communities—and indeed offenders— whether or not it offers a dramatic payoff in terms of crime control. The satisfaction typically expressed by victims and others involved in well-implemented restorative schemes[33] is justification enough.

THE AUDIT COMMISSION: A STRATEGY B PROGRAMME

The 1996 report of the Audit Commission entitled *Misspent Youth: Young People and Crime*[34] stands as an exemplar of a cost-conscious Strategy B approach to juvenile crime. One main thrust of the report was the need to bring about greater efficiency, speed and smoother running in youth justice by managerialist means such as encouraging different agencies to work together more closely and effectively and to streamline the hitherto notoriously delay-prone prosecution process. Another general message of the Audit Commission was that prevention is better (and in the long run cheaper) than cure of youthful offending. Whereas the (Strategy A-minded) Conservative government to which it reported had emphasised prosecution and custodial sentences in the shape of 'secure training orders' for persistent 12 to 14 year olds and militaristic 'boot camp' régimes in young offender institutions, the Audit Commission took a more pragmatic approach. It favoured diversion from prosecution by means of cautioning as a cheap and effective measure for non-recidivist young offenders and enthusiastically recommended *'caution plus'* schemes (in which a caution is combined with action to ensure that offenders make reparation to their victims and/or are challenged and confronted about their offending and the reasons for it) in these persuasive terms: 'If one in five young people accepted a caution plus programme instead of being processed through the courts, around £40 million a year could be released to fund services that challenge offending behaviour and prevent crime.'[35]

The Audit Commission's recommendations amounted to a *graduated* approach and response to juvenile crime. Most emphasis should be placed on validated crime prevention measures, which hold out the best prospect of cost-effective returns. (The Commission noted the often-quoted estimate that the 'Perry' or 'High Scope' pre-school programme in Michigan had brought about crime reduction and other benefits to the tune of $7 for each dollar spent.)[36] These crime prevention measures could include *voluntary* parenting programmes for parents in high-risk areas or who are identified as experiencing difficulties. Young people who do offend should normally be cautioned initially. The next stage should normally be a 'caution plus' programme of proven effectiveness rather than a court appearance. More persistent young offenders who are prosecuted should be supervised in the community wherever possible, with use being made of intensive supervision programmes of a kind likely to help them stop offending.

The Audit Commission was concerned that resources should be efficiently *targeted* in such a way as to achieve the maximum results. Firstly, crime prevention schemes should be concentrated in areas and on sections of the population where crime levels are high, since research evidence confirms the common sense perception that you can probably prevent more crime where there is more crime to be prevented.[37] Similarly, more intensive (and more expensive) programmes to tackle offending behaviour should be targeted on more persistent offenders. There are at least two good reasons for this. One is that it is a waste of resources to spend them on the majority of first-time or second-time offenders who will not reoffend anyway. Another is that the 'labelling effects' of the programme could well outweigh any positive effects. (One could also add that politically—with a small 'p'—it becomes less and less feasible to refrain from some more intensive intervention the longer a young person goes on reoffending, even if we were to subscribe to a minimum intervention approach.) Intensive parenting programmes should also be targeted on parents whose children are already seriously misbehaving or are clearly at risk, or who are otherwise having severe difficulties bringing up their children. Although the Audit Commission did not say so explicitly, it surely follows that the most expensive intervention of all—custody—should be reserved for those who have either committed very serious offences or who have continued to persist in serious crime despite having been through a graduated series of progressively more intensive treatments (and despite the passage of 'growing up time' which this implies).

In all of this, the Audit Commission relied on the '*evidence-based*' approach which we also favour, recommending that more research and pilot schemes should be carried out and systematically evaluated to discover 'what works' (and how well, and who with). Techniques which prove successful should be employed more widely, targeted on those with whom they seem to work. Monitoring and evaluation of the entire youth justice system should be a continuous process, with lessons learned being constantly fed back into practice.

The massive distance between this Strategy B approach and the Conservatives' Strategy A orientation was pointed up nicely by Home Office minister David Maclean's intemperate dismissal of the Audit Commission's report as 'pathetically defeatist'[38]—presumably meaning that we should not be deflected from a policy of maximum punitiveness towards young offenders by tiny considerations such as enormous cost and scandalous waste of public resources. The new Labour government's approach, however, is closer to that of the Audit Commission, as we shall now see.

NO MORE EXCUSES—THE NEW LABOUR APPROACH

No one could accuse the new Labour government of dragging its heels on the subject of young offenders. Its first few months in office produced a Task Force on Youth Justice, no fewer than three consultation papers,[39] a White Paper entitled *No More Excuses*[40] and a Bill (which became the Crime and Disorder Act 1998) containing provisions to implement many of the recommendations in these papers. New Labour's agenda for young offenders includes the following:

1. A new statutory 'principal aim' for the the youth justice system: to prevent offending by children and young persons. (Section 37 of the Crime and Disorder Act 1998).

2. A national *Youth Justice Board* to monitor the operation of the youth justice system, promote good practice and advise the Home Secretary on the operation of the youth justice system and the setting of national standards. (Section 41)

3. Multi-agency *youth offending teams* in each local authority area to provide, coordinate and run local youth justice systems in accordance with national standards and guidelines. (Section 39)

4. A statutory duty on local authorities to provide comprehensive youth justice services in their localities, including bail support services. (Section 38)

5. The replacement of cautions for offenders under 18 with a new system of *'reprimands'* and *'warnings'* to replace the current system of police cautions for young offenders. (Sections 65-66.) Normally a young repeat offender will only be able to receive one reprimand and one warning—previously referred to as a 'final warning'—before being prosecuted. Final warnings will be similar to existing 'caution plus' schemes: police officers who give warnings will refer the young offenders to the local youth offending team for assessment to see if they should participate in a programme to address their offending. The Crime and Disorder Act also provides that courts should only exceptionally pass a conditional discharge on a young offender who is convicted of an offence within two years of receiving a final warning.

6. *'Fast tracking'* of the prosecution of persistent young offenders[41] with the aim of halving the time between arrest and sentence from the previous average of 4.5 months. This was one of

Labour's five 'key pledges' in its 1997 General Election Manifesto. Fresh guidance has been issued to courts nationally,[42] and pilot 'fast-tracking' projects are under way in a number of courts as we write.

7. Abolition of the legal doctrine of *doli incapax*, the presumption that children aged 10 to 13 are incapable of committing a crime unless they can be shown to appreciate the difference between right and wrong. (Crime and Disorder Act 1998, section 34)

8. Provision for local *child curfew* schemes banning children under 10 from streets and other public places at night unless supervised by a responsible adult. (Section 14)

9. *Child safety orders* which magistrates' courts can impose on children under 10 who have committed acts for which they could have been prosecuted if over that age[43] *or if the child is thought to be at risk of committing such acts.* (Section 11.) These orders place the child under the supervision of a social worker or youth justice worker and require the child to comply with specific requirements made by the court, and can also lead to a parenting order.

10. Powers for courts to impose *parenting orders* on the parents of children who commit offences or act anti-socially or who are put under child safety orders. (Section 8.) Parents will be required to attend counselling and guidance sessions and comply with other conditions.

11. *Reparation orders* requiring young offenders to make reparation to the victim of the offence or the community at large. (Section 67)

12. *Action plan orders* requiring young offenders to comply with 'action plans' intended to address their offending behaviour. (Section 69)

13. Amendments to the existing juvenile *supervision order* enabling conditions requiring *reparation* to be attached. (Section 71)

14. Replacement of the custodial sentences 'detention in a young offender institution' and 'secure training order' by a new *detention and training order* for offenders aged 10-17 (Sections 73-79). Unlike detention in a young offender institution, this will be available for young offenders *under 15* as long as they are 'persistent offenders'. Eventually the Act envisages offenders as young as 10 being detained under these orders provided they are 'persistent' and the court thinks that custody is necessary to protect the

public from the child—a remarkable proposal, since even Michael Howard never suggested introducing penal custody for ten year olds who had not committed particularly serious offences.

15. The ending of the 'boot camp' young offender institution regime created by the Conservative government at Colchester military corrective training centre. The 'boot camp' was closed by the government in March 1998 on the grounds that, costing as it did around twice per inmate as a normal young offender institution, it did not represent 'value for money'.[44]

This flurry of proposals, initiatives and legislation represents a mixture of Strategies A, B and C. Final warnings, curfews and the abolition of *doli incapax*—not to mention the White Paper's title *No More Excuses* and much of the government's rhetoric—have clear overtones of 'zero tolerance'[45] and Strategy A, as does the notion of extending juvenile imprisonment to 'persistent' offenders as young as ten. The welcome emphasis on reparation and restorative justice, on the other hand, is redolent of Strategy C. And there is a great deal of managerial Strategy B—à la Audit Commission—in the mix: witness the thrust to routinise the youth justice system and ensure standard good practice nationally by means of the Youth Justice Board and local youth offending teams, and to make the prosecution process more speedy and efficient.

Consequently, as might be expected given our espousal of Strategy C and aspects of Strategy B, our own attitude towards the Straw programme is also mixed. We shall briefly indicate our attitude to some of these measures, and conclude by saying more about three crucial issues: diversion from prosecution, the youth court, and custody (and secure accommodation) for young offenders.

Strategy B measures in this package of which we approve include the introduction of a *Youth Justice Board* and local *youth offending teams*. For too long there has been a lamentable lack of direction and strategic management in youth justice policy at both national and local levels. In certain local areas the efforts of local practitioners, often influenced and assisted by the 'systems management' school of youth justice experts, have often achieved remarkable results in reforming local youth justice systems and bringing about inter-agency cooperation, but there has been little national backing for their efforts. (Moreover, cuts in local authority budgets in recent years have often led to decimation and disruption of youth justice services.) The new framework has the potential for promoting a systematic approach to youth justice throughout the country.

Nor do we have any quarrel with the desire to sort out Duck Boy and his like by 'fast tracking' the most persistent young offenders rather than constantly letting them go back to the end of the queue. Doubtless there is scope for improving the system in this respect, and at present it seems likely that the government's pledge to halve the time from arrest to sentence will prove realistic. We do have reservations, however. Given the government's rather broad definition of 'persistent' in this context[46] it is likely to catch not only offenders who are in the middle of a spree which needs interrupting but also others who are not actually in the course of a spree and might be about to grow out of crime fairly soon. But, if labelled as problem persistent offenders and rushed before the youth court, they could receive excessive punishment which, far from 'nipping in the bud' their offending, could ultimately lead to an amplification of it.

We have to admit to scepticism about the utility of *child curfews*. Of course it is undesirable, for all kinds of reasons, for children under ten to be out on the streets unsupervised at all hours, and it is sensible to amend the law so that police officers have a clear power to take them home and refer them to social services if there is any great cause for concern about their welfare. But the bureaucracy involved in the Act's provisions and the rhetoric with which they are associated makes us doubt whether the powers will be either widely used or, if used, enforced with either consistency, wisdom or effectiveness. It seems likely that those localities which implement curfews will do so as part of a strong-arm, zero tolerance, 'let's clean up the streets' approach which will have little to do with the welfare of children. Nor will it do much to reduce serious crime, little of which is committed by children under ten, let alone by children under ten at night on their own.

The thinking behind community-based *reparation orders* and *action plan orders* is essentially sound and is very much in line with the concept of 'restorative justice' which we favour.[47] Again, however, we see dangers. Such orders represent relatively severe (and expensive) interventions, and should be rationed by being targeted upon offenders who have already demonstrated a degree of persistence and intransigence. There are good Strategy B and Strategy C reasons for this. We have already mentioned the Strategy B reason, which is about being frugal with resources. The Strategy C reason is that excessive intervention in the lives of young people—especially those who are likely to grow out of crime anyway and therefore not benefit from these measures—is an infringement of their human rights.

We are also unconvinced of the need for these new court orders. Everything that could be achieved in the context of these orders could equally well be done in the context of juvenile supervision orders or probation orders, either under the law as it stands or with a modicum of legislative tweaking. The previous government made the mistake of suggesting a massive reduction in the number of different non-custodial orders which are available to the courts,[48] combining them into unwieldy generic sentences. The new government is in danger of falling into the opposite trap, creating a confusing plethora of poorly-differentiated sentences, which could paradoxically lead to their *under*-use by the courts if magistrates and other practitioners fail to fully comprehend all their options. (We find it disconcerting that the Crime and Disorder Act contains no fewer than eight new court orders which relate to young offenders.)

Our trepidation increases when we come to consider the *parenting order*. Anyone taking an 'evidence-based approach' must surely conclude that the evidence to support introducing such an order does not exist. Yes, poor parenting is a factor in juvenile crime; yes, some parental counselling and training programmes look promising; but there is no evidence at all that *compulsory orders* on parents will achieve anything, and they could even be counter-productive (as well as an expensive intrusion into the civil liberties of citizens). We may recall that the Audit Commission never claimed that parenting training schemes were of proven effectiveness as yet, and only recommended *offering assistance* to parents whose children were giving cause for concern. It does not seem sensible to us to go further than this in the present state of knowledge. Changing one's parenting methods is surely something which requires great commitment from the parent: not the kind of thing which can be imposed by a court order. Parents could indeed be required to attend counselling and training courses, but old sayings about leading horses to water spring to mind. Not only is there no evidence at all that compulsory parental training can be of any use with reluctant trainees, but the imposition of a parenting order could be damagingly stigmatising to both parents and child. (The same danger of adverse labelling also applies to the proposed *child safety orders* for children under ten who may not even have acted criminally.) Again, imposing an order could well have the effect of making parents less cooperative, not more.

It is some comfort, however, that the parenting order is one of the many measures in the Crime and Disorder Act which are currently being piloted and evaluated in local areas before being implemented nationally[49]—one indication of New Labour's welcome move towards an 'evidence-based' approach to criminal justice (see *Chapter 8*).

PROSECUTE, CAUTION, REPRIMAND OR WARN?

The decision whether to prosecute a young offender or take some alternative action represents a crucial moment in the criminal process—

and one where the opposing ideologies of 'minimum intervention' and 'zero tolerance' come sharply into conflict. For a long time the tide flowed in favour of minimum intervention, as throughout the 1980s and early 1990s the Conservative government lent its authority to the policy of diverting young offenders from prosecution.[50] Under the influence of the 'systems management' school, a 'gatekeeping' device in the form of 'cautioning panel' made its appearance in almost every locality. This is a multi-disciplinary body which advises the police when to prosecute and when to caution young offenders, normally with a bias towards cautioning wherever possible. Caution rates for known offenders under 17 rose from 49 per cent in 1980 to 82 per cent in 1992.

With the advent of Michael Howard, the tide inevitably turned, and new guidance to police and Crown prosecutors in 1994 placed severe restrictions upon the administration of cautions for either second offences or more serious offences. This development threatened the existence of the 'cautioning panel', whose effective ability to recommend a second caution was severely curtailed. The threat was increased by the 'Narey report', an internal Home Office review aimed at reducing delays in the criminal justice system published in February 1997, and which saw the cautioning panel as a source of undesirable delay in the prosecution process.[51] Cautioning rates for young offenders aged 14 to 17 declined significantly following Mr Howard's 1994 revision of the cautioning guidelines.[52] Then New Labour took power with their plans for 'final warnings' to replace cautions for offenders under 18.

To some extent, these proposals are an exercise in complicated relabelling: although the term 'caution' is to remain for offenders of 18 and over, for those under 18 'reprimand' is the new name for a first caution and 'warning' the new name for 'caution plus'. Michael Howard's crackdown on repeat cautioning also remains largely intact. However, one significant (and welcome) feature is the interpolation into the scheme of the 'reprimand' for less serious first offences. Previous Labour policy documents[53] gave the impression that a first caution would be a 'final warning'. This would have seriously intensified the response to a juvenile first offence by making 'caution plus' mandatory in all cases, and to a second offence by making prosecution automatic. The Crime and Disorder Act's provisions are closer to the Audit Commission's recommendations, which were to use caution plus as an alternative to *prosecution*, not instead of a simple caution.

The scheme as envisaged in the Act therefore represents a commendable step forward from the Michael Howard approach, in using diversion from court combined with action aimed at bringing about reparation and rehabilitation for cases where the Howard schema would have insisted on prosecution. The doubts that we still have concern the remaining rigidity of the new set-up, and in particular the lack of discretion for the police to administer a second reprimand or second warning in appropriate cases, bearing in mind that the empirical evidence suggests that at present it is only after the *third* juvenile caution that prosecution appears generally more effective in reducing reoffending. We also retain a (possibly over-sentimental) affection for the multi-disciplinary cautioning panel whose days look more and more numbered—but we have some hopes that the new youth offending team may replace them in our hearts.

THE SECRET GARDEN: THE YOUTH COURT

When offenders below the age of 18 are prosecuted, they normally go before the youth court,[54] a specialised version of the magistrates' court which usually sits in private with strict press reporting restrictions. Before 1992, this court was known as the 'juvenile court'; the Criminal Justice Act 1991 changed its name and raised the maximum age for its defendants from 16 to 17. Not only did this change bring the age at which young offenders appear in adult courts in line with the general age of majority, but it was also hoped that the less punitive ethos of the juvenile court could be usefully extended to 17 year olds. Some feared that the change could prove to be counter-productive[55] if the influx of 17 year olds led the youth court to adopt a generally harsher ethos than its predecessor the juvenile court, leading to more severe treatment for those *under* 17. It is hard, under the historical circumstances, to tell what has actually happened. Empirical studies show severer sentencing in the youth court in 1993 than in the juvenile court before the change, including a greater use of custodial sentences for children under 17.[56] However, 1993 was a year in which public concern and political rhetoric about 'law and order' went into hyperdrive, fuelling increases in sentencing severity for offenders of all ages (including adults), so it may not be correct to blame the invention of the youth court in particular for any of these changes.[57] Although the Home Office's internal Narey Report of February 1997 recommended a reversion to the prior cut-off point of the seventeenth birthday for the youth court's jurisdiction, this does not appear to be on the government's current agenda.

What does concern the government about the youth court—apart from delays in the prosecution process—is the secrecy of the court, described by Jack Straw as a 'Secret Garden';[58] the lack of involvement of victims and the parents of offenders; and the lack of attention to inquiring into the reasons for the young offender's behaviour followed by action to change it. The government has recently encouraged youth court magistrates to 'name and shame' persistent young offenders by lifting reporting restrictions more often, to invite victims and members of the local public to attend the court proceedings, and to engage in greater dialogue in court about the child's offending and how to stop it.[59]

We sympathise greatly with the government's view that what is needed is a forum in which real and useful dialogue takes place involving young offenders, their families, victims and others focused on the young person's offending and what to do about it. We strongly doubt, however, whether a court of law can ever really constitute such a forum. Law courts are an essential safeguard to ensure that citizens' basic rights are upheld: for example, that the innocent are not convicted, or that offenders do not receive punishment which is out of all proportion to their blameworthiness. But they do not excel as a locus for the kind of constructive, forward-looking dialogue between different parties which the government (and we) would like to see. In many other areas of law there has been a major shift towards 'alternative dispute resolution' (ADR) which takes place *outside* the courtroom, for this very reason—although disputes may be referred to ADR by a court, which may also be required to approve the solutions emerging from ADR.

Consequently, it makes sense for discussion about young offenders to be *diverted out of the youth court* and into new, less formal kinds of forum for dialogue; this would be a better way forward than trying vainly to turn the court into something it can never be. Various models for such a forum are already in existence, ranging from Scotland's children's hearings to New Zealand's Family Group Conferences (which were originally based on Maori traditions, and have recently been cited as an influence on restorative 'caution plus' schemes in Thames Valley[60] and elsewhere). Young offenders could be referred to such a forum either by the police or the Crown Prosecution Service (in consultation with a youth offending team) as an alternative to prosecution, or by the youth court following a guilty plea or conviction.

Encouragingly, the government now plans something not unlike this in the longer term strategy for less persistent young offenders. The Youth Justice and Criminal Evidence Act 1999[61] creates a 'youth offender panel' for dealing with young offenders who are prosecuted for the first time. The panel will seek to involve offenders, their families, their victims (with the victims' consent) and youth justice workers and draw up agreed 'contracts' (enforceable by the youth court) which would seek to achieve both reparation and the rehabilitation of the offender. We see this as one of the government's most imaginative and constructive innovations to date, and would hope that in time the panel's jurisdiction could be extended to include appropriate second and subsequent prosecutions as well.

We differ from the government, however, on the issue of secrecy. The youth offender panel's operations ought to take place in something of a 'secret garden'—although the principles it operates on should be open and accountable, and it should of course involve victims and perhaps other interested local parties in ways that the youth court presently fails to. But in the great majority of cases little would be gained and much might be lost if the proceedings were open to the public glare. For useful dialogue to occur in such a forum a relatively informal and stress-free atmosphere is necessary; and all the classic concerns about the dangers of publicly stigmatising young offenders remain as valid as ever. Secret gardens can nurture some fine flowers.

LOCKING UP CHILDREN: CUSTODY AND SECURE ACCOMMODATION

We British seem to have a particular *penchant* for locking up children, even though our young people do not seem to be any more delinquent than those elsewhere.[62] So unless we were hell-bent on Strategy A, one might think that we ought to be looking at ways of imprisoning fewer children rather than—as it seems—constantly looking for new custodial sentences for younger and younger children, such as Michael Howard's 'secure training orders' for 12 to 14 year olds or Jack Straw's plan to extend the new detention and training order to children aged 10 and 11.

Both the British and the international pictures are complicated, however, by the existence of legal methods of controlling misbehaving and problem children other than the criminal justice system. Children can also be taken into care or put under supervision via civil proceedings: in England and Wales this is done under the Children Act 1989 to prevent 'significant harm' coming to the child—and the 'harm' could be harm to their development as a result of their offending behaviour or its consequences. If a child in local authority care is likely to abscond and suffer or inflict harm as a result, he or she may be placed in 'secure accommodation'. Another route to secure accommodation involves both criminal and civil procedures. Sufficiently persistent young offenders aged ten upwards can be placed on supervision orders by the youth court with the condition that they live in local authority accommodation, and again they can be moved to secure accommodation if the criteria are met. Young offenders awaiting trial can also be remanded into local authority accommodation (which can again become secure accommodation) rather than being bailed or remanded into custody.[63] A common complaint has been the lack of secure accommodation places (unlike the old cliché about the prison system, secure units can put up a 'House Full' notice). An extra 170 places were planned to supplement the existing 295, but this is still said to be insufficient even to deal with pre-trial remands.[64] It looks as if something both horribly wrong and horribly inefficient is going on when a recent survey found that 31 per cent of secure places are currently occupied by children who do not need such a level of security,[65] with the knock-on effect that other children are finding themselves in Prison Service establishments (remand centres, young offender institutions and even adult prisons) as a result.

It may therefore be an encouraging sign that the government has instigated a review of the whole range of secure and custodial accommodation for young people[66] and will be seeking to rationalise use across the board. This coincides with a review by the Chief Inspector of Prisons of prison régimes for young offenders,[67] which seems likely to result in a separate system of young offender institutions for those aged under 18. We would hope that the result of this process might be that the expensive disruption of young lives which is juvenile custody could finally be minimised, by being targeted on those few young Duck Boys whose persistent and serious offending requires severe constraints on their liberty either for the protection of the public or (for the minimum possible period) to break their cycles of reoffending and allow a brief period of 'time out' to enable positive interventions to take place.

This is not about being 'soft' on juvenile crime—indeed, our preferred strategy would promise to be more effective in limiting the level of youthful offending than one which placed more store in punitive custody. Nor is it about 'making excuses' for young people who commit crimes. We are ourselves deeply sceptical of 'positivist' approaches which deny the responsibilities of offenders (and often their civil liberties as well).[68] It is right to bring home to young offenders their growing responsibility for their behaviour and to encourage them to be more responsible. But the way to achieve this is not by rejecting, excluding and punishing them as painfully and damagingly as possible—à la Strategy A. At the end of the day, we have to engage with young people as developing moral agents so that they grow out of crime and into responsible members of the community. Nothing else is likely to work.[69]

ENDNOTES: *Chapter 7*

1 Ricky Taylor and colleagues, *Cautions, Court Proceedings and Sentencing, England and Wales 1996*, Home Office Statistical Bulletin 16/97, Table 4.

2 David Farrington, 'Trends in English Juvenile Delinquency and their Explanation', *International Journal of Comparative and Applied Criminal Justice*, 16 (1992), 151-63.

3 Jack Straw and Alun Michael, *Tackling Youth Crime: Reforming Youth Justice*,

Labour Party consultation paper, May 1996.

4   See Roger Evans and Rachel Ellis, *Police Cautioning in the 1990s*, Home Office Research Findings No. 52 (1997).

5   Patrick Collier, *Police Disposals of Notifiable Offences Cleared Up, Following Arrest or Report by Age, Gender and Offence*, Home Office Statistical Findings 2/96 (1996); see especially *Table 6*. For example there were about 34,200 male offenders aged 10 to 13 known to the police in 1995 compared with 43,600 found guilty or cautioned in 1985.

6   This phrase was popularised by Andrew Rutherford's *Growing Out of Crime: Society and Young People in Trouble* (Harmondsworth, Penguin, 1986). This put forward Rutherford's 'developmental approach' which we discuss shortly.

7   Edwin Schur, *Radical Non-intervention: Rethinking the Delinquency Problem* (Englewood Cliffs, NJ, Prentice-Hall, 1973), 155.

8   See Michael Cavadino and James Dignan *The Penal System: An Introduction* (2nd ed, London, Sage Publications, 1997), 254-61; David Thorpe, David Smith, Chris Green and John Paley, *Out of Care: The Community Support of Juvenile Offenders* (London, George Allen and Unwin, 1980).

9   Rutherford, op. cit.; see also his *Growing out of Crime: The New Era* (Winchester, Waterside Press, 1992).

10 Home Office, *No More Excuses – A New Approach to Tackling Youth Crime in England and Wales*, Cm 3809 (London, Stationery Office, 1997), Preface.

11 *Criminal Careers of Those Born Between 1953 and 1973*, Home Office Statistical Bulletin 14/95 (London, Home Office, 1995). Female offenders have shorter criminal careers on average. It is of course quite possible that many people who are caught offending in their teens continue to commit the occasional undetected offence in later life, but the great majority of young offenders clearly grow out of any deep involvement in crime.

12 John Graham and Ben Bowling (1995), *Young People and Crime*, Home Office Research Study No. 145 (London, HMSO, 1995).

13 The peak age for males has risen from 14 in 1971 to 18 in 1995, and from 14 to 15 for females.

14 See further Iain Crow, Paul Richardson, Carol Riddington and Frances Simon, *Unemployment, Crime and Offenders* (London, Routledge, 1989: 6-12); Iain Crow, 'Employment, Training and Offending', in Mark Drakeford and Maurice Vanstone (eds.), *Beyond Offending Behaviour'* (Aldershot, Arena, 1996).

15 Donald West, *Delinquency: Its Roots, Careers and Prospects* (London, Heinemann, 1982: 104-11).

16 *The Criminal Histories of Those Cautioned in 1985, 1988 and 1991*, Home Office Statistical Bulletin 8/94. (London, Home Office, 1994), *Table F* and para 22. For further evidence that young offenders may be more likely to offend if charged and prosecuted, see Peter Jordan, 'Effective Policing Strategies for Reducing Crime', in Peter Goldblatt and Chris Lewis (eds.), *Reducing Offending: An Assessment of Research Evidence on Ways of Dealing with Offending Behaviour*, Home Office Research Study No. 187 (London, Home

Office, 1998): 63-81 at p. 67.

[17] *Persistent Young Offenders* (Northumbria Police, 1996).

[18] Cited in Home Affairs Committee, *Sixth Report: Juvenile Offenders* (1993): para. 18.

[19] Ann Hagell and Tim Newburn, *Persistent Young Offenders* (London, Policy Studies Institute, 1994).

[20] Hagell and Newburn, op. cit., p.123. The Audit Commission, not inconsistently, has calculated that five per cent of young males aged 14 to 17 are responsible for at least two-thirds of the *recorded and unrecorded* offences committed by males in their age group. Each offender in this persistent sub-group admitted having committed 20 or more crimes in the previous 12 months. (Audit Commission, *Misspent Youth: Young People and Crime*, Abingdon, Audit Commission, 1996, para. 7, drawing on Graham and Bowling's self-report research, op. cit.). It needs to be borne in mind that unrecorded crimes tend on the whole to be less serious than offences which are reported to and recorded by the police.

[21] Home Office, *Crime, Justice and Protecting the Public*, Cm 965 (London, HMSO, 1990): para 2.8 — a Conservative White Paper from the days of the 'Hurd approach'.

[22] Audit Commission, op. cit., para. 32.

[23] Hagell and Newburn (op. cit., p. 91) gained the impression that several of their persistent young offenders were already actively living up to their image; indeed, three had already been approached by TV companies doing documentaries on juvenile offending!

[24] See e.g. Mark W. Lipsey, 'The Effect of Treatment on Juvenile Delinquents: Results from Meta-Analysis', in Friedrich Lösel, Doris Bender and Thomas Bliesener (eds.), *Psychology and Law: International Perspectives* (Berlin, Walter de Gruyter, 1992), 131-43; 'What Do We Learn from 400 Research Studies on the Effectiveness of Treatment with Juvenile Delinquents?', in James McGuire (ed.), *What Works: Reducing Re-offending — Guidelines from Research and Practice* (London, Wiley, 1995), 63-78.

[25] Audit Commission, op. cit., paras. 56-7 and *Appendix 1;* see also McGuire, op. cit. and Julie Vennard, Carol Hedderman and Darren Sugg, *Changing Offenders' Attitudes and Behaviour: What Works?* Home Office Research Study No. 171 (London, Home Office, 1997).

[26] Vennard et al., op. cit., p. 3; D. A. Andrews, Ivan Zinger, Robert D. Hodge, James Bonta, Paul Gendreau and Francis T. Cullen, 'Does Correctional Treatment Work? A Clinically Relevant and Psychologically Informed Meta-Analysis', *Criminology*, 28 (1990), 369-429 at p. 382; Mark W. Lipsey, 'The Effect of Treatment on Juvenile Delinquents: Results from Meta-Analysis', in Friedrich Lösel, Doris Bender and Thomas Bliesener (eds.), *Psychology and Law: International Perspectives* (Berlin, Walter de Gruyter, 1992), 131-43 at p.138.

[27] See e.g. David Farrington, 'Human Development and Criminal Careers', in Mike Maguire, Rod Morgan and Robert Reiner (eds), *The Oxford Handbook of Criminology* (2nd edn., Oxford University Press, 1997), 361-408.

[28] Roy Walmsley, Liz Howard and Sheila White, *The National Prison Survey 1991: Main Findings*, Home Office Research Study No. 128 (London, HMSO, 1992).

[29] See Audit Commission, op. cit., paras. 88-95.

[30] Cf. Schur, op. cit., pp. 46-63. In other words, for such a programme to 'work' with any particular child, three things must hold true: (1) the child must be accurately identified as really likely to offend, or to continue offending; (2) the programme must have positive effects, rather than be ineffective or counter-productive in itself; and (3) the programme must not produce countervailing 'labelling effects' through stigmatising the child and family which nullify the programme's good effects. This may be a tall order; and even if all these factors are present it will not guarantee that the programme is a *cost-effective* method of reducing crime. It may simply cost too much per child to be efficient.

[31] *The Guardian*, 30 October 1997. More accurate figures can be found in Peter Goldblatt and Chris Lewis (eds.), *Reducing Offending: An Assessment of Research Evidence on Ways of Dealing with Offending Behaviour*, Home Office Research Study No. 187 (London, Home Office, 1998), 87.

[32] See e.g. James Dignan, *Repairing the Damage: An Evaluation of an Experimental Adult Reparation Scheme in Kettering, Northamptonshire.* (University of Sheffield, Centre for Criminological and Legal Research, 1991), ch. 6.

[33] See eg Dignan (op. cit., note 32), ch 5; Goldblatt and Lewis, op. cit., pp. 87-8.

[34] op. cit.

[35] ibid., para. 74.

[36] ibid., para. 96.

[37] See e.g. Paul Ekblom, Ho Law and Mike Sutton, *Domestic Burglaries in the Safer Cities Programme*, Home Office Research Findings No. 42, 1996, which demonstrated that anti-burglary programmes prevented one burglary for every £300 spent in very high-crime areas, but that the cost rose to £900 in very low-crime areas.

[38] *The Guardian*, 22 November 1996.

[39] Home Office, *Tackling Youth Crime* (September 1997), *New National and Local Focus on Youth Crime* (October 1997) and *Tackling Delays in the Youth Justice System* (October 1997).

[40] Home Office, op. cit., above n.10.

[41] The government has defined 'persistent' in this context as someone who has been dealt with by the courts on three or more occasions and commits another offence within three years of last appearing before a court (Lord Chancellor, Home Office, Department of Health, Welsh Office, Attorney-General and Department for Education and Employment, *Tackling Delays in the Youth Justice System*, October 1997, para 54 and *Annex C*). This definition is clearly much wider than the stereotypical 'spree offender' like Duck Boy.

[42] See previous note.

[43] Ten is the 'age of criminal responsibility' in England and Wales, i.e. the minimum age at which a person can be prosecuted in criminal proceedings. The Crime and Disorder Act also allows for a child safety order where the

child breaks a local curfew or acts in an 'anti-social' manner likely to cause 'harassment, alarm or distress' to others.

44 H. C. Deb. 22 January 1998.

45 Introducing the Bill, Mr Straw said it was 'about implementing a zero tolerance strategy' (*Guardian*, 4 December 1997), and other provisions in the Act, such as the 'anti-social behaviour order' also fit in with zero tolerance.

46 See above, note 41.

47 See James Dignan, 'The Crime and Disorder Act and the Prospects for Restorative Justice' [1998], *Criminal Law Review*, forthcoming.

48 Home Office, *Strengthening Punishment in the Community: A Consultation Document*, Cm 2780 (London, HMSO, 1995).

49 Other measures being piloted locally include child safety, action plan and reparation orders, youth offending teams, reprimands and 'final warnings'.

50 Cavadino and Dignan, op. cit., 258-9.

51 Home Office, *Review of Delay in the Criminal Justice System* ('The Narey Report') (Home Office, 1997), ch 8.

52 Caution rates for those cautioned or convicted of indictable offences declined from 62 to 54 per cent of males and 83.5 to 75 per cent of females aged 14 to 17 between 1992 and 1996 (Taylor, op. cit., *Table 5*); perhaps oddly, however, no such decline was seen in the figures for older offenders.

53 E.g. Straw and Michael, op. cit.

54 Certain particularly serious offences can lead to offenders as young as ten being tried before the Crown Court. It is also possible for young offenders to be tried as co-defendants with adults in the adult magistrates' and Crown Courts.

55 See e.g. Roger Evans, 'Cautioning: Counting the Cost of Retrenchment', [1994] *Criminal Law Review*, 566-575 at p. 569.

56 David O'Mahony and Kevin Haines, *An Evaluation of the Introduction and Operation of the Youth Court*, Home Office Research Study No 152 (London, Home Office, 1996); NACRO Youth Crime Section, *Sentencing in the Youth Court: The Effect of the Criminal Justice Act 1991* (London, NACRO, 1996; Iain Crow, Michael Cavadino, James Dignan, Valerie Johnston and Monica Walker, *Changing Criminal Justice: The Impact of the Criminal Justice Act 1991 in Four Areas in the North of England* (Centre for Criminological and Legal Research, University of Sheffield, 1996), *Appendix B*.

57 This conclusion, or lack of a conclusion, is supported by evidence that custodial sentencing for 15 to 17 year olds actually *decreased* in the first few months of the youth court's existence, which were the last few months of 1992 (NACRO Youth Section, op. cit., p. 10).

58 Speech to Labour Party Conference, 2 October 1997.

59 *No More Excuses* (op. cit.), paras. 9.1 to 9.10. New guidance along these lines was issued to courts in June 1988 (Home Office and Lord Chancellor's Department, *Opening Up Youth Court Proceedings*.)

60 Strictly speaking, the Thames Valley scheme owes more to a variant of the Family Group Conference idea implemented originally in Wagga Wagga, Australia: see Dignan, op. cit., note 47.

[61] See also *No More Excuses,* op cit., paras 9.20 to 9.59.

[62] Cavadino and Dignan, op. cit., p.267 note 4.

[63] The Crime and Disorder Act contains provisions which will allow a remanding youth court to directly *order* that offenders go into *secure* provision (at present only possible if the local authority applies to the court for this), and also to make it easier for youth courts to sentence offenders to live in local authority accommodation.

[64] *No More Excuses,* op. cit., para. 6.7.

[65] National Children's Bureau, *Safe to Let Out? Current and Future Use of Secure Accommodation for Children and Young Persons* (London, National Children's Bureau, 1995), 19.

[66] *No More Excuses,* op. cit., para. 6.3.

[67] *Young Prisoners: A Thematic Review by HM Chief Inspector of Prisons for England and Wales,* October 1997.

[68] See Michael Cavadino, *The Law of Gravity: Offence Seriousness and Criminal Justice* (Sheffield, Joint Unit for Social Services Research, 1997), ch. 2.

[69] See further *Children Who Break the Law, or Every body Does It* (Winchester, Waterside Press, 1999), which reaches similar conclusions to this chapter.

CHAPTER 8

Into the Millennium

> A map of the world that does not include Utopia is not worth even glancing at, for it leaves out the one country at which humanity is always landing:
> Oscar Wilde

THE REFORMER'S DILEMMA

Let us return to those armchairs in Anytown, where our wannabe reformers of criminal justice are still musing. They may find themselves torn between two different kinds of reform agendas, which we might call the *utopian* and the *realpolitikal*. In their utopian mode, they might each devise the ideal criminal justice system which they would like to see 'in an ideal world'. If their inclinations are similar to our own, their systems might be characterised by an absolutely minimal level of imprisonment. Incarceration would be reserved almost exclusively for the very small number of offenders whose extreme dangerousness means that it is vital to 'incapacitate' them from reoffending and whose characteristics and offences are such that no other method is likely to work. Additionally, confinement (typically for very limited periods) might remain necessary as a last resort for—again—a very small number of totally recalcitrant offenders who cannot be induced to accept any other form of sanction.

In this Utopia, criminal justice could operate almost entirely along 'restorative justice' lines. Offenders would make reparation for their offences to their individual victims wherever this is possible and appropriate; otherwise they would make reparation to victims generally and the community as a whole by performing community service and paying fines. Restorative measures would be designed to promote the reintegration of offenders into the law-abiding community—inclusion rather than exclusion—and within this generally restorative framework there would be a place for specific measures aimed at reforming offenders by getting them to examine their offending and encouraging and enabling them to pursue legitimate avenues rather than criminal ones. Little scope would remain in this system for the idea of 'retribution' in punishment: its main role would be as a limiting principle, to ensure that disproportionately excessive sanctions were not imposed on offenders for relatively minor transgressions.

Such an agenda would have much in common with those who call for 'the abolition of prisons'. This slogan is not actually quite as dramatic as it sounds once you interrogate one of those 'abolitionists' who are prepared to accept interrogation and ask them exactly what they mean. It usually transpires that they do not seek a complete end to the practice of confining people as a response to their crimes, but they do wish to see an end to the institution of prison as we know it.[1] Confinement should be restricted to the absolute minimum number of dangerous offenders for the minimum length of time, and when it occurs should be of an entirely different character to the oppressive phenomenon of contemporary imprisonment.

Our reformers are not näive. They fully realise that there is little chance of anything like this utopian agenda being pursued in the non-Utopia of Britain at the start of the twenty-first century. This is not to say that it could never happen at all: 200 years ago the abolition of capital and corporal punishment and their replacement by penalties such as imprisonment was at most a twinkle in the starry eyes of a few idealists. But such visionaries face severe problems of credibility when they posit a future which seems so far removed from the present that their ideas cause culture-induced shock, even horror, leading them to be written off as dangerous fantasists, more delusionary than visionary. It is also difficult for them to translate their utopian dreams into concrete proposals for reform. They can suffer from the 'If I were you, I wouldn't start from here' bafflement affecting the rural direction-giver in the old story. In short, the desire for revolution can impede reform.

So should reformers simply roll up and throw away the map of the world which includes Utopia and stick instead to the *realpolitikal* mode when campaigning, writing letters to the newspapers or to their MPs or the Home Secretary—or even when writing a book which they hope someone may take notice of? Should they merely push for piecemeal reforms which might make the system a little more humane, a little more rational, a little more restorative, but which do not connect with any broader vision of criminal justice beyond the horizon? Or is it possible to make the connection, in such a way that reforms presently demanded actually form part of a 'transitional strategy' for reaching Utopia?

Different reformers will reach, and have reached, different conclusions. Some choose to be visionaries and refuse to dirty their hands with *realpolitik*, in the desire to remain uncoopted by the system and the hope that they can inspire revolutionary fervour in others. Some go underground, keeping quiet about their long term aims but pursuing reforms which they hope will somehow bring us closer to Utopia. The radical Norwegian criminologist Thomas Mathiesen presented an original third solution to the reformer's dilemma in his seminal 1974 book *The Politics of Abolition*.[2] He urged abolitionists to avoid what he called 'the finished alternative', in other words a radical blueprint for a totally different system. Such a blueprint becomes a 'non-competing contradiction': abolitionists are 'defined out' by those in power or in the conventional mainstream: they are simply disregarded as irrelevant because their ideas are perceived as being so off the wall. On the other hand, conventional reformists (who are in 'non-competing agreement' with the status quo), are 'defined in' and coopted by the mainstream. They may be taken seriously; they may succeed in having some of their reform proposals adopted (although perhaps in such a watered down form that they are useless or even counter-productive); but they will be absorbed into the system and end up upholding it. Their reforms can only ever succeed if they accept that they must operate within the bounds of what is (conventionally regarded as) 'realistic' and 'desirable'; so they are forced to legitimate the system they should be seeking to abolish. Their reforms—Mathiesen gives the example of introducing treatment personnel into prisons—in the long run increase the power and legitimacy of an oppressive system.

Mathiesen's solution to this dilemma was to create a 'competing contradiction' by 'remaining unfinished'. Abolition is not to be seen as a complete blueprint for an end state we are aiming at, but as the *process* of overthrowing the established order. Abolitionists should and must pursue short-term goals and reforms, but these should be of a particular kind. They should be 'negative' or 'negating' reforms which undermine the power and legitimacy of the system. (For example, attacking prison censorship is a means towards 'unmasking' the truth about the oppressive nature of the prison system.) 'Positive' reforms—like providing treatment personnel in prisons—should be avoided because these legitimate and shore up the system you are trying to abolish.

We do not subscribe to Mathiesen's particular brand of radicalism. Nor do we call ourselves 'abolitionists'—partly because it is a misleading term which makes you sound more extreme than you are. Whatever the small print in your theoretical writings, there is surely a contradiction in political practice between wanting to be 'unfinished' and adopting a label which not only suggests a precise radical agenda (the abolition of prisons) but also makes it all too inevitable that many people will define you out as an alien from the Planet Wacko. This is not to denigrate the many abolitionists who have often done sterling and effective work in reform campaigns such as the one which achieved the closure of the psychiatric 'control units' which were introduced into English prisons in 1974;[3] but we venture to point out that such successes were partly gained by forging important alliances with more mainstream reformist elements within the establishment, and to suggest that the flag of abolitionism was not in itself helpful to the task of political persuasion required to achieve the reform.

Mathiesen's distinction between 'negating' and 'positive' reforms we also find problematic. For one thing, it is less than clear-cut. Would, for example, the setting up of a community-based restorative justice programme be 'positive' or 'negating'? We may not know in advance whether the scheme will actually have the effect of furthering the transformation of the system, or whether it will legitimate the *status quo*, widen the net of social control, or (through its perceived failure) set back the whole cause of restorative justice and give a boost to more punitive approaches. In a sense, the whole social world is 'unfinished' in such a way that it can be hard to draw such distinctions, let alone use them as a guide for practice.

We prefer an approach which operates—overtly and honestly—with an eye to different timescales and seeks to link desired immediate reforms with a longer term perspective. We would like to see minimal use of imprisonment in the long run—as a goal if not as a blueprint—and consequently we favour steps which seem likely to promote a reduced use of imprisonment in the short and medium term. Careful judgement may be required about specific reforms, for example whether introducing a new community penalty is likely to reduce the use of imprisonment or instead act as a bolt-on extra to the prison and serve only to increase the overall level of punishment by replacing less intrusive forms of community penalty and 'widening the net of social control'.[4]

In this connection, we are so far still less than convinced of the desirability and usefulness of electronic tagging as a high-tech fix for criminal justice. As we saw in *Chapter 4*, almost the only good things about tagging are negative, and derive from a direct comparison with incarceration. In this context, tagging is certainly cheaper and usually less inhumane than prison, so it is preferable if it can directly replace confinement in prison. But in comparison with most other community penalties, including 'high tariff' ones, it is unconstructive and (at least at present) more expensive. The latest research on the pilot tagging schemes suggest that simply adding the tagging option to the existing sentencing menu will divert some offenders from custody, but will probably divert just as many from other sentences such as community service.[5] Our preference at present would be to pursue diversion from custody to more positive and constructive community penalties and to reduce the general lengths of custodial sentences by means such as sentencing guidelines designed by the Sentencing Advisory Panel which should be given a reductionist remit (see *Chapter 3*).

We would like to see a system which was based on the principles of restorative justice rather than punishment in its traditional negative sense. Hence we are in favour of the introduction of restorative justice schemes, however small and piecemeal, which promise an opportunity to shift both practice and penal thinking in the direction of restoration. As we said in *Chapter 4*, it is important that these should not *simply* be grafted onto the existing punitive system, for they could end up being assimilated into normal punitive practice, legitimating it and themselves taking on a fundamentally negative punitive character. Restorative and other anti-custodial projects need to be developments which, despite all the pulls towards cooption which Mathiesen rightly identified, nevertheless retain something of the utopian about them, prefiguring a radically alternative way of responding to crime and contributing towards the creation of the kind of 'replacement discourse' about punishment which we previously identified as necessary (see *Chapters 1 and 4*). This requires practical skill and political nous on the part of practitioners and reformers, not just a politically correct theory (or pose). We are encouraged by the historical evidence which shows that, despite that nihilistically radical stream of theory which suggests that any form of anti-custodial reform short of revolution is doomed to failure, there are several clear examples of real and substantial 'decarceration' in the past, both in Britain and elsewhere, including a halving of the English prison population between 1908 and 1923 and a slashing of juvenile custody in the 1980s.[6] It is also encouraging that the philosophy of restorative justice—notwithstanding its utopian aspects—is currently a major influence on the thinking of real live politicians such as Jack Straw.[7]

We do not expect any government, whether New Labour or otherwise, to usher in a penal Utopia in the immediate future. But what hopes are there that they may take us in the right direction?

CRIMINAL JUSTICE, 2000 AND BEYOND

The three general strategies (A, B and C) which we have analysed and discussed throughout this book are 'ideal types', and none of them have ever been applied in a pure form by any government. Perhaps the nearest we have ever come to purism was Michael Howard's dogmatic pursuit of Strategy A between 1993 and 1997. With New Labour we have reverted to the more common picture of a mixed strategy with elements of all three. (Interestingly, no radically different Strategy D appears to be on the horizon).

Readers may have noticed a general historical pattern throughout *Chapters 3* to *7* of this book. For a long time, in all the penal realms covered in those chapters, the general policy could be described as one of relatively benign *laissez faire* with Strategy C overtones. Governments were mostly content to let the penal system drift along, letting practitioners get on with what they wanted to do, in the context of an ethos of rehabilitative optimism and the belief that gradual progress towards better ways of reforming offenders would come more or less naturally if allowed to develop. There were also some embryonic developments in the direction of managerialistic reform, such as the increased 'professionalisation' of the probation service in the 1960s and the incorporation of prison administration into the Home Office. But by the 1970s the world was changing rapidly, and so was punishment and its politics. The rehabilitative optimism of the 1960s collapsed, and into the vacuum rushed a variety of competing ideas,[8] ranging from Strategy A calls for tougher measures of deterrence and incapacitation to Strategy C notions of just deserts and restorative justice. All the time, however, the managerialism of Strategy B was making quiet headway.

This continued into the 1980s. Although the decade may be best remembered for its high profile 'short sharp shocks' and other such manifestations of Mrs Thatcher's Strategy A instincts, a more interesting and perhaps more significant long-term trend was the continued forward march of managerialism. Nor was this confined to government and its agencies such as the Home Office; the 'systems management' approach to criminal justice (and especially to youth justice) was an outstanding and successful example of managerialism being applied from the practitioner level. The high water mark of penological managerialism in the 1980s and early 1990s was the 'Hurd approach', which as we have seen contained aspects of Strategies A, B and C but should probably be regarded as most crucially embodying a managerialist attempt to contain the penal crisis of the time.

Despite the virulence of the resurgence in Strategy A after 1992—especially, of course, while Michael Howard was Home Secretary—the overall underlying trend can clearly be seen as one of apparently *inexorably increasing managerialism* over a period of several decades. There may have been occasional blips: for example, Michael Howard's Strategy A instincts conflicted with managerialism in some respects, leading him to interfere with prison management to an extent which was the subject of implicit strong criticism in the Learmont Report.[9] But—although clearly the current mood is far more punitive than it once was—we think it makes much more sense to see managerialism as the most dominant long-term trend in penality.

Nor should this be surprising. It is entirely in line with Max Weber's theory that, as societies become more complex, there is likely to be a progressive movement towards 'legal' authority as opposed to 'traditional' or 'charismatic' leadership.[10] Legal authority appeals to rational legislative processes to legitimate itself rather than to traditional customs or the personal qualities of those in power. The administrative form which corresponds to legal authority is 'bureaucracy', a concept closely related to that of managerialism. Increasingly it is likely that public bodies, state systems and people providing public services will have to justify their existence and their activities not by saying, in effect, 'trust us, we know we are doing the right things' (let alone 'this is the way things have always been done') but by reference to rational criteria and logical systems of management and accountability. Not only is this true of criminal justice as it is of any other realm of public life, but we can clearly see it happening.

Weberian bureaucrats would of course pursue a Strategy B approach to criminal justice. If they were suddenly placed in charge of a criminal justice system formerly run by (say) Michael Howard, they would want to know what were the most cost-effective and administratively rational options open to them. So they would doubtless institute a review of the system with a view to assessing what works, what doesn't, how expensive everything is, and how things could be done more rationally and cheaply. In other words, their initial actions would have much in common with those of the New Labour government, which on taking power set up several reviews of criminal justice policy and practice (and acted similarly in several other policy areas outside the realm of criminal justice, including a Comprehensive Spending Review covering all areas of government expenditure).

Hence, *inter alia*, Jack Straw set up a Cross Departmental Review of the Criminal Justice System, which in turn instituted a working group on the effectiveness of dealing with offending behaviour, which commissioned a wide-ranging report on the subject. This report was published by the Home Office Research and Statistics Directorate under the title *Reducing Offending*[11] on 21 July 1998.

Reducing Offending is of significance not just for its findings (which were mostly a compilation of existing research), but for the manner of its reception by the government. A Strategy A Home Secretary (mentioning no names) might have never allowed the report to be commissioned, or might have suppressed or delayed its publication, distorted its findings, picked out only those which seemed to support his own position, denigrated its authors, or completely ignored it. Mr Straw's actions were very different. He published it with an official fanfare, including a statement to the House of Commons, praised it as 'a pivotal step towards developing an effective crime reduction strategy for the next decade'[12] and announced a £250 million Crime Reduction Programme based on its findings. The Home Office's Director of Research and Statistics, Chris Nuttall (who directed the *Reducing Offending* review) confessed to being 'stunned' by this ministerial endorsement of the report and the government's shift towards an evidence-based approach. [13]

It was perhaps especially stunning when the *Guardian* could (without too much distortion) headline the story of the report's launch as 'Prison doesn't work: official'. [14] The report did not actually say this. It said that 'the cost-effectiveness of imprisonment in terms of crime control cannot be assessed with any degree of reliability',[15] pointed out that while prison has some incapacitation effect there is little evidence of increased imprisonment achieving greater deterrence, and drew a cost comparison between imprisonment and crime prevention schemes in terms of their effectiveness which was staggeringly unflattering to the prison. [16] The overall thrust of the report was against reliance on punitive measures such as custody and in line with some of the *desiderata* we outlined in *Chapter 2* about refocusing on crime prevention rather than punishment as a means of reducing crime and attempting to identify and implement effective preventive and reformative measures rather than trust to deterrence and incapacitation.

This is not only good news for Strategy B and bad news for Strategy A. It does indeed mark a step forward for rational managerialism and a more open-minded approach to policy-making in criminal justice, and—hopefully—an end to blind punitiveness. But the rational managerial approach, if pursued logically in its own terms, actually points towards the desirability of taking on board many elements of Strategy C. We suggested briefly in *Chapter 2* that a 'pure', utilitarian or amoral, version of Strategy B would be likely to fail if not allied to a human rights perspective. In a field as emotive as criminal justice, people need to be convinced that what is being done is not only cost-effective but right—and if the positive morality of rights, justice and inclusion[17] is not present the vacuum will almost inevitably be filled by the negative, punitive morality of Strategy A. At best we will have a version of 'punitive managerialism' (see *Chapters 2* and *4*) in which pragmatic and fiscal concerns limit the unbridled imposition of harsh punishments, but which is still considerably more expensive and less cost-effective than an approach which employs managerialism in the service of human rights. As we write, there are some signs that New Labour may be beginning to see the need to pursue and sell criminal justice policies which at least contain a stronger leavening of Strategy C.

If we were being ultra-optimistic, we could say that the logic of historical development points towards the adoption in future of a Strategy B/C approach of the type we would favour. We are not such Polyannas as this, however, nor such historical determinists. It may be—God or history willing—that in retrospect Michael Howard's tenure of the Home Office will come to be seen as both the high-water mark and last dying thrash of Strategy A, but in our more sober moments we have to admit that there remain countervailing social and political tendencies which could still favour Strategy A in the future. It may be that the decline of traditional communities and the consequent 'disembedding' of social relationships from their traditional contexts[18] has led, not only to higher crime levels but also increased insecurity in the psyche of the modern individual, feeding a tendency to reward those politicians who offer a punitive fix for crime. At the same time, modern politicians have increasingly tended to consult opinion polls and focus groups in an attempt to find and adopt those policies which are (often superficially) attractive to voters. But here again, the dramatic political fall of the Conservative Party (and of Michael Howard in particular) in 1997—see *Chapter 2*—might suggest to the wise politician that this may only work on a temporary basis. Maybe you really can't fool all the people all of the time. Those who seek to introduce less harsh policies may also be buoyed by research (rehearsed in *Reducing Offending*)[19] which shows that the general public are not so much inexhaustively punitive as misinformed about how harsh punishments currently are.

As Tony Bottoms has noted, popular punitiveness is an unpredictable factor—and, we would add, one which is itself heavily influenced by the discourse of politicians—and it can be quite hard to guess when politicians will choose to adopt any particular penal stance. It may, as he says, 'depend more on the particular political situation (and indeed on the particular politician) than on any objective analysis of the crime problem in the country in question'.[20] When pursuing less punitive policies, politicians need to do their best to take the public with them, and are of course acutely conscious of the possible adverse electoral consequences of failing to do so—perhaps especially those who have made the journey from Old to New Labour. But at least at present the government seems quite bullish about putting across its law and order policies, confident that they can be popular and relatively undaunted by the prospect of being attacked for being 'soft'.

As we write, one remarkable—and perhaps temporary—facet of the current situation resembles Sherlock Holmes's curious incident of the dog that didn't bark in the night. In this case, the curiously silent dog is the Conservative Party. Since losing power in May 1997, the Conservatives under new leader William Hague have been uncharacteristically quiet on law and order questions, only occasionally taking the opportunity to fling their usual 'soft on crime' jibe at Labour. This may prove to be only a temporary respite, with the Conservatives simply calculating for the time being that their own recent record on crime control is a stick too easy for Labour to beat them with; as time passes the Tories could easily revert to their recent Strategy A type. But for the moment, Labour can afford to be bullish on law and order while their opponents seem so cowed (to mix our animal metaphors somewhat).

From our point of view, New Labour's balance sheet on criminal justice is mixed but on the whole favourable (especially when compared with their predecessors in power). The government has adopted a strongly evidence-based approach, dropped the 'prison works' mantra (for which of course there was no evidence), dropped the catastrophic plan to all but destroy early release, watered down 'three strikes and you're out', and shown interest in restorative justice. On the downside, it has so far taken no significant action to stop the rocketing expansion in prison numbers, has performed a U-turn on creating more private prisons, has partially implemented 'three strikes and out', and in general still seems recurringly (albeit—thankfully—inconsistently) to equate 'toughness on crime' with harsh punishment rather than effectiveness.

One relatively bright spot concerns the new policies towards young offenders. We detailed in *Chapter 7* some of our reservations about the package of measures in the Crime and Disorder Act 1998, which for our money retains far too much of a Strategy A flavour. (For example, the provision including ten year olds within the new 'detention and training order', and the over-rigid reprimand/warning/prosecution scheme which brings 'three strikes and out' into the juvenile prosecution decision.) Nevertheless, the commitment to encouraging restorative justice principles within youth justice is impressive; it is only disappointing that so far the government shows little interest in applying the same principles further up the age range. One other reservation of ours on this point concerns the way in which restorative justice is currently being viewed in perhaps unrealistic terms as a brilliantly 'effective' way of dealing with young offenders. While we have every hope that it will prove to be at least as rehabilitative as other measures and a great deal more cost-effective than custody, there is a danger that restorative justice may be set up to fail if expectations are raised any higher than this. A few poor evaluation results could lead to the government turning its back on this line of development for years, as the Conservatives did at the turn of the previous decade. Restorative justice needs ultimately to be seen as a 'replacement discourse' for punishment—for adults as well as young offenders—and not marginalised as one particular technique which works as a useful fix for certain young and relatively minor miscreants.

Having said that and perhaps paradoxically—the main reason for hope at present may be the onward march of rational 'Strategy B' managerialism. As governments increasingly perceive a need to pursue fiscal efficiency in order to please voters by keeping taxes down while providing acceptable public services and still building up their 'election war chests', it surely makes pragmatic sense for the staggering waste of public finances caused by excessive imprisonment to come under scrutiny. We mentioned in *Chapter 1* the moment at Leeds Castle in 1987 when the Conservative government's policy changed direction from Strategy A towards Strategy B as soon as ministers and officials were faced with the prospect of an unmanageable rise in prison numbers. Perhaps for New Labour the publication of *Reducing Offending* in 1998 could come to be seen as its own 'Leeds Castle moment'; or perhaps such a moment is yet to come.

The biggest, most immediate and most expensive problem in the criminal justice system—and the one representing the greatest injustice— remains the massive overuse of imprisonment. Although occasionally expressing a desire to reduce prison numbers and have more offenders dealt with by community penalties (see *Chapter 4*), Jack Straw's main strategy to achieve this appears to be a re-run of the old 'strategy of encouragement' and 'punishment in the community' combination: trying to ensure that community punishments have a tough enough image so that sentencers will more often use their discretion in this direction. Quite apart from the fact that this has always failed miserably in the past, it is not compatible with a policy which seeks tighter regulation of sentencing (see *Chapter 3*) and a general approach which stresses cost-effectiveness, modern management of the system and evidence-based measures.

Sentencing remains the key to the use of imprisonment in the medium term. Here so much depends on the way in which the new system under the Crime and Disorder Act—whereby the Court of Appeal advised by the Sentencing Advisory Panel creates comprehensive guidelines for sentencers to follow (see *Chapter 3*)—turns out to operate in practice. If the government and senior judiciary were to work together, there is no reason why they could not ensure that the new guidelines had a beneficial, reductionist effect on the prison population—as would only be proper, given the court's duty under the legislation to have regard to the cost and effectiveness of different sentences. If this could be achieved in the medium term, it could only assist the prospects for a longer term transformation of penal practice and discourse into something which was not only more humane, but more rational and more effective. And much cheaper.

This is what wise politicians and judges would do. Unwise politicians will still be tempted constantly to reach for instant crowd-pleasing Strategy A rhetoric and measures. They should remember, however, that it is all too easy to store up trouble for yourselves in this way, since it seems from recent history to be much easier to ratchet up levels of punishment than it is to bring them down again: that way lies disaster both penal and political. The fate of the Conservative Party in 1997, and the state of the criminal justice system they bequeathed to Labour, should stand as a horrible warning. Let politicians beware—and let penal reformers take heart.

ENDNOTES: *Chapter 8*

[1] See Joe Sim, '"When you Ain't Got Nothing you Got Nothing to Lose": The Peterhead Rebellion, the State and the Case for Prison Abolition', in K. Bottomley, T. Fowles and R. Reiner (eds), *Criminal Justice: Theory and Practice* (London, British Society of Criminology, 1992), 273-300 at p. 296; 'The Abolitionist Approach: a British Perspective', in Anthony Duff, Sandra Marshall, Rebecca Dobash and Russell Dobash (eds.), *Penal Theory and Penal Practice: Tradition and Innovation in Criminal Justice* (Manchester, Manchester University Press, 1994), 263-284 at p. 280.

[2] London, Martin Robertson, 1974.

[3] See Sim, op. cit. (1994).

[4] See Michael Cavadino and James Dignan, *The Penal System: An Introduction* (2nd edn., London, Sage, 1997), ch. 8.

[5] See Ed Mortimer and Chris May, *Electronic Monitoring in Practice: the Second Year of the Trials of Curfew Orders*, Home Office Research Study No. 177 (London, Home Office, 1997), 26-9.

[6] Cavadino and Dignan, op. cit., chs. 8 and 9, especially pp. 241-2.

[7] It has also not only influenced but fundamentally reshaped the entire youth justice system in New Zealand. See e.g. Fred McElrea, 'Justice in the Community: The New Zealand Experience', in Jonathan Burnside and Nicola Baker (eds.), *Relational Justice: Repairing the Breach* (Winchester, Waterside Press, 1994), ch. 7.

[8] See Anthony Bottoms, 'An Introduction to "The Coming Crisis"', in Anthony Bottoms and Ronald Preston (eds.), *The Coming Penal Crisis: A Criminological and Theological Exploration* (Edinburgh, Scottish Academic Press, 1980), 1-24.

[9] Sir John Learmont, *Review of Prison Service Security in England and Wales and the Escape from Parkhurst Prison on Tuesday 3rd January 1995*, Cm 3020 (London, HMSO, 1995), especially paras. 3.83 to 3.86.

[10] Cavadino and Dignan, op. cit., p. 72; Max Weber, *Economy and Society* (New York, Bedminster Press, 1968), chs 1, 3 and 11.

11 Peter Goldblatt and Chris Lewis (eds.), *Reducing Offending: An Assessment of Research Evidence on Ways of Dealing with Offending Behaviour*, Home Office Research Study No. 187 (London, Home Office, 1998).

12 '£250 Million to Develop an Effective Crime Reduction Strategy of the Future', Home Office Press Release, 21 July 1998.

13 *The Guardian*, 22 July 1998.

14 Ibid. We are also perversely cheered by the *Daily Telegraph* leader article of 23 July 1998 stating that (from their Strategy A viewpoint) the report's acceptance meant that 'at the Home Office it is the soft-on-crime, liberal consensus that is back in charge.'

15 Goldblatt and Lewis, op. cit., pp. 94 and 98.

16 Ibid., p. 135; see above, *Chapter 2*, note 45.

17 Anthony Bottoms has summarised some of the other social trends towards consumerism and the discourses of individual rights and community which could also be seen as historically favouring Strategy C, in 'The Philosophy and Politics of Punishment and Sentencing' in Chris Clarkson and Rod Morgan (eds.), *The Politics of Sentencing Reform* (Oxford, Clarendon Press, 1995).

18 Anthony Giddens, *The Consequences of Modernity* (Cambridge, Polity Press, 1990); Bottoms, op. cit., pp. 44-49.

19 Goldblatt and Lewis, op. cit., pp. 95-6; Michael Hough and Julian Roberts, *Attitudes to Punishment: Findings from the British Crime Survey*, Home Office Research Study No. 179 (London, Home Office, 1988).

20 Bottoms, op. cit., pp.47-8.

Index